I Am a Teacher

I know you have long interest in Macalester. Here is a view from the inside

Wayne

WAYNE ROBERTS

Copyright 2023 by Wayne Roberts

Copies available at Amazon.com

Cover photograph courtesy of Macalester College

Dolores

Her involvement in my various enterprises has been the principal joy of my life.

PREFACE

Everybody likes a good story, and having spent more than 50 years on campuses with college-age young people and those who profess to teach them, I have many stories, true ones, to tell.

My stories are literally tales out of school, many schools: two-year colleges, four-year colleges, and graduate schools. They are about professors, some of whom could light a mind on fire, others who were clinkers. And they are about students, most of whom learn from their classes, all of whom learn from each other during their time on campus. They include comic events, incidents that can be instructive, and sometimes the pathos that can be found in enclaves of college-age young people.

In another sense, however, this is one story—my story. It begins in Cicero, Illinois, at a time when our most famous citizen, Big Al (Capone) was in Alcatraz. It covers my formative years, when our town was still governed in ways that Al would have approved. Owing to a naivete that almost ended my academic career before it got started, I followed a zig-zag path through a variety of educational institutions before serving, near the end of my career, as the provost of a highly selective liberal arts college.

I have, in telling my stories, not hesitated to suggest ways I think the educational system that served me so well could yet be improved. Indeed, I must admit that these stories have been chosen not only to be entertaining but also to provide a context for suggestions, many of which have the following objectives:

- Improve articulation between secondary and postsecondary schools.
- Make much better use of community colleges.
- Address the escalating costs that increasingly distance private liberal arts colleges from public schools.
- Modify the publish-or-perish syndrome.
- Make the tenure system more friendly to those whose forte is classroom teaching.

In these and other ways, I believe we can and should respond to current calls for relevance and affordability in our institutions of higher learning.

Finally, I have included stories related to the place of Christian faith in my life—moving from my early training in a fundamentalist church in Cicero to a career in one of the nation's highly respected liberal arts colleges. Unlike many who simply jettison such early training, I tried to embrace the best of Christian faith in an academic climate that provides a long view of history, an appreciation for advances in science, tools for critical thinking, and a skepticism that discourages one from settling for trite answers. I hope what I have written might be helpful to young people who, in the course of their education, encounter ideas in conflict with their early training.

Contents

I.	Training in Want of Perspective	1
II.	A Wider View	29
III.	Introduction to the Liberal Arts	53
IV.	The Bumpy Road to My First Sabbatical	87
V.	Settling In	125
VI.	A Math League for Minnesota	159
VII.	The Middle-Aged Professor	191
VIII.	Some Lessons in Academic Leadership	219
IX.	The Trials of Administration	267
X.	The Joys of Administration	295
XI.	The Joys of Teaching	353
	Epilogue	391
	Acknowledgements	395

I. Training in Want of Perspective

My training was good, but a lot of what I learned
needed to be seen in a much larger context;
I needed perspective so badly that
I didn't even know I needed it.

Ah, Cicero

I was raised and received the first 14 years of my formal education in Cicero, an inner-ring suburb of Chicago. Named, I suppose, for the famous Roman statesman, the town sometimes got mentioned in political science or history textbooks as a model of corrupt government. Corroborating evidence existed to support our claim to such distinction.

Al Capone spent 4 ½ years in Alcatraz.

Big Al Capone, our most famous citizen, was in Alcatraz during my most formative years, but his legacy lived on. As a teenager I could direct any inquirer to a nearby bookie. (For younger people, a bookie was someone who ran a clandestine business where one could place a bet on a horse race, illegal before gambling became a tax-raising enterprise of the state.) Similarly, I could point out houses of prostitution or put you in touch with a precinct captain who could fix a traffic ticket or other citation inadvertently issued to a local citizen. One day the newspaper I delivered on my route carried the story of a reform candidate who was riddled with bullets shortly after being elected to the town board.

Bob Konovsky, the son of our police chief, was a friend of mine who attended Wilson, a grade school a mile or two from Goodwin, where I attended. When Wilson's baseball team came to play us in our schoolyard, kids would throw barbs from the (appropriately named) foul territory behind third base, where Bob played. They would loudly read from the *Chicago Tribune*: "Cicero Police Chief Irwin Konovsky reports that he can find no gambling in Cicero." This was followed by calls that everyone knew to be true, even if not meant to be helpful. "Hey Bob, doesn't your old man know about Chico's across the street?"

Bob would stand for this for several innings before flying into the crowd to forcibly silence whomever he could lay hands upon. Some years later, Bob reigned for three successive years as the Big Ten heavyweight wrestling champion. We knew where he got his start.

Those of us who lived in Cicero knew that our police had a tough job. It was obvious that while maintaining their authority on the streets, they surely had to overlook a variety of illegal activities that flourished all around us. For citizens, the trade-off was that we felt very safe. Petty crime (home burglary, store robbery, street mugging, etc.) was almost nonexistent in our town. One assumed that the payoff that came from winking at gambling, prostitution, and

Morton High School graduate Bob Konovsky won three Big 10 wrestling championships at the University of Wisconsin.

other activities of organized crime was too great to risk facing an alarmed citizenry at the polls, and that those at the top of organized crime themselves kept small-time thugs at bay.

Only once do I recall our police coming under real criticism, and that came not from those of us who lived there but from the national press. In 1951, a Black family moved into an apartment in Cicero—for a few days. The great majority of our residents were certain that if one Black family was allowed in, our tidy neighborhoods would quickly be converted into slums just like those on the east side of Cicero Avenue, the street that served as a color-proof shield separating us from Chicago. A mob attended to the problem by trashing the apartment. In reporting the event, the national press was highly critical of our police, accusing them of making no effort to thwart the obvious intent of the crowd.

I was on a camping trip with two teenage friends at the time of the riot. We were passing through Madison, Wisconsin, on our way home when we saw a newspaper headline that seemed to shout at us: "Race Riots in Cicero."

Soldiers hold back the crowd at a July 11, 1951 riot in Cicero, Illinois.

I was stunned. Of course I knew that Cicero Avenue had long served as the color divide between Chicago's Westside community of Black people and our all-White town, but I never thought much about it. That's just the way it was.

The church in which I was raised was at the time the largest Protestant church in Cicero. Its membership included a number of men who had been converted from workers in the Capone organization to law-abiding fundamentalists. I wondered as we hurried home to hear first-hand accounts of the rioting what role our church might be playing in the effort to restore peace.

As we expected, our friends had joined the thousands who gathered in front of the building that was housing a Black family. Their account of the proceedings was conveyed in the high spirits of teenagers who had been part of a great deal of excitement. It was widely reported that one of the bigger kids from our church had lent his heft to pushing a grand piano out of a second-story window. By all accounts, it made a splendid crash when it hit the street.

I don't know what I would have thought or done had I been in town on that fateful day. I was preserved by distance from getting caught up in the fervor of a crowd that sometimes causes people to do things they wouldn't do if acting on their own. I do know that with the opportunity to think, which the passage of time allows, I was confused by the light-hearted hilarity of my friends.

I was more confused, feeling that something was out of kilter, the next Sunday at church, when I heard adults, gathered in little clusters, agreeing that it was too bad such a thing had happened, but after all, "property values had to be protected."

I have given a lot of space to this incident because I believe it was the first time, but certainly not the last, when I felt a bit out of step with the church in which I was raised.

Christianity has always been important to me. I like to think that it provides the light by which I try to live. It is true, of course, that a person living in the world of academia encounters many challenges to embracing religious faith, but they are philosophical, posing problems to the life of the mind. Problems that come when trying to guide one's life by Christian principles are of a different kind. They come with particular force, I believe, when you realize that you're part of a group that's finding it difficult to live up to the ideals of their faith.

Uneasiness about the attitudes of my church and my friends was a first step in coming to grips with my own racial prejudice, but it was just the start to a long process. Our community was more than willing to forgive what the national press said were deficiencies of our police. And sad to say, it would take a lot more than one incident to force me into anything like a realization of the deplorable role the Christian church has played in the treatment of Black Americans. By the time school began in the fall, the neighborhoods in which I lived had pretty much returned to the way Cicero liked them: White.

High School

Morton, the high school to which I returned, served about 5,000 kids from Cicero and several neighboring suburbs of Chicago. It was a four-story building that covered an entire city block. The curriculum had strengths in mathematics, physics, chemistry, and vocational courses intended to prepare us to work at Western Electric or one of the less-well-known factories in our heavily industrialized area. Social sciences were understandably less robust in a school serving a community like ours where, in addition to corrupt city officials, constant rumors suggested that service on the school board was a financially rewarding avocation.

The intention to prepare us for work in the highly industrialized Westside of Chicago led to what now strikes me as a peculiar practice in our high school. Those of us who demonstrated interest and some aptitude in science were all directed into the school's vocational program. When required in 8th grade to investigate and then write about a career I would like to pursue, I wrote about electrical engineering.

Morton High School

Totally oblivious to any distinction between an engineer and a technician, I cheerfully accepted guidance into our school's four-year vocational electric shop program. I learned to identify faulty tubes and other components of a superheterodyne radio, rewind a motor, and perform other tasks soon to be outmoded by changing technology.

This is probably the place to say something about the role of my parents in guiding my education. I cannot recall a time in my life when it was not understood that I was to go to college.

My father, abandoned on a doorstep as an infant, was taken in by a family named Roberts (so the roots of my family tree go underground very quickly). The breadwinner of that family was a railroad engineer who worked out of Chicago, evidently commuting on weekends to Watertown, Wisconsin, where his wife and my dad lived.

My dad was 11 or 12 when his adoptive mother died. I know very little about his life for the next five years, except that his formal education ended with 8th grade. During a period of his life about which he seldom talked, he evidently found himself very much on his own. It wasn't until he was about 17 that his adoptive father remarried and only then brought my dad to Chicago. My dad was determined that I get the education he missed.

Besides his determination that I go to college, I now recognize that my father's awareness of his abbreviated education had other benefits for me. My dad was very much in awe of my mother's achievement of having finished high school. He had unfeigned admiration for her ability to manage the family interaction with what he called "officialdom." Whenever an official-looking letter (say from the city, a lawyer, an insurance company, the bank) arrived, he would simply set it aside and explain to me, "That's skull practice. Your mother will handle that." And when I began coming home from school with good report cards, he would say to me with great pride, "You get that from your mother."

All this accounts, I believe, for the fact that I never had to overcome the idea, so prevalent in males of my generation, that men were just naturally superior to women in matters of business and running the affairs of a house. Though he was a good automobile mechanic, my father even maintained that my mother was a better driver than he was.

So, though I had a good home with parents who loved me and each other, and though I respected them both, neither was prepared to offer me much advice when the time came in 1952 to enter college.

Morton Junior College

Fortunately for me, the top floor of our high-school building housed a junior college that enrolled about 400 students. Though I had made honor rolls in the high school, it was in junior college that I blossomed as a student. I discovered that even though I didn't have the potential necessary to make any of the sports teams in our huge high school, I could play on teams in the junior college. Teachers actually had time to visit with students. My freshman rhetoric teacher stopped me after class one day to encourage me to join the staff of our school newspaper, an example of the kind of individual attention I needed but never got in high school.

I learned a great deal in the junior college, not only about the subject matter I studied but also about the enterprise of higher education. To make clear just what I learned about the latter, I must do all one can do with words to introduce Miss Tucker, the woman who taught calculus to me. She, more than anyone else, inspired in me the idea that teaching mathematics might be one acceptable way to escape the assembly line at Western Electric.

Alice Tucker

Alice Tucker surely set standards to which I later aspired: unquestioned command of the material, clarity of presentation, return of papers the day after they had been submitted (always carefully read and annotated), an evident love for her subject, and a never-mentioned but always-present expectation that we would develop the same personal integrity that she set before us every day. Yet for all that I admired and wanted to emulate, I later learned that she skipped entirely one important part of her job, and to understand her error is to understand an important component of college teaching—to which I'll return after I've attempted to underscore her strengths.

Alice Tucker had the appearance of a country schoolmarm. With her coarse gray hair pulled back in a severe bun, attention was drawn from her thick stature to her thick glasses. Those glasses somehow focused the piercing stare with which she could make you regret every wrong thing you ever did or thought about doing.

One's first impression on seeing her stride into the classroom was that she would be intense, efficient, quick to see through humbug, and intolerant of anything less than your best effort. As you got to know her better, you realized that your first impression was right in all respects.

She was not mean-spirited. If you were stuck on a problem, you could take the work you had done to the mathematics study center, where she presided virtually every minute of the day when not in a classroom. She could spot your difficulty and explain it to you without sugar coating. "Mr. Roberts, I've noted several times now that you aren't grasping the combinatorial significance of the binomial coefficients." Of course, if you had no written work to show as evidence of having made a serious effort on the problem, you didn't even consider going to her. Lack of understanding was tolerated; lack of effort was not.

Effort was assessed each day. Each student came to class with a report listing each of the previous night's assigned problems in one of three categories: problems solved, problems attempted but not solved, and problems not attempted. Class began with a five-minute quiz calling for some skill that was required to complete one or more of the homework problems. By the time the quiz was over, she had scanned the reports. People who reported solving a problem that others didn't get were asked to go to the board and show how to solve it. Those reporting that they worked on but couldn't solve a problem might also be called upon to go to the board and show what they did so the rest of us could try to spot the difficulty.

Students who reported a problem solved but could not produce a solution when called upon, or those who reported trying a problem but had no work to support the claim, were not reprimanded. They were frozen by a penetrating stare that could make one long for some other form of punishment, like a good thrashing. By the end of the second week of classes, very few tried to misrepresent their effort on a report. Along with calculus, we learned that there was a sense of well-being accompanying honesty.

Classroom time was planned to the minute. The quiz, discussion of the quiz and review of the homework, some well-conceived questions to probe understanding of the last lesson and lead into the next topic, perhaps some time to work on a challenge problem while she walked the aisles to see what ideas were developing, a few minutes of lecture on the next assignment, and the hour had flown by.

Quizzes and tests all received a red grade that was based on what was right and what was wrong, and a blue grade that gave generous credit if your method was correct but was marred by an error of the kind that so easily creeps into mathematical work. Just how these two grades were weighted in determining one's final grade for the class was never explained, but most of us knew that it was done as God would want it done and did not question it. We did know that if we went to talk to her in the study center, she could peer at her grade book and point out what types of problems we tended to miss, whether Monday quiz grades indicated not enough attention to homework over the weekends, and more. One came away simply amazed at the details that could be pulled up from tiny marks and symbols that she could, with the aid of those thick glasses, decipher in the meticulous records she kept.

Convinced that I learned more mathematics from her than from any other teacher in my undergraduate experience, I tried to adopt a good many of her methods when I began my own teaching career. I realized that I would not have, indeed would not want, her intimidating presence in the classroom, but I did try, for instance, to use the reports and daily quizzes. I quickly learned that I could not keep up with reading the hundred or so reports and quizzes I was carrying home each night. Even allowing for the fact that she had no family obligations at home and virtually no social life, I could not imagine how she had kept up with the workload she imposed on herself.

It has already been said that her handling of the daily reports helped us see that great peace of mind accompanies habitual honesty. She seized other opportunities to instill in us some of the disciplines she regarded as essential for responsible living. I vividly recall a very snowy morning, more than 60 years ago, when she entered our first-hour calculus class, took note of the number of chairs not filled, and addressed us thusly: "This snowstorm was predicted last evening. The less conscientious take such predictions as an announcement that they won't be expected to get anywhere on time, perhaps even as an excuse for sleeping in the next morning. The conscientious hear such predictions and make plans for an earlier start that will get them to their appointments on time. I congratulate each of you who are here this morning." And then we turned to the daily quiz.

Alice Tucker saw the junior college where she taught as a place that provided an opportunity for a college education to students who, for lack of money or encouragement from their blue-collar homes, would not otherwise have continued education beyond high school. Aware that most of us were getting our introduction to college in the same building where we had gone to high school for four years, she did everything in her power to make the experience different. We were addressed as adults: Mr. Kuskowski, Miss Paginini. She could be counted upon to take our side against an administration that found it inconvenient to grant to us privileges denied to the high school students in the building (a place to smoke, the right to come and go in the building's one cafeteria, the right to bring cars to school, etc.).

In these and other ways, she implanted in us the expectation that our two years at the junior college were but the first half of an education that would continue at some four-year school, and it hardly needs to be said that she intended to have us academically prepared to do well in the school of our choice.

She was not a political person and did not meddle in the unsavory politics that occasionally came to light in Cicero. We never doubted, however, the contempt in which she held members of the school board who had found ways to make off with resources that could have been used to make our experience on the fourth floor of our old high school building more like a college.

She headed a committee that used such funds as she could get to sustain a college convocation program that included musical performances, dramatic readings, comedy, and more. Students would judge a comedian by whether he could get Miss Tucker to break into a laugh. Believing that weekly events would foster an esprit de corps among us, she exerted great energy in trying to get everyone to attend. People (college faculty as well students) leaving the building when they could have been heading to a convocation exerted some of their own energy trying to avoid her on their way out.

Because she was committed to ensuring that students had a genuine college experience, Tucker was always pleased when one of her students entered into other aspects of college life. It was natural, therefore, for her to engage me from time to time in conversation about a weekly column I had begun writing in the student paper as one result of the prompting of my rhetoric teacher.

She appreciated it when I occasionally pointed out another indication that the administration was running the college as a kind of afterthought in a building primarily serving the high school population. She also appreciated my references to the problem community politicians had in giving lip service to prevailing social mores of the 1950s even as they presided over the profitable gambling and prostitution rings that operated quite freely in the community.

What I wrote was by no means a column on religion, but my religious views were evident from time to time, so religion often came up in these conversations. Over time, she inadvertently taught me something very important. It was from her that I first realized that there are fine people who have a good understanding of Christianity but find it intellectually impossible to embrace.

That may seem an odd thing not to have understood, but the church in which I grew up placed a heavy emphasis on the kind of lifestyle that members felt was demanded by Christian living. We understood, of course, that there were people who had not embraced the faith but thought that they probably rejected it because of the attractions of this present world, whether in unsavory business activities or riotous living. There were examples enrough in our town to make those explanations entirely plausible. But in Miss Tucker I found a person who clearly had high expectations, some would say impossibly high expectations of individual integrity, and no one could imagine that riotous living held any attraction for her. For her, the barriers to religious faith were clearly intellectual.

I believe that in this way she prepared me for a lifetime of working with and respecting people who simply could not accept any version of Christian faith, people who in fact helped me develop what I now believe is a more mature understanding of my own faith. Her willingness to enter into such discussions, indeed the willingness of many of my junior college teachers to enter into far-ranging discussions, illustrated for me an important component of good teaching.

It was also in the junior college where I was first redirected from the vocational program I had been following. I mentioned electrical engineering as an ultimate goal to the person signing me up for courses in the junior college, and he steered me into the pre-engineering curriculum. I was no better informed as to what engineers did, but at last someone put me on the track to find out. I've tried to remember in raising my children as well as in counseling my students that it isn't necessary to tell young people everything you want them to know. Sometimes it's more effective to simply point them in a direction in which they will discover these things for themselves.

Getting a Little Perspective

During the summer between finishing at Morton Junior College and transferring to Illinois Institute of Technology, I finally got a good introduction to at least one phase of electrical engineering. I participated in a summer program run by Chicago's electrical utility, the Commonwealth Edison Company, for students who had completed a pre-engineering curriculum. It was a wonderful program, a precursor to what in later years were called internships. For the first time, I came to understand what engineers actually did, and it gave the company a chance to see what some aspiring engineers could do.

We began with a month in the drafting department, where we learned what great care had to be exercised when adding new information to drawings, some of which had been in company files since the days when electrical equipment was first installed in Chicago. In the second month, we worked with engineers who decided what new equipment had to be installed in vaults under and on poles over the city's streets. The final month was spent working alongside the engineers who were then designing Chicago's first nuclear generating plant.

A friend of mine, also from Morton, liked what he learned, and Commonwealth Edison Company liked him. It was the beginning of a long career for him, one in which I am quite sure he made a great deal more money than I did as a teacher.

It was also a very good program for me. I learned that eight hours at a drafting table seemed much longer than eight hours. I learned that crawling into a manhole to make a drawing of how new equipment should be installed had to be followed by crawling into the same manhole some weeks later to make a new drawing of how the equipment was actually installed. I learned that manholes are not ideal places to spend an afternoon. I learned that designing a generating station was necessarily the work of hundreds of engineers, making it unlikely that one could ever point to something and say, "I did that."

I learned that maybe engineering wasn't what I wanted to do.

Most young people would not feel compelled to pursue a course of study through the second year of college because they wrote a little paper about it in eighth grade. I hate to think of what it says about me if Emerson was right when he wrote that a foolish consistency is the hobgoblin of little minds.

Even so, my experience has made me cautious about pressing students at any level about what they intend to do when school days are over. I've had many conversations with parents who lament "that kid of mine has absolutely no idea of what he (or she) is going to do after graduation." That, I have come to think, is better than having a young person follow a consistent path into something that he or she really dislikes. It's often effective to ask parents if they're doing what they envisioned when they were 21.

I also have become a strong advocate for internships or other programs that allow a student to get a first-hand look at a particular field. It's time well spent, sometimes giving a young person a springboard into a satisfying vocation, and sometimes helping a student understand that a change in direction would be an excellent idea. These things are hard to teach in a classroom.

Illinois Institute of Technology

Illinois Institute of Technology (IIT), formed in 1940 as a merger of Armour Institute and Lewis Institute, had, by 1954 when I got there, become one of the largest engineering schools in the country. It was said at the time that IIT aspired to be the MIT of the Midwest. It had attracted several internationally respected faculty members, two of the most famous being the architect Mies van der Rohe and the mathematician Karl Menger.

Its goals for its residential undergraduate school were not realized, however, partly because its location in the heart of Chicago's infamous highrise and high-crime housing projects made it a dangerous place to reside, and partly because it had trouble escaping its image as an evening school serving a large clientele of people working full time in Chicago's loop, just north of the campus.

Old Main at the Illinois Institute of Technology

For me, IIT was a school to which I daily made the approximately 10-mile commute from Cicero, attended my classes, and went home. I started at IIT as a major in electrical engineering, but having just completed my summer at Commonwealth Edison, I began to think about majoring in mathematics to prepare for a career as a high school mathematics teacher.

Not knowing anyone on the faculty at IIT to whom it would

seem natural to go for guidance, I returned to Miss Tucker to discuss the idea with her. She scowled and pulled down a book on mathematical logic that had full pages of symbols uninterrupted by words. Was I prepared to try to learn to read such things as this? Fortunately, I reasoned that although I couldn't make any sense whatever of musical scores I'd seen, I knew there were people of average intelligence who had learned to read them. Perhaps, then, I could learn to understand the symbols in a book on logic.

Her warning about logic was prophetic, however. It wasn't long after that conversation that I entered a course in mathematical logic taught by Karl Menger, a world-famous mathematician who wound up at IIT as a Jewish refugee from Hitler's Europe.

Menger had great enthusiasm for his subject and was unencumbered by any idea of how his approach would hit a young American student fresh from spoon-fed calculus and the courses that follow directly from it. He entered the room on the first day of classes, told us we would not be using a text, and plunged in with his heavy accent to announce that we would assume (among other things) the axioms,

$$a \times a = a$$
$$a + a = a$$

There are several approaches Menger might have taken that would have mitigated the shock that those two lines engendered in the mind of a kid accustomed to having some idea of what was going on in the classroom. He might, for example, have digressed to say that for two sets of objects A and B, we would define

$A \cap B$ = {the set of objects in both A and B}

$A \cup B$ = {the set of objects in either A or in B or in both}

Then, using $\cap$ and $\cup$ instead of x and +, the statements

$A \cap A = A$

$A \cup A = A$

might have made a little more sense.

As it was, I might have given up my mathematics major right there if I had not been determined to prove Miss Tucker wrong in expressing skepticism about whether I could learn formal logic. It took me a week of combing through the library even to find the right books to read in order to make any sense at all of what appeared to me as gibberish on the blackboard.

Karl Menger was rightfully regarded as a mathematician of the first rank, and no one could hear him lecture without immediately seeing his enthusiasm for his subject. He would arrive with his mind focused entirely on what he wanted to say, and would begin his lecture as he moved from the classroom door to the board, apparently oblivious to whether all the students were yet in the room, much less on whether they were prepared to pick up with him in the midst of the topic on which he had been thinking during the hour preceding the lecture.

Karl Menger

Most memorable was his unconscious struggle with trousers that threatened throughout his lectures to slide off his pear-shaped frame. He'd feel them slipping, and so grab at them without really thinking about what he was doing, because he was totally focused on the mathematics at hand. And because he evidently dressed in the morning by tucking both his undershirt and his dress shirt inside his shorts, he often tugged up not his south-bound trousers but rather his shorts. One fascination of the class was to see just how high above his midsection he could pull the elastic band of his shorts over the course of the hour.

Menger's international reputation as a mathematician was unknown to me at the time, and while I enjoyed the multiplied instances of his classroom enthusiasm, these things did not in my mind make up for his obvious failings as a teacher. I was accustomed to Tucker's daily check to see that we'd assimilated yesterday's lesson, the review of what we seemed to have missed, and her efforts to motivate the next lesson. Most of all, I had come to expect that my teacher would know something about me and provide regular feedback about my progress. What I learned most from Menger was how to dig information out of the library. While this proved enormously useful in the future, I didn't appreciate it at the time, and I don't think of it now as something he was consciously doing for us.

I did fare better with him in a second course, by which time I'd gained a little maturity and an understanding that one must accommodate to the fact that different people have different styles. One could learn to appreciate Menger's enthusiasm, his occasional departures to give an account of some experience he had while consulting with Chicago's industrial community, and the basic decency of the man. In time, I came to owe him a great deal.

Perhaps it is because I had so little interaction with other students at IIT that an incidental 20-minute conversation I did have stands out as a watershed incident in my memory. It occurred during my senior year.

I was one of several hundred temporary employees that the U.S. Postal Service hired in those days to handle the Christmas rush of packages and greeting cards. Somehow, I got into conversation with another temp, a student at the University of Illinois Chicago campus, who was majoring in international relations. Still very much influenced by the political as well as the spiritual guidance of my fundamentalist church, I one day parroted to him the thought that the United States would be better off if it withdrew from participation in the "United Notions."

Wisely, he did not respond with a similar witticism or generality. Instead, he asked if I was not grateful to be a student instead of a soldier in Korea, where I would likely be if not for the role of the UN peace-keeping mission in that country. He followed that up with references to the World Bank, the battle against smallpox being waged by the World Health Organization, UN efforts to establish international rules with its Civil Aviation and its Maritime Organizations, its Telecommunications Union, and more. When he learned that a lot of my ideas were coming from the conservative church I attended, he mentioned that it was the UN that had created Israel in 1947.

I had never considered such questions, hadn't even heard of most of the things he asked about. I was fast coming to realize how little I knew about things for which I promulgated dismissive little quips. It was not that I became an instant supporter of the things he mentioned. It was the realization that in just a few minutes, I'd been shown to be intellectually naked, bereft of any defense for the opinions I held about the United Nations.

And there's this: It had been accomplished by a Black student about my age!

I wish I could say that in just those few minutes, I learned not to blithely accept opinions, even opinions of people I greatly respected, on topics about which I knew very little. I also wish I could say that the experience eradicated all my racial prejudices. Unfortunately, both of these laudable goals are the work of a lifetime, but that conversation with an individual I never met again made a powerful contribution.

Failure to have much meaningful interaction with other students was one price of being a commuting student. Another was that I had almost no contact with faculty members outside the classroom. When I decided in my senior year that I would like to be a high school teacher of mathematics, I was in need of a lot more guidance than I realized.

I somehow had learned that there were salary schedules for secondary teachers, and that teachers with a master's degree earned more. As I approached graduation from IIT, therefore, it seemed logical to me that I should get an M.S. before looking for a job.

Applying to Graduate School

If someone had been counseling me, I probably would have been told to get a teaching job first and then pursue an advanced degree during the summers. It was probably as true then as it is now that while school administrators talk glowingly about their efforts to provide students with the best possible education, they prefer to hire teachers with a bachelor's degree, which will start them lower on the salary schedule.

Also, with the aspirations I had, I would have been counselled to seek a master's degree in mathematics education from a school of education. I doubt if I knew one could get such a degree. I no doubt figured that a master's degree in mathematics should be earned in a department of mathematics.

In deciding where to apply, I certainly did not think about the possibility that graduate schools might have reputations for strength in a certain field, making one a better choice than another. I applied to the University of Wisconsin because it was easily accessible from Chicago, I was somewhat familiar with Madison from family vacations in the area, and—well, probably because Miss Tucker had often talked about her wonderful experience in studying there. Only later did I learn that the Graduate School of Mathematics at Wisconsin was consistently rated among the top dozen such schools in the country.

Neither did it occur to me that I might have trouble getting admitted, or getting a teaching fellowship that I'd need to survive financially. I'd established a record of good grades, reliable work habits, and good character, all of which I imagined to be important in being selected for a position that would ultimately involve teaching high school students.

I fashioned my application along these lines. I stressed that I looked forward to the experience of being a teaching fellow because I wanted to be a high school teacher, and that I thought I might want to take some education courses to be a better teacher. For references, I listed Miss Tucker, who, better than anyone else, could describe my mathematical aptitude; the paint store owner for whom I had worked all the way through college, who would describe my work habits; and my pastor, who would say good things about my character. I should have signed my application, "Naive Kid Without a Clue."

In retrospect, it's not surprising that I heard nothing in response to my application. At the time, I was perplexed. When the date for notification went by, I decided to drive up to Madison to talk to the chair of the department to assess my prospects. In due course, I was ushered into the office of Cyrus Colton MacDuffee for what was to be one of the revealing conversations of my life.

Professor MacDuffee was dressed very formally in a three-piece suit (unusual, I was to learn, for a faculty member in that department), and his courteous, gracious manner entirely masked the steely resolve with which, I learned in the years to come, he held to certain opinions.

When I explained the purpose of my visit, he set about looking for my application. After a few futile minutes of searching through file drawers, he went to a cardboard box in the corner containing applications obviously never to be looked at again, except possibly for rejection letters after all positions had been filled. There he found my application. A gentle smile crossed his face.

Cyrus Colton MacDuffee

"So you're the guy," he must have been thinking, but his courtesy and kindly manner did not desert him.

He started with the essay in which I told of my plans to teach. Why, he asked, would someone who had good grades in all the courses I had taken in mathematics at IIT want to take education courses in graduate school? Did I know that graduate students in mathematics were expected to take all their courses in the department of their major? Did I know that teaching fellowships almost always went to students aspiring to a Ph.D. in mathematics? (I don't remember if he added that master's degrees were primarily consolation prizes for those who weren't going to be able to complete the Ph.D., or if that was scuttlebutt I was to learn from other students later on.) Each question underscored for me just how inept my application looked.

I was to learn later that the gentle man sitting at the desk before me was at war with the education establishment, including the School of Education at the University of Wisconsin. He was of the firm opinion that training schoolteachers had gone too far in the direction of pedagogy at the expense of subject matter content. Many times I would later hear him demand that we be able to reproduce proofs of certain key theorems by intoning, "My friends in the Education Department tell me that memorization without understanding is useless, but I tell them that understanding without memorization is hopeless."

All this was in the future then, but it was clear in just a few minutes that I had better downplay my interest in teaching and focus on my desire to learn mathematics if I was to have any chance of getting a teaching fellowship in this department.

The subject turned to my choice of references. The pastor's note was, I was told in a kindly but firm way, predictable and useless. "Ministers always say good things; don't use them as references." End of discussion on that topic. I felt foolish. The letter from a former employer was equally useless. The issue here was whether I could learn mathematics, a subject about which a man who ran a paint store was most likely incompetent to make a judgment.

Miss Tucker was all I had left, and I eagerly assured him that she was the best teacher I ever had, that she was rigorous and demanding, and that she was indeed competent to make a judgment about her students. Wisely, he did not argue the point, but moved quickly to show me the problem.

"You know that," he said, "but I do not. When I read her good letter about you, I wondered who she was. I looked in the membership lists of the Mathematical Association of America and the American Mathematical Society. She belongs to neither. I inquired of members of our departmental admissions committee, people who do get to mathematics meetings in the Chicago area. No one could remember having heard her give a talk, or even meeting her. Her good letter doesn't mean much because we don't know anything about the writer."

I felt that my case was clearly hopeless. It was, until Professor MacDuffee himself offered me some hope. "You have been at IIT. Haven't you had a course from Karl Menger?"

I allowed that I had in fact had two courses from him, but I explained that I doubted Menger would know who I was. "I understand that he may not know you, but I know him." He asked me what grade Menger had given me, and I told him I had two A's from him. That surely meant, MacDuffee pointed out, that Menger would have a grade book with some records of my work. A letter from Menger, I was told, could put my application in a whole new light.

I was in Menger's office the next day. As I expected, he didn't recognize me, but when I explained the situation, he dug out a grade book and was actually able to recall a few details about some work I'd turned in. He agreed to write a letter of recommendation, and about 10 days later I had a letter offering me a teaching fellowship at Wisconsin.

And so I have come to Alice Tucker's great mistake as a teacher. She let herself get isolated from the larger mathematical community. When I sought her counsel about a mathematics major, she could offer no more help than to say it would be hard. She could offer no counsel about choosing a graduate school or how to apply, and her own alma mater could not identify her when she wrote a letter in support of one of her students.

Academics have argued for many years about the "publish or perish" syndrome, and it has been suggested that we need to revisit the notion of what constitutes scholarship when college and university faculty are evaluated. I find myself sympathetic to the idea of broadening the scope of what we recognize as professional growth, particularly for those who teach at the undergraduate level. But I have, ever since that day in MacDuffee's office, felt very strongly that every faculty member should participate in the professional activities of one's discipline so as to be visible to colleagues outside one's own school.

Many years later, when serving as provost of Macalester College, I got into discussions with faculty members who wanted more recognition (i.e., bigger raises) for work they'd done in their department, or on a special assignment within the college. They often had a good case, but somewhere in the conversation I always asked what they'd done to make themselves visible in the professional circles of which they were a part outside the college. And along with this question, I asked how they contributed to making Macalester College visible in a way that supported our effort to attract students from all over the country and internationally.

I would explain that we certainly wanted our students to have an excellent experience in the classroom and in the entirety of their on-campus experience. But we also wanted them, as they moved into the off-campus world, to encounter people who had heard of and thought highly of Macalester College.

Alice Tucker was a wonderful classroom teacher. In many ways, I modeled my own teaching after the things she did. I have always been grateful for the things she taught me, and I remained in contact with her throughout her long life. In the important aspect of remaining active in professional life, however, I did not want to emulate her. Devotion to the classroom to the exclusion of all else is not a good idea, and will ultimately be a disservice to your students.

The Need for Perspective

Alert to the corruption that surrounded us in Cicero as I grew up, it took me a long time to realize that there are people of integrity who run for public office with the aspiration of providing good government.

Taught in a well-organized Sunday School by competent teachers, I have throughout life been able to surprise people with the Biblical stories I know and the passages I can quote. It took a memorable conversation with a college student I did not know, however, to make me realize that along with learning my Bible, I had absorbed a lot of political ideology that needed to be examined in a wider context.

With intentions of becoming an electrical engineer, I completed a four-year vocational program as an honor student in high school, learning things that every electrician should know, and it wasn't until I completed two years in college that I learned enough about electrical engineering to know that it was not something I wanted to do.

I was in good command of elementary calculus when I left Miss Tucker's classroom, and after Professor MacDuffee scanned my IIT transcript, he assured me that I knew more mathematics than many students when starting graduate training in the subject; but my naivete regarding what graduate schools were looking for in prospective students very nearly got me turned away from graduate study.

My training was good, but a lot of what I learned needed to be seen in a much larger context; I needed perspective so badly that I didn't even know I needed it.

II. A Wider View

I have sometimes said that four years of college
and two years of graduate school at Wisconsin
provided excellent training,
but my broader education began
in the Carley living room.

A Quick Way to Expand Your Horizons

Unaware as I was of my need to see the world in a broader context when I graduated from IIT, there was one way I knew that I did want to widen my experience. Having graduated from IIT on a Friday night, I got married on Saturday night.

The quick plunge into married life was not quite so impulsive as it sounds. I began dating Dolores when she was a sophomore and I a senior in high school. She graduated from Morton High the same weekend that I graduated from Morton Junior College. By the time I graduated from IIT, we had been dating for five years. It seemed to us anything but impulsive to finally get married.

Getting married is one quick way for any young

Dolores Jensen and Wayne Roberts

couple to expand their horizons. In our case, we immediately settled in Madison, where I would be entering graduate school in the fall. Starting life together in a university town enabled us, perhaps I should say forced us, to very quickly realize that we had a lot of ideas that needed to be reexamined. That's a subject to which I'll return.

Graduate School at the University of Wisconsin

Perhaps Professor MacDuffee had decided on the basis of one interview that I was a young man in need of all the guidance I could get. New graduate students were, upon arrival, handed a sheet of paper telling us who was to be our faculty advisor. I was one of very few who got the chair of the department as advisor.

He was ready for me when I arrived for my appointment. He told me he would be glad to serve as my advisor on one condition. I must forget about taking any courses in the Education Department. Coming from an institute of technology, I had taken more mathematics courses than most entering students, and "There is no point in wasting that advantage by taking education courses." He signed me up for his abstract algebra course and Creighton Buck's advanced calculus. I never saw the inside of the education building.

MacDuffee had very firm ideas about how one comes to understand mathematics. He followed up with his students and tried to encourage them through what he anticipated might be rough spots along the way.

For instance, sometime in the first several weeks of my first semester, MacDuffee called me in, ostensibly to ask how things were going but in fact to make it clear that he expected me to attend the department's weekly colloquium series. He explained that in my first year, I probably would not understand much that was presented. Nevertheless, I would pick up technical vocabulary, get a sense of the direction of current research, hear some famous mathematicians who regularly appeared for guest lectures, and get to know the department's faculty.

So charged, I went to the next colloquium. A famous French mathematician, Jean Dieudonné, was the guest lecturer. No sooner was I seated than MacDuffee came over and sat next to me. We weren't far into the lecture before I found myself taking such comfort as I could in MacDuffee's warning. It was an understatement of monumental proportions to say that I probably would not understand much. I hoped desperately when MacDuffee leaned over to speak to me after the lecture that he wasn't going to ask me what I learned. I need not have worried.

"Do you know what I learned from that?"

Jean Dieudonné

I don't remember if I mumbled an answer, or whether I was too concerned that his next question might ask what I had learned. Fortunately, he answered his own question in a way obviously intended to put me at ease.

"I learned what 'Lie algebra' sounds like when pronounced with a heavy French accent."

Not every faculty member attempted to ease us into new experiences. Those of us who had teaching fellowships were notified a few days before classes were to begin of a meeting we were to attend. If we went to the appointed meeting place feeling honored to have been chosen from a national pool of applicants, we were quickly disabused of any sense that we were a favored few. We were herded into an oversized lecture room where there was standing room only. There were no name tags, folders with our names on them, or attempts to dispel a general sense of disorder as we milled around.

The professor in charge of courses for entering undergraduates came in a bit late. He distributed sheets listing the names of students in our classes and telling us where and when the classes were to meet, and he gave us one piece of advice: "The University of Wisconsin is a public university that must accept most students from Wisconsin who apply. We compete with private schools like Harvard. If you feel that half of the students in your class should fail, fail them. "

That advice was given to recent graduates of undergraduate institutions from across the country, young men and women who had never taught a college class. Whether that attitude prevailed in all major public universities, whether it even prevailed at

Wisconsin, I don't know. It certainly made clear to us that our first priority was to make good progress in the graduate courses we were taking and that we need not worry too much about the progress of the students we were assigned to teach.

That introduction to undergraduate education in a major university made me appreciate the attention I received in junior college and would later confirm that I wanted to teach in a small school that valued the teaching of undergraduates. I think that introduction was extreme, even for the time, and in the aftermath of the student rebellions of the early 1970s, I don't believe such a thing would happen anywhere today.

It remains the case, however, that in many highly rated graduate departments of mathematics, a low premium is placed on undergraduate education. Mathematical research is regarded as the primary work. Just a few years ago, I visited one of the nation's top graduate schools. I was hosted by a prominent member of the department who really was interested in teaching undergraduates. As we walked along the corridor of senior faculty offices, he said, "I'm sure it wouldn't surprise you to know that if we went into any one of these offices, the occupant wouldn't know what text we are using to teach undergraduate calculus, but it might surprise you to know that he or she would be proud of not knowing."

Today I do understand this focus on research. Success in research is the activity most admired by one's colleagues, the activity that gets recognition, grants, and promotions, and the activity most demanding of deep understanding, insight, and creativity. I did not appreciate this so fully when I started grad school, and attitudes toward undergraduate teaching surprised me. There was another aspect to life in graduate departments that surprised me more, however.

I did not anticipate that so many graduate students would be so competitive, so willing to engage in overt one-upmanship. It was common to be stopped in the hallway and asked, "Want to hear a good problem?" Usually, without risking an answer of no, a problem would immediately be posed. The intent was to stump you and then offer a really clever two- or three-line solution that left you feeling dumb and showed the proposer to be ever so clever. These were the same people who liked to raise questions in classes, colloquia, and seminars that started out, "I was recently reading an article about [enter obscure topic here], and I'm wondering if there is a connection to [topic under discussion]." This ethos was described well in *A Beautiful Mind*, Sylvia Nasar's book about the mathematician John Nash, who was a combative presence at Princeton in his early days.

> The atmosphere was, however, as competitive as it was friendly. Insults and one-upmanship were always major ingredients in teatime banter. The common room was where young bucks sized each other up, bluffed and postured, and locked horns. . . . Back in their undergraduate days, most of the young men had gotten used to being the brightest and the best, but now they were bumping up against the brightest and best from other schools. One of the graduate students who entered with Nash admitted, "Competitiveness, it was sort of like breathing. We thrived on it. We were nasty."

People of this mentality intimidated me in the early days. I was slow in coming to understand that there were others who, like me, were annoyed but simply plugged away. I especially appreciated, however, those who would occasionally express their irritation.

One day an office mate and I were standing in front of a blackboard (the laboratory equipment of the Math Department in those days) puzzling over a question that had come up in a class we were both taking. She perfectly fit the image of a pert young woman from Brooklyn: quick-witted, feisty, not easily diverted from whatever was on her mind.

The office door opened, and a local version of John Nash stuck his head in to ask, "Want to hear a great problem?"

Before I could think of a suitable way to turn him aside, she shouted, "Hell no; I've got enough of my own problems." And for emphasis as she spoke, she wound up and let fly the eraser she was holding. The white puff of chalk dust left on the door where his head had been just before he had quickly slammed it was testimony to her good aim.

It probably took a semester or two for me to realize that these individuals—possessed of such confidence, quick wit, and loud mouths—were often less than stellar in classroom work. Gadflies, they found it hard to settle down to mundane things. Once in a while, it would occur to me that one of the more obnoxious of these no longer seemed to be around.

Happily, there were a good many students of a different mindset around the department. Quicker than most of us to understand new material, to see connections with other ideas, and to point out implications, they quietly exercised their gifts.

It was not unusual in advanced classes to have some of the department's young faculty members in attendance. On the basis of his useful and insightful contributions as a participant in one of my classes, I assumed George Glauberman was such a person. I learned in time, however, that he was a student just like me, only not like me at all. He often took time to help me grasp a concept. He went on to a distinguished career at the University of Chicago. Getting to know him helped me understand my place in the rarified atmosphere of higher mathematics.

There was no blustering about George. He understood that he had a better grasp of things than did most of us and was willing to help others who needed additional coaching. It seemed to me that to succeed in the department, you had to understand and accept your place in the world of mathematics. I, and many other students of rather ordinary talent, came to believe that contributions could be made by those of us who were captivated by the precision of mathematics. We simply had to be willing to work hard to understand the contributions that gifted people have made to create the beauty of mathematics.

One can in many respects forget while in graduate school that he or she is a student in a huge university. All one's professors, all one's courses, virtually all one's friends and acquaintances are in the same department. To my taste, the graduate faculty maintained an admirable balance of humor, encouragement, and challenge. I got into Creighton Buck's advanced calculus class during the semester in which he was writing a text that, when published, became a national standard for the course. We in the class felt respected when we made suggestions for improving an explanation or introducing a new problem, and real competition developed in trying to identify a mistake or even a misprint in the notes being used in class. It was an environment in which I prospered.

A Wider View for Two

As previously noted, Dolores and I began married life in Madison. After finding an apartment, a place to park our car, and a grocery store, we turned our attention to finding a church where we might meet some new friends. We visited several churches that summer before happening into a class of university students being taught during the education hour preceding the morning service. The teacher was David Carley, himself a graduate student. It was evident from the first visit that he was no ordinary teacher.

Many of the students who normally attended this class were out of town because of the summer break. Being part of the small group attending the class that summer, we got to know David and his wife, Adele, quite well. From them we were to learn a great deal, and they ultimately became very close friends. I have sometimes said that four years of college and two years of graduate school at Wisconsin provided excellent training, but my broader education began in the Carley living room.

When the fall semester began, David's class took on the character of a theological free-for-all. It was clear that those in attendance could interrupt with questions at any point. David seemed to thrive on questions challenging some aspect of Christian faith. Responding extemporaneously, he was usually able to begin with some historical perspective, making it clear that the interrogator was not the first to grapple with the question. He would then cite Biblical passages relevant to the topic, summarize what commentators from various branches of Christendom had said about them, tie the ideas to what was being said in some university course if possible, and conclude with his own thoughts on the matter. The erudition was often astounding.

In time, we learned a number of things about David. He came from a Plymouth Brethren background, a group that eschewed paying a minister, relying instead on members of their assembly (the word preferred over church) to take turns sharing insights from their personal study of the Bible. David was a voracious reader. He subscribed not to religious magazines but to theological journals, the periodicals one finds in seminary libraries. (He also subscribed to and read medical journals, but that's getting ahead of the story.) His wife, besides having a master's degree in chemistry, was an accomplished singer. She sang in a civic chorus and led the church choir.

These things were impressive, but there was nothing there that would startle us. There were other things, however, that we thought very surprising to find in a couple that seemed to have Christian beliefs so similar to ours.

David was close to getting his Ph.D. in political science. Kids who grew up in the Chicago area, and particularly in Cicero, knew that politics was a dirty business avoided by all but the most unscrupulous characters. Who would expect to find a gifted Bible teacher intending to enter politics? But even more was true. He was a Democrat, someone whose name frequently appeared in Wisconsin papers because of his activism in the liberal wing of the Democratic party. In the church where I grew up, Christian faith and conservative Republican politics went together like peanut butter and jelly.

My wife and I were one of the few married couples that

attended his class. In time, it became a regular pattern for us to go to the Carley home on Sunday evenings, after their kids were in bed, for an evening snack. Then began the discussions in which most of the things Dolores and I thought we knew were challenged, often demolished. Sixty years later, it is still painful to recall some of the notions we tried to defend, even though handicapped by having so few facts at our disposal.

- I never should have mentioned an article I once read defending slavery of Black people on the basis of the passage in Genesis saying that Canaan (and by inference, all descendants of Ham) was to be a slave to his brothers. David had no trouble destroying that nonsense. Very few times in life have I more regretted something I said.

- None of our attitudes regarding race fared much better. Numerous Sunday evenings covered segregated housing, perceived differences in ability among racial groups, intermarriage between racial groups, and more. These discussions started us on the long task of confronting the racism that had become a part of us so naturally in our youth.

- Our home pastor made it clear that the Marshall plan was one more example of "Uncle Sap" giving away money that should be used to strengthen our military, since the Bible says there will always be wars. David wondered if I agreed that repatriation burdens placed on Germany after WWI had paved the way for the rise of Hitler; I'd never heard of repatriations. He also wondered if I took the warning of war to mean we should not bother trying for peace. Were we to pray for peace while preparing for war?

- When I found David to be a great admirer of Franklin Roosevelt, I asked if he agreed with the *Chicago Tribune's* accusation that FDR actually wanted to get America involved in WWII. He looked at me with great astonishment. "Of course he did. You're a Christian. How long do you think we should have sat on our hands while Hitler marched across Europe killing Jews?" I knew frightfully little at the time about the Holocaust. That was another time when I much regretted having introduced the topic of the night.

• The pastor of my youth was troubled by the welfare programs used to support people who didn't work. He was particularly distressed by the Social Security program FDR introduced. We were warned (circa the 1950s) that because of ever-increasing government deficit spending, the Social Security system would collapse before we ever collected a dime of what we paid in. David could end most of these discussions by reminding me of all that Jesus said about caring for the poor, the widows, the hungry, etc., and then asking me how I thought these people would fare if their fate were left to people in churches like the one in which I grew up.

There were, over that two-year period, far more topics that were worked over than are mentioned here. It's worth emphasizing that much as David disagreed with us, he was always ready, even eager, to put his viewpoint in the context of the historic Christian faith. And though we began to realize how much political and social philosophy found its way into its teaching, we remained appreciative of the church of our youth, where we learned what the Christian Scriptures had to say.

We did not overestimate David's ability. Our friendship with the Carleys continued for many years, during which time David served as Democratic National Committeeman from Wisconsin, and served as president of a mortgage insurance company, later as president of the Medical College of Wisconsin, and near the end of his career, as president of the National Association of Public Television Stations. In between these jobs, he ran for governor of Wisconsin. His losing campaign put him into deep personal debt, a problem that he solved by starting a company that ultimately made him a multi-millionaire.

It is for us an interesting exercise to try to identify what we learned from the association with the Carleys that began during our first two years in Madison.

The first big lesson was that one should not thoughtlessly buy into the social, economic, and political views so often presented as if they are a part of Christian faith. David never demeaned an attempt to take the Bible seriously; indeed, he could quote Scripture in defense of most of what he believed.

Those years also created a much-needed antidote for the idea that politics is intrinsically a crooked business practiced by charlatans whose only goal is to enrich themselves. Through the Carleys, we met others who were involved in politics for quite altruistic reasons, and we learned that it is possible to meet and converse with such people.

That latter point is a lesson that started just weeks after we met the Carleys. Adele picked Dolores up one evening for a women's event at church. I began to worry when Dolores wasn't home by 11:30 p.m. It turned out they had stopped for some pizza on the way home, met David and Gaylord Nelson, who was then running for governor, and got into a discussion. The idea of being able to talk to state leaders about an idea certainly served me well years later when I was trying to start a Minnesota State High School Mathematics League. If we had come to Minnesota straight from Illinois, I doubt that it would have occurred to me to seek an ally in the state's governor.

Our marriage was greatly enriched by our association with the Carleys. We saw their willingness to acknowledge what they learned from one another, their unconscious way of taking on family responsibilities according to respective abilities instead of traditional gender roles, and the way their associations reached far beyond a few neighbors, church friends, and business associates.

It's ironic that we should think of our association with the Carleys as having contributed to our uncommonly happy marriage because in time their marriage ended in divorce. In a conversation that came after many years of our friendship, David ruefully summarized his life this way: "When Adele and I got married, three things were important to me: my church, my goal of someday being governor, and my family. Now the energetic promulgation of my liberal views has alienated me from the church, I was rejected in my run for governor, and my family life is in ruins." Once more I was forcefully reminded that soaring intellect and great financial success do not guarantee happiness.

From this sad conclusion, there is one more lesson we have drawn upon repeatedly and yet need to consciously refresh in our minds: Don't discount things you can learn from others just because they aren't able to live up to the ideals you would like to see in your teachers and mentors.

Back to Cicero

I certainly needed more counseling than I got when applying for graduate school. There was no lack of advice when I prepared to leave Wisconsin with my M.S. to teach at the secondary level. Several of my professors encouraged me to stay. Creighton Buck, who would eventually play a large role in my career, called me to his office and was particularly forceful in encouraging me to accept a proffered extension of my teaching assistantship that would allow me to work toward a Ph.D.

I listened to encouragement from a different source. Alice Tucker decided to retire just as I was finishing my M.S., and I was invited to take her position at Morton Junior College. With gratitude for what she and the school had meant to me, the appeal to return to my roots in Cicero was irresistible—and instructive.

Having seen and participated in undergraduate instruction at Wisconsin, I saw instruction at MJC in a new way. Beside the obvious difference of not having graduate students as teachers, the full-time instructors at MJC were different in ways I never thought about in my student days. They were not teaching out of obligation while their attention was focused on something else, forever frustrated with having to teach basic skills when they would rather be teaching the advanced elements of their discipline. They saw instruction in the basics as their job, an opportunity to open the eyes of beginners to new ideas and new skills. Except for a few clinkers such as work their way onto any faculty, they were genuinely interested in their classroom work, drew on their long experience, and still looked for ways to improve at what they regarded as their full-time job.

Seeing the school from the point of view of an instructor, I realized that besides greatly reduced costs, MJC afforded me some benefits that had not occurred to me in my student days. Moreover, as the years have passed and I've become acquainted with a wide variety of educational institutions, I've come to believe that there are many good reasons to begin one's higher education at a two-year college.

An Endorsement for Two-Year Colleges

For more than 50 years, even in a highly selective four-year college, I've faced many disgruntled students asking, "Why must I study _____ (Greek philosophy, novels, calculus, art appreciation, etc.)? What use will I ever make of this stuff?" I was ready 25 years ago to agree that not every student should be forced into a B.A. program, that many of them thought the B.S. degree was appropriately named.

Today, two-year colleges have a plethora of programs designed to prepare their graduates to enter the workforce. These programs have responded to the charge that not all students need or want the traditional B.A. or B.S. but that they need more training than their high schools provide if they are to have the skills needed in the modern workplace. To make clear that their focus has changed to preparing students for the kind of jobs to be found in their communities, two-year colleges (including the one I attended) call themselves community colleges today.

There is a clear need for schools offering the training needed for today's workplace, and many good two-year community colleges admirably fill that need. My hope, however, is that all such schools might still include in their curriculum a path that offers sound preparation for continued work in a four-year college or university.

The program I envision would be as intellectually demanding as the first two years of any four-year degree program. Many students who start college today drop out during their first two years, having discovered that they don't have the interest, the aptitude, the perseverance, or the money needed to finish. These students should make the same discovery in the two-year program for which I advocate.

There are other advantages to consider. The administrative and support staff of a community college focus their attention on programs that meet the concerns and needs of students largely drawn from a surrounding community. At a university, the administration and staff are charged with providing support for four-year and graduate programs, which bring in research grants. They're also burdened with providing for the needs and putting up with the antics of a sizable residential community of students who are at an age where, as one wag put it, "they sow their wild oats, then go home and pray for crop failure."

Finally, a community college can provide students with the first two years of a quality educational experience at a much lower cost, both to the student and to the state. As the soaring expenses of higher education become more and more a concern, it seems to me that greater reliance on community colleges that include the programs of the old junior colleges offers an alternative that should be more widely utilized.

I did, in time, see some drawbacks to making a lifelong career of teaching at MJC. The culture of a junior college never quite fit into a building in which schedules, rules, and allocation of space were necessarily attuned to the needs of a very large high school. I was convinced from the way Tucker's recommendation for me was treated at Wisconsin that I should be active in a professional organization, but I didn't find one that fit my situation. The National Council of Teachers of Mathematics was an organization for secondary teachers; the Mathematics Association of America focused on college teaching in which one was always aware that most members had a Ph.D. (The American Mathematical Association of Two-Year Colleges nicely fills that gap today.) I was also getting some ideas about texts I'd like to write and finding out that publishers pretty uniformly expected authors of college-level mathematics books to have a Ph.D.

The National Science Foundation (NSF) had, after the Russians launched Sputnik, introduced a variety of fellowships that enabled those who had studied mathematics in college to go on to graduate training. With Creighton Buck's continuing encouragement and financial support from NSF, I decided to return to Madison to work on my doctorate. I did so, however, with a keen appreciation for the two-year college.

Back to Graduate School—Ramped Up

Several surprises awaited me upon my return to graduate school. The most obvious was that a greatly enlarged mathematics department had moved out of old North Hall into Vleck Hall, a new eleven-story building set on the main hill of the campus, just behind historic Bascom Hall. The first two floors contained a multitude of classrooms and the mathematics library. Being an old mathematician, it seems natural to say that the expansive two-story structure was surmounted by a splendid tower.

Old mathematicians recall an enduring calculus problem that invariably used the word *surmounted* to describe a Norman window, probably making mathematicians the last of English-speaking people to use the word. The memory testifies to how long calculus books borrowed from one another as they continued to propose antiquated, irrelevant problems, masquerading as applications. (That's a topic that will come up later).

The tower housed the offices of faculty and graduate students, whose office keys also operated the tower's elevators. Undergraduates determined to see their instructor had to climb the stairs, evidence, I thought, that undergraduate education still had a relatively low priority in the department. I held generous office hours in the library on the lower level. The key system was done away with during the student revolts in the early 1970s. Mere undergraduates were allowed to use the elevators just by pushing buttons—a real concession.

I was also surprised to discover that graduate courses had been redesigned to move through material much faster. The two-year sequence in real and complex analysis that I completed during study for my master's degree was being taught as a one-year course. Several second-level graduate courses proved very difficult for me because they built on material that had not been in the first-level course when I took it four years previously.

Difficult or not, I did well with them. Put material in front of me and I will eventually master it, perhaps even to the point of being able to improve the explanations from which I learned. The real challenge for me came not from course work but from the requirement that I complete some original research in fulfillment of the Ph.D. requirements.

People who have no reason to think about it sometimes ask me how one does research in mathematics. It's a natural question to people whose personal mathematical training stopped with Euclidean geometry, and who suppose that whatever Newton did pretty much ends what a mathematician needs to know. They don't realize that computers, geographic positioning systems, video games, the encoding of multiple messages on the same coaxial cables, magnetic resonance imaging (MRI), sorting systems, encoding, and much more all operate using mathematics developed in recent years.

Mathematical research is demanding, exacting work that excuses no lapse in one's reasoning. When I was looking for a suitable research problem to solve, Professor Buck (by then my major

North Hall

Vleck Hall

professor) suggested that I look at a theorem first proved in 1850. He noted that Joseph Liouville, who discovered the theorem, had called attention to a problem, and then written, "I have obtained, benefiting from a sort of chance, the complete solution."

Buck's idea was that no better proof had yet emerged, and he felt that a proof that flowed out of a natural context rather than from "a sort of chance" would give useful insights into other problems as well. I worked for months to find a context that would give insight. I finally found a new proof, but it depended on using a result from an area of mathematics called lattice theory. Though that result seemed highly intuitive, I could not prove it.

One morning, on the shuttle bus coming in from the parking lot used by those of us perched on Bascom Hill, I described my problem to a senior professor who knew a lot about lattices. He thought about it, and by the time our bus dropped us at the top of the hill, he had sketched an approach he was quite sure would work.

Imagine my euphoria when, using the idea I'd been given, I developed a proof. It seemed quite complicated for so intuitive a result, but a proof nevertheless. I left my work with Buck just before the Christmas break. I knew it fell far short of a providing an insight into the original problem, but it was a new proof, and I went on the holiday a happy young man.

When I returned to campus in January, I went, full of expectation, to see what Buck thought of my work. He told me that he had great difficulty following my proof of the theorem from lattice theory, and that he finally figured out why it was so difficult. "Consider the following counter example."

Nothing is more devastating to a mathematical theorem than a counterexample to what the theorem says is true.

The result I needed from lattice theory wasn't true in general. Eventually, I altered the approach, looking for what additional conditions would make it true. Those conditions were satisfied by my original problem, so I limped through to a proof, but it surely did not make the result seem a natural consequence of anything.

Even now, 50 years later, proof of the original problem still seems entirely dependent on "a sort of chance."

Besides learning a good deal of mathematics during my years in Madison, I, together with my wife, learned several things less technical but very important to our future happiness. One big insight, something we'd never thought of while growing up in Chicago, was that we were children of the city.

That knowledge came to us slowly.

• It came when, having heard about a very attractive fountain in front of Madison's Oscar Meyer plant, we drove across town one night to see it. With visions of Buckingham Fountain on Chicago's lakefront dancing in our heads, we stared in disbelief when we realized that the spigot in front of us was what we had come to see.

• It came when, having heard that Madison had a nice zoo, we paid a visit to Vilas Park. Since it had been described to us as a "nice little zoo," we weren't expecting the Brookfield Zoo. We thought it might be more like the Lincoln Park Zoo. In fact, it was more like a display of animals we once paid money to see at a traveling carnival when we were dating.

• It came when my wife told me one evening about a pair of shoes, perfect for her outfit, that she saw in a store on Madison's downtown square. Though rather new to marriage at the time, I already knew her well enough to expect this to be a lead-in to showing me her new shoes. When it turned out that she didn't have the goods to stand on, I asked how she had resisted. "They already sold the pair they had in my size," was the rueful response she meant as a commentary on the depth of stock available.

Madison, even in the mid-60s, was not Podunk, but to two young people raised in Chicago, our experiences conveyed a clear message. We wanted to live in a city substantially bigger than Madison, Wisconsin.

Another thing I learned was more a confirmation than a revelation. Two years at an institute of technology, coupled with the intensity of five years in graduate school, made clear to me how much I appreciated my two years as a student at the junior college. It was there, in the only small school I attended after 8th grade, that I'd been able to participate in sports, serve as editor of the school paper, and generally enter into the life of the campus. It was there I was first attracted to the idea of teaching, and it was there as a faculty member that I realized students thought I was a good teacher. It also seemed to me after the ordeal of finishing my thesis that my greatest satisfactions were probably not going to come from mathematical research.

My interests and talents pointed in the same direction. I wanted to teach in a small college.

The year 1965 was a good one for a mathematician to look for a job. The space race with the Russians had driven a national interest, if not in science, then at least in beating the Russians, and that, people understood, required building up the sciences in our schools. One university sent me a contract solely on the basis of a telephone interview. But none of that changed the fact that there are not a lot of good, four-year, undergraduate colleges located in major metropolitan areas.

The Wisconsin Department of Mathematics maintained a book of ads and letters of inquiry from schools hoping to hire mathematicians. It was in this book that I came across Macalester College. It attracted my attention because it was a small college, it combined unusual resources with aspirations of academic excellence, and it was located in the Twin Cities of Minneapolis and St. Paul, a large metropolitan area. The description mentioned that it was a liberal arts college, a point I skipped over in my application letter, principally because I had no clue what was meant by a liberal arts college.

Like most quips, that one is not entirely true. A few of my

high-school friends had gone to liberal arts colleges, and through summer vacation discussions with them, I had some idea of what courses they took. I even realized that the required courses in philosophy and English literature that I'd taken at IIT would qualify as important to the liberal arts. I at least had the idea that had there been more freedom for electives in the mathematics curriculum, I would have enjoyed more courses of this sort. At any rate, I did not let my shortcomings in the liberal arts deter me. I applied.

In due time, my wife and I were invited to visit Macalester. We were impressed with the cultural attractions of the Twin Cities, and we liked the residential area where the college was situated. We learned that Macalester had recently been made aware of the possibility of very generous financial support if it would take steps to become one of the nation's leading liberal arts colleges. There was an aura of excitement on the campus, and I decided I would like to be part of it.

Macalester College Old Main

III. Introduction to the Liberal Arts

It was (and still is) my belief that Christian faith
is a matter of personal conviction,
not corporate participation,
and certainly not forced participation.

The excitement that accompanied the decision to accept a position at Macalester became tinged with apprehension as the time approached for us to move to the Twin Cities. I increasingly dwelt on the fact that I'd spent four years in a high school vocational program, went to college at an institute of technology, and never strayed outside the Mathematics Department in graduate school. What about that background made me think I was equipped to teach in a liberal arts college?

Then there was the matter of Macalester's Presbyterian heritage. I was certainly aware that I needed to sort out my religious training from the cultural ideas that came with it. I wasn't certain that I wanted to do it on a campus where it might be expected that the faculty would in at least some nominal way be expected to embrace a Presbyterian outlook.

I need not have worried. If I came wondering what influence the Presbyterian heritage would have, most of the newly hired faculty came determined that it should have no influence. But I am getting ahead of a story that requires some context.

Some History

Founded but not funded as a classic church-related liberal arts college in 1886, Macalester quickly transitioned from its founders' vision as a place for fiercely rigorous study to one that emphasized survival—an accommodation to what was possible.

A mathematician reading the early catalogs is struck, for example, by the original intent to require calculus of every student. This ambitious goal gave way quickly as four different professors of mathematics over the four academic years, 1891-92 through 1894-95, progressively weakened the mathematics requirement. By 1900, there was no mention of it.

The swings between aspirations and accommodations continued throughout the first half-century of the college's history, though it must be said that each swing brought the college closer to its ideal, until two world wars made their peculiar demands.

The college remained a friendly, Presbyterian-related school serving students from the upper Midwest, but to serve the influx of students after World War II, a good many vocationally oriented programs were added. Mac still claimed the liberal arts mantra, but its curriculum included both two-year and four-year programs in everything from accounting to elementary teacher training, from nursing to secretarial and related business programs.

Senior faculty were proud of the fact that the college had been cited in one study as a school that made a significant difference by inspiring its graduates to lives of service. The one distinguishing feature that really set it apart from many similar schools, however, was the fact that one of its early presidents, James Wallace, had a son, DeWitt Wallace, who founded *The Readers Digest*. Having no children, and having accumulated an immense fortune, DeWitt evidently decided in the late 1950s that father shall not have labored in vain. He made it known that if Macalester would take steps to become a liberal arts college nationally recognized for its academic excellence, he would fund the effort.

DeWitt Wallace

Several conferences in 1959 and again in 1961 developed the plan. Programs tinged with vocational overtones were jettisoned, and along with them, of course, the faculty who taught them—making some hard feelings, even among their friends who were retained. A new calendar was adopted, providing for a fall term, a spring term starting in February, and an interim term in January during which students were to take just one course, required, but graded on a pass/fail basis. That interim course had to be in an area different from the student's major interest. It was intended to produce graduates not only well-trained in the area of their primary interest but (in the liberal arts tradition) having developed an understanding and appreciation for other disciplines as well.

With major changes accomplished in the calendar and curriculum, the college began a major effort to attract a faculty that would be expected to lead the way to national standing. I was part of the wave of faculty hired between 1963 and 1966. Attention was also given to attracting a strong student body. Mr. Wallace established generous scholarships for students who, having achieved high ranking in the national Merit Scholar program, chose to come to Macalester. For a few years, the school was distinguished among the nation's colleges for having in its student body one of the highest percentages of Merit Scholars.

My first official duty at Macalester was to help register students during Welcome Week. I quickly saw that there was substance to the reputation that Macalester students had as volunteers to the larger community. A bazaar-like atmosphere developed on the north end of the campus, with booths set up by every organization in the Twin Cities that made use of volunteers: the Red Cross, several animal shelters, foundations to combat most diseases known to humanity, Meals on Wheels, Scouting organizations, suicide prevention hot lines, and many more.

I learned in talking to recruiters in the booths that they regarded their visit to the Macalester campus as the most productive of the stops they made around the city. The faculty of the old Macalester took justified pride in saying that instilling students with an obligation to serve was one of the college's distinctions

Another distinction about which one heard a great deal was internationalism. I learned about SWAP, the Student Work Abroad Program, which enabled students of ordinary means to spend a summer or longer working abroad. I learned that the admissions office made a conscious effort to attract international students (this being done years before it became common in undergraduate institutions). I learned that faculty members were encouraged to take sabbaticals or accept short-term teaching assignments abroad.

The international emphasis owed a great deal to Charles Turck, who had been president from 1939 to 1958. He was the one who decided that Macalester would fly the League of Nations flag at the center of the campus, not a popular decision in the Midwest in those days. There was a story of how Turck had, without campus consultation of any kind, hired Ya Ya Armajani, a Persian professor, because he thought the campus needed the influence of some foreign-born professors. When I arrived, Armajani was one of the most popular professors on campus and was a promoter of international interests.

Charles Turck

Turck promoted student participation in a mock League of Nations, an effort that would produce highly visible results years later when one student participant, Kofi Annan (class of 1961), became secretary general of the United Nations.

The Presbyterian Connection

I had asked when interviewed for a position at Macalester if I would be expected to attend a Presbyterian church. The question seemed to puzzle Lou Garvin, who was charged with building an academic powerhouse, much as it would have if I had asked if I could wear yellow shoes while teaching. He assured me that my job was to help raise the academic reputation of the school, and that there would be no effort to coerce anyone on campus into any religious position.

In fact there was still a good deal of religious coercion on campus that had somehow survived the axe wielded at the conferences that revamped the school. Chapel was still required.

Several religion courses were required for graduation. Faculty meetings still opened with a prayer.

It wasn't long after I joined the faculty that, having been identified as someone who had a religious bent, I was asked to offer the opening prayer at a faculty meeting. I'd noticed that most of my colleagues endured these prayers with furtive glances, rolling eyeballs, and other actions not generally associated with reverence. I refused the honor.

It was (and still is) my belief that Christian faith is a matter of personal conviction, not corporate participation, and certainly not forced participation. When students, faculty, and staff are invited to join a college community with no expectation that they come with Christian faith, it makes no sense to me to expect them to suddenly join in prayers, worship, and study of the tenets of the faith.

My colleagues spent a good deal of time during my first few years trying to eliminate vestiges of the Presbyterian faith. I was surprised in those days at what seemed to be the disrespect directed toward our Presbyterian-leaning president during faculty meetings. Discussion included a lot of wit. During a debate on the value of required courses in religion, a colleague from the Department of Religion, tired of facing resentful students, rose to tell a story about Oscar Wilde.

Wilde had boasted at a party that he could make a pun from any word. Someone challenged him with horticulture. After a little thought, so the story went, Wilde responded with, "You can lead a whore to culture, but you can't make her think."

I contributed very little to these debates. If I had no appetite for trying to force the old traditions of the college on its new clientele, I had even less taste for offending the old-time Presbyterians still on the faculty. They were few in number but unified in their disappointment with how the college was veering from its Presbyterian roots. They were disappointed that I did not join their fight to preserve the past but were nevertheless welcoming to me, inviting me to their weekly Bible study.

Attendance at the Bible study varied from four to six. It was a new experience for me to be in a group of men (they were all men in those days) who knew their Bible well, were serious about their own faith, but interpreted some things much differently than had been the case in my tradition.

Most of the discussions in which I felt isolated came back to one's understanding of what it means to say that the Bible is the word of God. In the tradition in which I was raised, saying that the Bible was the inspired Word of God meant that the words of the Bible were the unequivocal words of God. Others in the group told me I was embracing a paper pope. Perhaps it was in this group where I first heard that in defining inspiration of the Bible, it was easier to memorize someone else's definition than to try to fashion one for yourself. Several years in this company certainly added yet another reason to think that I needed to seriously appraise my own understanding of the faith.

This Bible study was led by Max Adams, who had been chaplain of the college for a long time when I arrived. Max had a daughter, Joan, who had attended the college, and as such things happen, she married a Macalester student. Nothing special there, except that the young man's name was Walter Mondale. He went on, of course, to be one of the best known of young men who attended the college and ultimately one of its most devoted boosters. I have heard Mondale more than once say that he had skipped chapel so often that the only way out was to marry the chaplain's daughter.

There is a related story here that I think should be preserved. Some years after retirement, Max and his wife, Eleanor, moved to a house in a heavily wooded area along the St. Croix River. One night they invited Dolores and me for dinner. After dinner, Max and I settled in the living room to decide what should be done about the troubles of the world, a discussion enriched by the fact that by then, Max's son-in-law was vice president of the United States. While we talked, Eleanor took Dolores on a tour of the house.

When we got in the car to return home, Dolores told me that Eleanor had taken her into what had been an ordinary basement until it was remodeled as a place for the Secret Service to stay whenever "the kids" came for a visit. "And," Eleanor had added in a lowered voice, "Walter likes a cocktail before his evening meal, but Max won't stand for serving alcohol, so Walter sneaks down here to have a drink with the Secret Service guys."

Where in the world, I wondered, would the vice president of a country have to repair to the basement for a drink because his father-in-law wouldn't tolerate alcohol at the dinner table?

My First Book

Though the new arrivals on the faculty thought it important to shed Macalester's image of a religious college, it must be said that this was, in their mind, a small part of creating a school to be known for its academic prowess. The challenge to become a leading liberal arts college naturally provoked a lively debate about what a liberal arts college should look like if given an opportunity to reconstitute its program. This was the real focus of their energy. Their discussions made Macalester an excellent place for a young man with a vague feeling that he might be interested in the underlying philosophy of a liberal arts college if he understood it better.

Much aware that I had little to contribute to forming a liberal arts curriculum, and even less to contribute to the pervasive international spirit on campus, I wondered if I should be applying to some of the programs then available to attract college faculty to teach in developing countries. I asked one of my older colleagues if he thought someone so new to the faculty should consider such a thing. As it turned out, he was one of the disgruntled old-timers who thought Macalester was selling its soul to pursue the holy grail of academic excellence as it was currently defined. "Forget the distinctions like service and international concerns," he told me. "Write a book."

I was not unhappy for his sardonic advice. Half of my salary during my first year on campus was paid by the Research Corporation of America, enabling me to devote only half of my time to teaching, the other half to publishing my thesis or otherwise preparing materials for my career as a teacher. And I did have an idea for a book.

When I was going through college, the usual sequence in mathematics for engineers and students in the physical sciences was three semesters of calculus, followed by a semester of differential equations. Those who went further in mathematics would soon encounter a course in linear algebra. By the time I got to graduate school, however, there was a trend at the undergraduate level to incorporate ideas from linear algebra into the differential equations course. They made it much easier to understand certain techniques used to solve differential equations.

It was while doing research for my doctoral dissertation when it occurred to me that there would be similar advantages to incorporating ideas from linear algebra in the third-semester calculus course. In particular, a useful theorem that appears utterly unmotivated in the traditional course appears as an obvious consequence of a well-motivated theorem in linear algebra.

As is usual in my experience, I learn after exploring some idea that is revolutionary to me that others noticed the same thing years ago. Indeed, Jean Dieudonne (the mathematician McDuffee had cajoled me to hear in my first weeks in graduate school) had written in one of his books that

> the fundamental idea of calculus [is] the 'local' approximation of functions by linear functions. In the classical teaching of calculus, this idea is immediately obscured by the accidental fact that on a one-dimensional vector space, there is a one-to-one correspondence between linear forms and numbers, and therefore the derivative at a point is defined as a number instead of a linear form. This slavish subservience to the shibboleth of numerical interpretation at any cost becomes much worse when dealing with functions of several variables.

It was clear that Dieudonne was far too involved with high-level mathematics to bother with an introductory calculus text. I thought, therefore, that I might try writing a calculus text that would free the subject from the "slavish subservience to the shibboleth of numerical interpretation."

The first problem for a would-be author, especially a first-time author, is to find a publisher. The Dieudonne quote above was taken from a book published by Academic Press, a well-respected publisher of high-level mathematical books. Somehow I had learned that Academic Press was intending to venture into publication of undergraduate textbooks in mathematics. It was natural to send to them a description of my idea.

I thought when they quickly agreed to publish my book that it was because I was setting calculus in the context recommended by Dieudonne, one of their most esteemed authors. Later, when I met Sam Saslow, who had been hired to guide Academic Press's entry into the undergraduate market, I learned that my theory had nothing to do with their agreement to publish my book. Sam told me he was attracted to my book because "you write with piss and vinegar." He would repeat that compliment when we met with others, so I tried to get him to refine it a bit. I told him that I tried to mind the Scriptural admonition to "let your conversation be seasoned with salt, never insipid." Sam preferred "piss and vinegar."

My book, *Introductory Calculus*, was published in 1968. It did not make me rich. It turned out that mathematicians who choose texts to be used in their college prefer slavish subservience to numerical interpretation over an emphasis on the local approximation of functions by linear functions. I have often wondered if Dieudonné bought a copy of my book.

Though the book was not a great financial success, it did accomplish several things. It lifted me out of the category of first-time authors, making it easier to get a publisher the next time I wanted to write a book. It taught me how important it is when writing a mathematics text to hire someone else to verify the answers you put in the back of the book. And finally, reviewers were kind to me for writing a calculus book that actually had something new in it, making it a book that counted for something when I was evaluated for tenure.

An Uncertain Approach to Teaching a Liberal Arts Course

I did not forget during the writing project that I still wanted to fit into a liberal arts college. One innovation of Macalester's new curriculum was that every first-year student had to take a course titled Man and his World, which would, according to one college brochure, "expose students to the best that men [sic] have thought and written, challenge them to develop personal ideals, and then express these ideals in clear writing."

Each department was expected to assign one member of the department to teach this course, in this way providing enough teachers for the many sections required to serve all the first-year students. Classes would come together to hear weekly lectures by faculty with expertise in the topic under consideration that week, and then meet with their individual instructor, who leant maturity and a point of view, though not necessarily expertise, to discussions.

The opportunity to hear knowledgeable colleagues teach history, philosophy, literature, religions of the world, art—everything associated with a liberal arts education—was made to order for me. I asked to be the volunteer from our department.

During this experience, I came to realize anew the paucity of my own education. Even when we came to the field of science, and I read for the first time Thomas Kuhn's *The Structure of*

Scientific Revolutions, I was impressed with how little I had thought about my own field in the larger context of human thought. I did perk up when we came in one of the assigned readings to Plato's assertion that

> in every man there is an eye of the soul which, when by other pursuits is lost and dimmed, is by these [arithmetic, geometry] purified and re-illuminated; and is more precious far than ten thousand bodily eyes, for by it alone truth is seen.

I had seen that quotation in an undergraduate philosophy course. I remembered discussing then the idea that a deductive argument that seems logical to one human will seem logical to another, regardless of race, gender, or culture. Anxious to be a full participant in teaching Man and his World, I offered to give one of the weekly lectures, using the concept of a finite geometry to explain the nature of deductive thinking.

A finite geometry is a simple mathematical concept in which very little background is needed for proofs of theorems, allowing one to focus on the ingredients of any deductive argument: undefined terms, assumptions (usually called axioms), and the deductive proof of things implied by assumptions. The problem is that the initial concept, an undefined term, is itself a very sophisticated concept.

Geometers take *point* to be an undefined term. One grasps quickly that *point* might conjure up different images: a dot representing a city on a map, the location of a surveyor's stake, your location on the screen of a geographic positioning system (GPS) in your automobile, a star used to map out constellations in the sky, etc. But what about having no image at all? A famous mathematician, David Hilbert, once said, "One must be able to say at all times, instead of points, lines, and planes—tables, chairs, and beer mugs." What he meant is that the logic of one's proof cannot depend on a preconceived idea of what a point is.

A writer strives to make things clear, of course, but to what extent the preceding paragraph may seem clear, it masks an idea that I, at least, failed to grasp for years. Having only 50 minutes for the lecture I wanted to give, I decided to circumvent the problem of preconceived notions entirely by using the nonsense terms *poke* and *loke* instead of point and line. I hope that gambit succeeded for some of the students. I'm afraid that for some, having a math professor using nonsense terms may only have confirmed what they believed about mathematics.

A More Certain Approach to Teaching Mathematics

Buoyed by the reputation I had developed as a good teacher, both as a teaching assistant at Wisconsin and then for four years at MJC, I certainly began teaching mathematics at Macalester with more confidence than I had when trying to contribute to Man and His World.

My confidence was buoyed in part because I had developed a few unusual classroom procedures that always proved popular with students. It's odd to say, but one thing that set me apart from a good many teachers is that I gave a lot of thought to how I would use the board.

Material written or drawn on the board should be easy to see and comprehend. That's obvious. It's also obvious to anyone who has been attending lectures for years, however, that many speakers give very little thought to making board work useful. I printed on the board, not only because printing is more easily read but because it slowed me down, something always appreciated by anyone taking notes. I wrote big enough so people in the back could see what was written. I have seen senior mathematicians scrawling in cursive, seeming not to realize that they would run out of board before they ran out of what needed to be written. All too often, the difficulty is met by using small, illegible writing as they come to the all-important conclusion.

Instructors who arrived for the next class before I had finished erasing boards at the end of my class (a courtesy that should always be given) often commented on the board work. They seemed to think that I was lucky to be able to draw a circle that looked like a circle instead of an egg. It seemed never to occur to them that part of doing a good job was practicing. It is possible to improve at things you want to do better.

Another easily accomplished improvement addresses the common complaint of teachers that their students don't know how to read a mathematics text. I was myself guilty of that lament, until one day it occurred to me that since it was true, I as a teacher should do something about it.

I began looking in the textbook we were using for passages I thought might be misunderstood. I occasionally asked someone in the class to read it aloud, and then to explain what it meant. I suggested that members of the class work out an example on scratch paper as the passage was read. Working out examples is probably not necessary when reading a history book. It can often be useful in mathematics and ought to be encouraged. Why not encourage it?

I wanted my classroom to be a place where students would have a good time, where they would make some good friends, where they would feel free to interrupt with questions—a place where there is sure to be laughter.

Toward this end, I planned the first class of a semester with great care; it sets a tone. I began by walking straight to the board, carefully printing my name and my home phone number, and then telling the class that there would come times when they'd need help with homework. In such times, I said, they should feel free to call me. I told them that I was a night owl, so it was okay to call until midnight; after that, I added, they should not call unless they had a crisis in their love life, in which case they should ask for my wife. That last comment brought some of the light-heartedness I wanted.

Though intended to provide help to students when they needed it, these phone calls also helped me establish personal relationships with my students. They came to realize that I had a family, stories about which often provided some of the humor I wanted in the classroom. When my daughter Chris was in elementary school, her service in answering the phone at home contributed to the goal. Always loquacious, she would sometimes answer the phone and ask if her dad was their teacher; there was no predicting what she might say next.

Many years later, I spoke to an alumni gathering of Malaysian students in Kuala Lumpur. I was surprised at how many former students remembered Chris's name when they came up to tell me what they remembered of my cute little daughter, and to ask what she was then doing.

The academic and social value of phone calls aside, I would in the first class meeting stress things I expected of them, and things I expected of myself. I told them, for example, that I try never to casually select homework problems—say by glancing at the text at the end of class and assigning the odd numbered exercises on a certain page. Rather, part of my preparation for class is to select a few problems that embody the specific skills stressed in class. I then expect that these problems will be tried by the time we meet again, so that if the students had trouble, their questions would be focused.

I told them that I would not collect homework because I had found that I could not keep up with reading everyone's work. Instead, I promised them that there would be a 15-20-minute quiz every Friday covering aspects of the week's homework, and that I, not a student assistant, would read each quiz paper carefully, write notes trying to analyze the reasons for mistakes when I see them, and always return it on Monday. In this way, I would over the semester get to know each student's work.

I told them that most students need some help in getting organized. I did my best to convince them that the proper equipment to bring to class would be a sharp pencil (never a ball point pen), a good eraser, and a scientific calculator. We all make mistakes. If you make one with a ball point pen, scratching it out is the only option. The result when you look at your notes later that evening is to be discouraged before you start. At least until you have mastered using a scientific calculator, it is very helpful to have it with you in class, where you can ask someone how to enter the limits on an integral, rather than trying to read the manual later.

I encouraged students to use a loose-leaf notebook (never a hard-bound one). The need for a loose-leaf notebook was a hard sell. I told them that if you start a problem and get stuck, it may be a day or two before you get the help you need. The completion of the problem should be inserted right where the problem began, not several pages later. Quizzes should be inserted with the material they cover, not accumulated in a pile somewhere. Handouts should also be inserted at points where they are relevant, not on the floor under your bed where they dropped when you fell asleep reading them.

In more advanced classes, where class size was smaller, I had students periodically bring their notebooks to my office so we could review them together. It wasn't until I retired and got letters from former students that I learned that some students actually appreciated these one-on-one lessons on getting organized.

The procedures outlined up to this point were well received. My next point invited a little (sometimes more than a little) pushback. I told them that in addition to quizzes, there would be at least two problems given during the term on which they would have about a week to work at home. Solutions to these problems, I told them, had to consist of more than just calculations. They were to include explanations of what was being done and why, much as their textbook explained a solution to a problem, and on these papers, their use of the English language would enter into my evaluation of the paper. Mathematics, I said, free from political terms and ambiguous terms, is an ideal place to learn to depend on the clarity, not the charity, of the mind of your reader.

When I made this point by actually correcting some of their prose, I often heard something along the lines of, "I'm taking this course to learn mathematics, not English." I replied that I didn't see them as having a little corner in their brain labeled mathematics that I am to train. I see them as whole persons whom I am to educate using the medium of mathematics. Mathematics, I reminded them, is a wonderful discipline in which to learn to say exactly what you mean, because if you say a thing incorrectly, it's often easy to provide an example showing how a carelessly worded argument can be misunderstood. I closed my case with two quotations:

> The study of mathematics is wrongly divorced from the practice of speaking and writing good English. For the essence of good mathematics, like good language, is first to know what to say, and then to be able to frame words which express exactly that and nothing else.   —E. Cunningham

> In rigorous proofs one must either establish his point beyond doubt, or else beg the question inexcusably. There is no chance of keeping one's feet by invoking limitations, distinctions, verbal distortions, or other mental acrobatics. One must with a few words and at the first assault become Caesar or nothing at all.   —Galileo

Another Invitation Back to Chicagoland

Sometime during my second year at Macalester, I got a call from Wheaton College, asking if I would be interested in coming to chair their Department of Mathematics. That was a school I would have been interested in when I was a high school senior selecting a college, except that it was completely out of range financially and had no engineering program. A number of my friends from our church had gone there. I knew it to be a premier evangelical school that attracted very good students from all over the country.

The offer certainly carried some attractions. In addition to our parents and extended families, we had a lot of close friends in the Chicago area. I did visit the Wheaton campus and was aware of how much the western suburbs felt like home.

On the other hand, I was struck by how many casual remarks and little jokes I heard during my visit suggested an underlying agreement at Wheaton on issues that had become questions for me. I was reminded of how secure I felt about a variety of issues before I tried to defend my ideas in the Carley living room, in faculty Bible studies with the old Presbyterians at Macalester, even with fellow students met at different stages of my schooling. The visit made me aware that I had questions that would never have occurred to me if I had not been challenged in so many ways.

I'm not sure I can identify all that went into my decision to stay at Macalester, but certainly the lingering influence of professor John Alexander played a roll. John was chair of the Geography Department when I was a graduate student at Wisconsin. He was highly respected in his profession as well as at the university. I met him because it was his practice to invite to his home one Sunday evening a month as many graduate students as he knew that had an interest in Christian faith.

John was a Christian who loved the university. He saw it as an arena of competing ideas in which Christian faith should be competently represented as a viable option. Sometimes participants in his Sunday evening discussions told stories of encountering anti-intellectualism in their churches.

He would in his very gentle way lament that there were indeed Christians who felt that Biblical passages calling for separation from the world meant one should withdraw into social circles consisting entirely of like-minded people. He liked to remind us that Jesus did not limit his own contacts in this way, and in the prayer recorded in John 17, He said, "I do not pray that You should take them out of the world, but that You should keep them from the evil one." Many well-meaning people, he argued, frustrate that prayer by taking themselves out of the world.

He always spoke well of Christian colleges. He stressed the importance of the interface between Christian thought and the ideas of current scholarship. He even allowed that some of us in his living room should perhaps consider teaching in one of them. He never failed, however, to make the point that there were also many fine secular schools teaching some very fine young people, and they also should have some Christians on the faculty who could thoughtfully and intelligently make the case for Christianity.

The invitation from Wheaton was not a turning point in my life, but it was an incident that made me realize that I was more thoughtful than I was when I left Cicero. I was examining my own faith at Macalester to a depth I would probably not have undertaken if not forced to by the skeptics among whom I lived. Things were going well as the college entered a new phase, and I decided that I was happy to be a part of it.

A Conference to Remember

In my second year at Macalester, it was announced that the annual conference of the Minnesota Academy of Science was to focus on science and faith. Since I had been identified as a person interested in religion, the dean asked if I would represent the college. I was the only one from Macalester who attended. It was a memorable event.

In tune with the times, the keynote speaker, starting with the then-popular premise that "God is dead," thought a new understanding of the word *God* was in order. His idea was that theologians could learn something from the way scientists had embraced the word *atom* after it fell out of use from meanings it once had.

He then traced the meanings that a long string of ancient thinkers had attached to the word *atom* before it was gradually abandoned. In recent times, he said, the scientific community, seeing some similarities between the ancient use of the word and the ideas that they were developing, had infused the ancient word with new meanings.

That, at least, is what I was able to make of the presentation.

For the rest of the afternoon, the audience was broken into small discussion groups. Short as I was on epistemology and the terms of theology used in the discussions, I was feeling increasingly left out of the conversation.

I hoped to get a better understanding of what was meant in saying that God is dead. I had once read a book titled *Your God is Too Small*, which argued that it is stifling to think of God in terms we use to describe humans: a benevolent grandfather, a great physician, a teacher. Even the use of fictional personages (Father Time, Atlas, etc.) was too limiting. Was it the paucity of our ability to imagine God that caused modern thinkers to say that God was dead? Or did they mean that there simply was no knowing, guiding power in the creation/sustaining of our world?

Several times it seemed quite clear to me that I disagreed with meanings discussants wanted to attach to a new concept of God, but whenever I tried to express myself, the moderator somehow managed to phrase it as another good idea that he added to the list being developed on a blackboard.

By dinner time, my frustration knew no end, and we still had one more talk, a response to the morning speaker, scheduled for the evening. The speaker was a Catholic priest, Father McMullin.

To my surprise, the good Father spoke in terms I understood clearly. He began with a thorough refutation of the paper, concluding that it was little more than a resurrection of pantheism that had been refuted by Christian thinkers

Father Ernan McMullin

long ago. I was filled with admiration for the presentation, even as I was dismayed to think how little prepared I was to argue in this company.

Near the end of his talk, in what I took to be an effort to soften his attack on the principal speaker, McMullin said something to the effect that he hoped he did not sound as if he thought we had nothing to learn from scientists. After all, he concluded, without the work of scientists, we would never have been able to open, much less read, the Dead Sea Scrolls.

The keynote speaker was given time to respond. He came to the microphone, and the whole of his amazingly short response was to say that Father McMullin agreed with his main point, that theologians can learn a great deal from scientists. That said, he concluded, "I think Father McMullin and I are in basic agreement." Then he sat down.

I could hardly believe my ears. By that time I had learned a little of the lingo being tossed about, and I could not contain myself. I was seated in the back of a large room like they have for dinners in hotels, so I stood up as I waved my hand. I got the floor, and I think I said something like this:

"All day I have been aware of my deficiencies in trying to express disagreement with things I heard, so I have been pleased to listen to what I thought was a thorough refutation of your paper. But now I'm confused again by hearing you say that you and Father McMullin are in basic agreement. Let me ask, Do you think there is a God, with attributes describable in terms we associate with personhood, who intersected time as we understand it to reveal Himself to us in the person of Jesus Christ?"

The speaker went to the microphone and said, "That's a pretty hard question to answer."

Before he could say any more, McMullin rushed to the microphone and said, "No, it's not hard to answer. The gentleman has asked the question perfectly, and the answer is yes or no."

When the program ended, I made my way to the front of the room and told Father McMullen that all of my life I had thought

I was a Protestant, but that he made me question it. I told him, "I have never felt more Catholic in my life."

To finish this story, I must skip many years ahead. Dale Varberg, a friend and fellow mathematician (about whom I shall have much to say later), had already retired and had spent part of a winter in Florida. Sometime the following summer, he and I were out walking along the beach in Door County, and he began to tell me about a wonderful talk he'd heard while in Florida. It had been by a professor from Notre Dame. I asked if he remembered the man's name. He did not, but he said that because he intended to tell me about the talk, he'd brought along a brochure he picked up after the talk. When we got back to our cabin, he gave it to me.

The speaker was, as any reader will have guessed, Father McMullin. I wrote him a letter. I told him that I didn't suppose he would recall an incident that occurred more than 30 years ago, but I told him how much his talk had meant to me that night.

He responded with a very nice letter, and with the letter was a short, hand-written note. It said, "Yes, I remember the night very well. You're the guy who said he was a Protestant thinking of becoming a Roman Catholic. How are you coming on that?"

A Church for Questioning Academicians

By the time Dolores and I left Madison for life in the Twin Cities, we fully understood what people meant when they referred to a church located in a university town as having a town/gown split. A goodly number of students came to our church in Madison to hear David Carley (the gown) in his Sunday School class, and then left without attending the church service led by our kindly old country preacher. David's confrontational style did little to heal the resentment felt by the more permanent members (the town) who supported the regular activities of the church.

Unlike most students attending David's class, we were

married, and during our second sojourn in Madison, had children. We still enjoyed David's class greatly, but the children inevitably drew us into the mainstream of the church; and we were inclined in church, as we were everywhere else, to hear people on both sides of a divide, hoping to serve as a bridge. Maintaining good standing with the relatively small group of town people, however, involved being present for more activities than were allowed by the demands of graduate school. Moreover, attendance at these events regularly involved defending the views and activities of that liberal university crowd, of which we were members.

We decided when we left Madison that we not only wanted to live in a large city but we wanted to be members of a large church. We wanted to go to a church where one did not have to give an explanation for every event missed. We wanted a church where we could admit that we were holding in abeyance some questions brought along from our days in Madison, some generated by life at Macalester—a church where we might even be helped as we grappled with questions.

Nothing in these desiderata suggested a Baptist church, and we did make a tour of a good many churches in the Twin Cities before we eventually visited the First Baptist Church of Minneapolis, located in the heart of downtown.

The service began with a formality we didn't expect, especially in a Baptist church. Precisely at 11 a.m. doors near the front of the sanctuary opened, and in filed about 15 men (yes, all men), taking seats in the first row. We learned later that the lineup included senior officers of some of the biggest firms in Minnesota, and that the last one in line, the senior pastor, Curtis Akenson, was himself a major player in the recent renewal of downtown. That formal beginning presaged all that was to follow, even to the chimes that punctuated the lines of the benediction.

Akenson began a series on the Apostle's Creed that morning, unusual in a denomination that often revels in being noncreedal. He began, naturally enough, with the first line: "I believe in God the Father, creator of heaven and earth." Though we didn't know it, one of his predecessors in that pulpit was W. B. Riley, who had been a loud national voice on the side of a seven-day creation during the famous Scopes trial on the teaching of evolution. I can still, more than 50 years later, give a close paraphrase of Akenson's introduction:

> We have had, in this pulpit, men who were convinced that the seven days in the Biblical creation story were literal 24-hour days. We have had others, competent scholars who wished to be faithful to the Scripture, no less devoutly Christian, who thought the days referred to epochs of time. Still others have understood the account as a story similar to what a father might tell his young child about how he built the garage behind the family house—that one day he poured the floor, the next day he built the walls, etc. And I myself have a viewpoint. Perhaps, if you and I have an evening in front of a fire in a cabin up north, I'll share my thoughts with you. This morning, however, I have a question for you. Suppose that by eloquence of speech, force of argument, or great intellectual erudition, I persuaded you that my view of the first few chapters of Genesis was indeed the correct view. What, in a world where great numbers of people question the very existence of God, would have been accomplished for the sake of the gospel?

In that first visit, both Dolores and I felt that we had found a church home. The dignity of the service, as well as the clarity of the ideas presented, appealed to Dolores. These things, and the ability of the pastor to see merit in different viewpoints, certainly appealed to me.

Akenson held a Ph.D. in political science from the University of Minnesota. That accounted in part for the role he played when Minneapolis undertook a major renovation of its downtown. It also accounted for the number of university faculty, some avowed agnostics, who occasionally showed up on a Sunday to hear what

Curtis had to say. His sermons, always rooted in a Biblical text, were never predictable repetitions of familiar pieties associated with the passage under consideration. They were thought-provoking, frequently applicable to questions of the turbulent, anti-Vietnam war, anti-establishment days in which we then lived.

We came to appreciate the sense of anticipation that permeated the sanctuary before services began, the wonderful renditions of sacred music, and of course the consistently helpful sermons. We appreciated the people we met, and the freedom and civility with which they sometimes discussed views quite at variance with one another. I thought in those days that we could not have come across a better church experience, planting as it did at a critical time in our lives the idea that Christian faith could flourish among thoughtful people who were fully involved in the life of their community and the issues of the times.

Curtis Akenson merits mention in this account of my education because of his leadership style. I referred above to the manner in which members of the church felt free to disagree with one another. Akenson was included in the ranks of those with whom you could disagree.

In time I was elected to the board of that church, and my first meeting was a shock. I forget now the issue, but the debate was lively. Eventually, Akenson got the floor. He began by saying that as usual, he would not be exercising his right to vote, but he did want to express his opinion on the matter. When he finished, a man who had been expressing himself on the other side of the issue stood to address Akenson. "Curtis," he said, "I have told you before that I wish you would exercise your vote and keep your mouth shut."

Addressing the senior pastor by his first name and telling him to keep his mouth shut breached all the rules of my church experience. It took me a long time to accept this behavior in others. I could never bring myself so to address the pastor. I heard stories from others who were quite amazed at how Akenson responded to critics. One such story illustrates my point.

Along with pastoring the church, Akenson headed a Christian radio station. In this capacity, he had contacted the pastor of a quickly growing church in the metro area to point out that in radio broadcasts of his services, he was spending more time appealing for money than was then allowed by FCC rules. The good man's response had been to denounce Akenson on the air as a liberal (the most derisive term known to fundamentalists), and to proclaim that "I am not ashamed to ask support for the gospel." He followed that up by saying that his growing church would do all it could to drive Akenson and First Baptist out of business.

At a social event sometime after I heard this story, I decided to ask Akenson if the story as I had heard it was accurate. I began by asking if John Doe (there is no point in dredging up the man's real name 75 years after the event) had really implied on the radio that Akenson was ashamed to ask for money for the gospel, and that he intended to drive Akenson and First Baptist out of business. "Where," he asked me, "did you ever hear that story?"

He laughed as he slapped his hands in his lap, evidently intending to make no comment. I persisted. "Is it true?" I asked.

"Yes, John did say that once." And there the story ended. He could have gone on to make some allusion to the fact that it was John's church that no longer existed. He didn't. Neither did he feel any need to explain the circumstances that led to John's irritation. It was clear that our conversation on that topic was over.

As I heard these stories and saw for myself the way Akenson accepted disagreement and the disagreeable, I decided it was a trait I'd like to emulate. It was a wonderful example to keep in mind many years later when I served as provost at Macalester. A former provost told me when I took the job that I would find that friends come and go, but enemies accumulate.

Curtis Akenson was widely respected for the financial acumen he brought to the church. When he assumed the helm of First Baptist, their financial problems were overwhelming. I was told of an instance in which a truck driver refused to empty the coal he was delivering until he was first paid. When Akenson retired some 25 years later, the church was debt-free and owned outright the entire downtown city block on which the church stood.

I happened to visit with Curtis several days before he died. When I told him his preaching had ruined me for most of my succeeding church experiences, he said he was afraid that young pastors placed too much emphasis on the idea that it is what we say spontaneously that comes from the heart. Too many preachers, he thought, trust in their ability to speak with insufficient study and preparation. "In that respect," he said, "I was fortunate because I loved to read and study, so the preaching came easy. In my mind, I was paid to manage the business affairs of the church; the preaching was free."

I reveled in the freedom we had at First Baptist to be encouraged and strengthened in our Christian lives on Sunday morning, but to give our time to maintaining a Christian presence on a campus where the focus on building academic excellence had overridden all vestiges of the college's past Christian commitment.

A Christian Presence on Campus

It was clear from my first year on campus that Macalester's ties to the Presbyterian Church were being severed. That was okay with me, but I thought that among the plethora of ideas on campus, Christianity should still be represented as a viable option. I was drawn to the Macalester affiliate of Inter Varsity Christian Fellowship (IVCF) as one way to maintain a Christian presence on campus that avoided the coercive aspects of the Presbyterian past. The chapter at the University of Wisconsin, and especially its faculty advisor, John Alexander, had been very helpful to me when I was trying to sort out the basics of Christian faith from the context of conservative politics, economics, and social policy in which the faith had been presented to me in my youth.

In his book, *The Secular City*, after making it clear that he found many IVCF people held to a theology that he regarded as indefensible, Harvey Cox wrote of IVCF:

IVCF on many campuses sometimes provided the only place where a student Christian-movement program went on entirely without benefit of adult staff supervision. On the campus where I was an undergraduate (the University of Pennsylvania in Philadelphia), IVCF sponsored scores of student-led Bible studies, where the discussions were often hotter and more valuable than those carefully supervised by clergymen. They sponsored lectures and conferences whose content often left much to be hoped for but which attracted people because they were obviously student affairs and not foisted upon them by their all-knowing elders. Furthermore, IVCF meetings and discussions were visible. Lacking the facilities of a foundation house, they often met in dormitories, student union lounges, and the like. In short, IVCF was a lay-led, highly visible, and extremely mobile organization which did not have enough money to erect separate facilities, so was forced to live in the same world with everyone else.

That last phrase, "live in the world like everybody else," has resonated with me ever since I read it. Perhaps it's just a succinct reminder of professor Alexander encouraging us not to take ourselves out of the world, but it often comes to mind. Engage with those around you.

The visibility of Macalester's IVCF was illustrated one morning for those of us attending a breakfast committee meeting that was interrupted by news of violence in an off-campus apartment the previous night. The dean of students recognized the apartment building as a center of drug activities, but I was the only one present who recognized a name from the list of students involved.

It turned out that a member of the IVCF group had been leading a Bible discussion in an apartment next to the scene of the trouble. He rushed into the middle of the fray to play peacemaker when he heard a shot. That qualifies as living in the same world with everyone else.

Talk had been underway when I arrived on campus of phasing out the requirement that student organizations must have faculty advisers. I was more than willing to become advisor to the IVCF group. It was a position I listed as one of my activities on campus for my entire career, long after it was no longer considered a faculty duty.

I found that involvement with a student organization not only provided opportunities to participate in many aspects of education that occur outside of the classroom but it also helped me appreciate some of the difficulties that deans face in dealing with a large population of inquisitive, immature, energetic young adults. An experience early in my career at Macalester gave me an insight into the tough side of a dean's job. I've never forgotten it.

One Long Day

As a kickoff event to the new academic year, the IVCF group planned a retreat at a Presbyterian campground still available to the college in those days. I wondered at the time if I, as faculty advisor, should accompany the group, but in the absence of any college pressure to do so, I had decided to use the last weekend of the summer to go camping with my family.

Just as we were about to leave on Saturday morning of the Labor Day weekend, however, I got a phone call from the president of our IVCF group. He reported that a member of the group, George Berman, had drowned the night before and that dragging operations would soon be started to find the body.

I contacted the dean of students, busy on campus settling new students into the dorms, presiding over meetings for parents, etc. He asked if I could drive out to the campground to represent the college and to keep him informed of developments.

I pictured George as I drove out to the camp. I didn't know him well, but one didn't have to know him well to guess that high school had probably not been a happy experience for him. He was not athletic, wore thick glasses, and was socially hesitant. Several members of the IVCF group had made a point of befriending him, and he had responded, regularly attending weekly meetings.

By the time I arrived, the county sheriff was on the scene, and dragging had begun. The sheriff pointed out that a command post had been set up on the opposite side of the lake. This was done, he explained, so that when the body was found, it would not be brought back where a group of young people would be subjected to the trauma of seeing a dead friend. He was very businesslike, very efficient. I was not.

I called the dean to let him know I had arrived. He too was very efficient and gave me a lot of helpful advice. Did I know for sure that George had drowned, that he had not just wandered off into the woods and gotten lost? I told him I had talked to some girls that George had been helping to get their canoe beyond the rocks along the shore. He had paddled alongside the canoe until they were underway, but when he left them to return to shore, he suddenly vanished from sight.

The dean gave me contact information for the parents on the East Coast, but counseled me not to call until the body had been found and I was able to answer questions that he anticipated would be asked.

In time, the sheriff provided me with more details. The lake dropped off very quickly. George had laid his glasses on the dock, had probably misjudged how far it was back to shore, and probably did not realize how quickly the bottom dropped off. Moreover, since he had disappeared the previous night, the body had probably rolled along the bottom into water too deep to be retrieved by dragging. The sheriff had sent for divers.

It was a long day. I couldn't help thinking about George's parents, perhaps out with friends enjoying a holiday weekend, having no idea of the unfolding tragedy. I dreaded the time when I'd have to call them. At the same time, I questioned the wisdom of not warning them of the impending news. It was a very long day.

I had joined the students for evening dinner when the sheriff summoned me to identify the body just recovered. On the way down to his boat, he asked me if I'd ever seen a body after it had been submerged for a day in very deep water. I told him I had never seen a drowning victim under any circumstances. He warned me that the pressure in deep water forces blood from all seven natural openings in the head, that it was not a pretty sight.

Our power boat arrived at the command post just prior to the rowboat bringing the body to shore. As several men in diver's gear clamored from the boat, I heard a thumping sound that turned out to be George's rigid body rolling back and forth on the floor in the rocking aluminum boat. The sheriff's effort to prepare me for the ordeal of identifying the body proved to be totally inadequate.

I was asked to talk to the coroner, who arrived shortly. Here was another man, businesslike, I thought even brusque as he recorded my replies to his questions. I noticed that he actually got ahead of my reply when he checked "yes" to the question "Alcohol involved?" on his form. I interrupted his efficiency by telling him that I had not been present the previous night, but that I doubted that alcohol had been involved.

For the first time, he raised his eyes from his clipboard to look at me. "College kids, holiday weekend, no adult supervision, and you think there was no alcohol involved?"

The sheriff intervened. "He may be right. It's an odd bunch of kids. They invited us up for lunch today. Somebody said a prayer. I didn't see any beer."

"Sorry," said the coroner. "The last kid we pulled out still had his hand clenched around a beer can."

I made my way to the camp administration building, from where I could make the dreaded call. I have no recollection of how I stumbled through that obligation. I do remember that when I told the dean a few days later that I was woefully aware of my inexperience in such circumstances and was sure that I had been awkward and inept, he simply said, "It never gets any easier."

I would never wish such an experience on a colleague, but I

will say that it gave me a new respect for the difficulties with which a dean of students must cope.

Some weeks later, George's parents came to campus for a memorial service. I was apprehensive about meeting them. I wondered if they would wonder why I, the advisor of the group, had not accompanied them to the campground; why I had not called them sooner; why? why? why?

I could not have been more surprised or relieved. They thought that Macalester had been a wonderful experience for George. They told me they took comfort that George had spent his last hours in the company of the best group of friends he had ever had. They appreciated that I had gone out to the camp. They made a sizable gift to the college in George's memory.

A Third-Year Review

By the end of my third year, I had learned quite a bit about the ideals of a liberal arts education and even gotten involved in the course required of all entering students. I was feeling good about my math courses, and my first book had been published. Dolores and I had settled into the Twin Cities, and the future looked bright.

IV. The Bumpy Road to My First Sabbatical

*I should always remind myself when I have
a disagreement with someone
to focus on the point of disagreement;
don't allow yourself to begin questioning
the motives or the character of the person
just because you disagree.*

By the end of my third year, there was reason for the trustees to be pleased with the progress being made toward the goals envisioned in the planning conferences of the early 60s. With a new curriculum, the recruitment of a faculty charged with making the school one of the nation's leading liberal arts colleges, and the arrival of a student body brimming with National Merit Scholars, attention turned to attracting a president of national stature. The trustees felt that they had their man when they brought in Arthur Flemming as president in the fall of 1968.

The Fleming Era

Arthur Flemming had been president of Ohio Wesleyan, served as secretary of Health, Education, and Welfare in the cabinet of President Eisenhower, and left the presidency of the University of Oregon to come to Macalester. He was also serving a term as president of the National Council of Churches when he arrived.

He came to Macalester with an agenda. Flemming believed public service to be the highest of human callings, and it was his idea that at Macalester, he could open wide the doors of a fine liberal arts college to significant numbers of American minorities. He was impressed with the fact that Macalester had produced such leaders as Hubert Humphrey, Walter Mondale, and Kofi Annan, and his vision was that we might be part of providing leaders that the nation would need as minority people moved into positions of leadership.

Arthur Flemming

The ambitious program that he outlined in his very first talk to the faculty was to be known as Expanded Educational Opportunity (EEO). It included generous scholarships for students of color, a summer program to prepare these students for a rigorous academic experience, review of existing courses and perhaps a few new courses to be sure that topics of special relevance to minorities were included in our curriculum, and vigorous recruitment of faculty members of color.

Well aware that the great changes at Macalester were being funded by DeWitt Wallace, and that Mr. Wallace's educational advisor had been involved in recruiting Arthur Flemming, the faculty assumed that the costs of the proposed program were part of what Mr. Wallace had agreed to fund. With most of the rest of my colleagues, I thought it sounded like a wonderful opportunity to be involved in a worthy altruistic effort.

A few paragraphs cannot do justice to the troubles that ensued. It was naïve in the extreme to think that students coming out of high schools in Black ghettos could in one summer be prepared for the curriculum being developed for the majority of students we had been aggressively recruiting. Having just divested ourselves of courses not in the liberal arts tradition we were trying to cultivate, we suddenly realized that we needed to add remedial courses.

Who would have guessed that racial integration takes more than just putting groups from very different backgrounds into the same classrooms, dining hall, and dormitories? Or that we would find ourselves in such competition to find people of color with a Ph.D.?

In addition to the self-generated difficulties that came with our well-intentioned EEO program, we shared fully in the campus turmoil then sweeping the country. With a vision of the college as a training ground for public service, Flemming's natural inclination was to be supportive of student involvement in the Civil Rights Movement, of student's rights to be heard in the furious debate over the Vietnam War, and of student efforts to get involved in the electoral politics of the larger society. "In loco parentis," the idea that colleges were to exercise some parental roles for students living in college residence halls, was soon to crumble across the country. It crumbled faster at Macalester under the benevolent direction of a president who believed that if students were treated like adults, they would act like adults.

Supporters would say that Flemming was ahead of the curve, that he saw that the days of colleges setting curfew hours, enforcing dress codes, and dictating sexual mores were over, and he quickly abandoned what could not be defended. Critics would say that he was constitutionally unable to say no to anyone, and that he and like-minded administrators failed the country when firm direction was needed. Both things were being said. Loudly. Hubert Humphrey's return to Macalester after the bitter presidential campaign of 1968, together with our location in a major urban area, guaranteed that everything on our campus happened in the glare of continual local and national publicity.

In the transition the college accomplished in the early 60s, we had lost many faculty members who might have provided leadership during these turbulent times. As it was, campus leadership devolved to newly minted Ph.D.s, some of whom were themselves inclined to join the student protests.

Inclined by nature to be conciliatory in the midst of conflict, I soon found myself serving as chair of the faculty's principal committee, the Faculty Advisory Council. This position entailed a weekly breakfast meeting with Arthur Flemming, and ultimately meetings with members of the Board of Trustees. It added another chapter to the education that Macalester provided me.

Like many of my colleagues, I was impressed with Arthur Flemming's ideals as I was coming to understand them. I wanted to see him succeed, but as his unflinching pursuit of his goals alienated one group after another, I began to feel that he was his own worst enemy. We talked a lot in our private meetings about original sin. I tried to argue that his policy of always expecting people to make good choices was not taking into account the human tendency toward self-gratification, self-aggrandizement, and promotion of their own self-serving interests. He thought me far too influenced by the fundamentalists among whom I had grown up, and wanted me to see more of the potential of human beings created in the image of God.

From the many interactions I was privileged to have with this remarkable man, I have selected two that illustrate the consistency with which he pursued his ideals, and the things I admired about him even as they ultimately destroyed his presidency.

It was at one of our morning meetings that he told me that student activists had approached him about bringing to campus Abbie Hoffman and the Chicago Seven for an anti-Vietnam War protest. This was a group nationally prominent at the time for the way they had disrupted the Democratic National Convention that ultimately nominated Hubert Humphrey. Flemming said they had demanded (nobody asked in those days) that they be allowed to

Six members of the Chicago Seven: Abbie Hoffman, John Froines, Lee Weiner, Jerry Rubin, Rennie Davis, Tom Hayden

use the gymnasium. Thinking that their presence on campus was the last thing we needed, I was almost afraid to ask how he had responded, but my worst fears did not anticipate his reaction.

He had responded with a suggestion that must have caught them completely off guard. "Why the gymnasium? Why not use the football stadium?" He certainly caught me off guard. Sensing my incredulity, he explained it this way: "If I resist them, they've got a cause with which to stir up the campus. But this way, they risk embarrassment over the likelihood that the group they've invited will face yawning stands that will drain the energy right out of them."

Insofar as his analysis went, he could not have been more right. People experienced in planning a rally to agitate for a cause would have known not to plan it in a facility they couldn't be sure of packing.

Anticipating (correctly) that the event would in one way or another generate the kind of controversy that found its way to one of our morning meetings, I decided to see it for myself. I don't have the experience that enables me to recognize from half-way up in a stadium whether those on the stage are under the influence of drugs, but I do recognize when things are going wrong. From the viewpoint of the student organizers, they went very wrong that night.

Those on the platform seemed to be wandering around aimlessly, occasionally getting close enough to the microphones so we could hear some of their cursing, or the screeching feedback when they got the microphones too close to each other. Shouts of the crowd disappeared into the night air, and it didn't go on too long before people in the stands, themselves looking a bit aimless, began to drift off.

As a rally, it was exactly the washout the president had anticipated. But the effect on the surrounding neighborhood was what he had not anticipated. The lights stayed on well past midnight, while the amplified cursing and squealing PA system washed over several blocks of homes. Those who had come to the rally hoping for a major disruption that never occurred took their energy to the nearby residential neighborhood, where they boisterously roamed the streets for a couple of hours.

The neighbors who expressed themselves in letters to the newspapers and to the trustees failed to appreciate the genius with which Flemming had handled the matter. That same inability of observers to see the whole picture is even more evident in a second incident.

It took place as the board was getting increasingly anxious about the college's mounting debt. A Monday morning meeting of campus leaders was called in anticipation of a meeting of the Finance Committee of the board to be held that afternoon.

Our emergency meeting was occasioned by the fact that in the building (a converted apartment building with a quite narrow staircase in those days) housing our business office, a single student was staging a sit-in to block the staircase. He'd been there since Friday, and being only one, he couldn't completely disrupt traffic. It was simply something of a nuisance to step around him, his coat, books, and backpack. The question before us was whether to call in city police to forcibly remove him.

Procedures in place at the time called for the college president, the student body president, and me, representing the faculty, to agree before city police were called onto campus. None of us, not the three of us nor anyone in the larger group present, knew what the student was protesting. He had no evident support for his lonely vigil, but he would not respond to the campus security people who asked him to leave.

Thinking of the trustees who would be making their way up that stairway later that afternoon, trustees already quite sure that the president was letting the kids run the institution, I was quickly in favor of having him forcibly removed. The student body president, a strong supporter of Arthur Flemming and very much aware of the increasing impatience of the board, was as quick as I was to vote for removing the student.

Then Arthur had his turn. Did any of us know the student?

No one did. Well, he didn't either, but he had taken the trouble to learn something about him. He had come to campus on Sunday afternoon, talked to the student a bit, learned his name, and then used his pass key to get into the office of student records. There he found the young man's personnel folder.

Did we know that while in high school the young man had been hospitalized for a time because of mental problems? Of course no one knew that. Arthur then pulled out a copy of the college catalog and read to us from the mission statement, that lovely prose with which every college catalog begins. He gave special emphasis to the part that said we try to help every student reach his or her full potential.

After a dramatic pause to let these seldom-read words sink in, he said something like this: "Here we have a young man who already has a confinement for mental problems on his record. He is now partially blocking a stairway for reasons he himself cannot fully explain. I fail to see how we can keep our promise to this young man and his family by adding a police record to his file. He isn't hurting a thing, and will surely leave of his own volition in time. I say, let him stay. The trustees can step around him like everyone else is doing."

Few people heard the explanation, involving as it did the privacy of the individual involved. For the increasing number of presidential critics, it became just one more story of Fleming's unwillingness to exercise any discipline whatsoever on students. And for his supporters, it was one more exasperating example of Arthur's unwillingness to act prudently in even small matters in order to stay in a position from which he could still maintain the larger vision.

Those holding out hope for a dramatic announcement from Mr. Wallace to the effect that he was backing President Flemming's great experiment with increased giving were the ones most shocked when an announcement finally came. Wallace was, at least for the time, no longer going to support the college with the annual gifts to which we had become accustomed. The faculty, most of whom had been brought to the college with money Wallace had provided, were stunned. There was widespread suspicion that this was all the doing of Paul Davis, a consultant who advised Wallace on his philanthropy, often appeared surreptitiously about campus, and was widely disliked.

It was about this time that Archie Jackson, chairman of our Board of Trustees, invited me downtown for lunch. It was not my first trip to the St. Paul Club; it was in that posh dining room that I had learned first-hand of the grief that Mr. Jackson and a few defenders of Arthur Flemming were taking from the St. Paul business community. It was also where I had formed the opinion that Archie Jackson greatly admired Flemming and would support him to the end. I was to learn that day that it was the end.

Archie told me that he knew the faculty held a low opinion of Paul Davis, and he admitted to some of the same feelings. But, he was careful to point out, it was not all one way. Paul had, after all, been advisor to Mr. Wallace during the early years of Macalester's drive to excellence, and he had come up with some very helpful ideas that had gotten things off to a great start. He had been helpful in bringing Macalester to the attention of some key people in academia, as well as to some besides Wallace who had given major gifts.

It had been Davis, according to Jackson, who first suggested Arthur Flemming as a possible president, and who first told him about the great things going on at Macalester. The board merely followed up on Davis's suggestions when they interviewed Flemming. They were, to be sure, very impressed with Flemming, and there was broad support for bringing him in as the next president.

Then, just before an offer was to be made, Davis flew into St. Paul, went to Archie Jackson, and pronounced Flemming a disastrous candidate. He claimed he had been so enamored with Flemming's resume that it had not occurred to him to undertake visits to Ohio Wesleyan and Oregon to talk to faculty and administrators who worked under Flemming's leadership.

Davis had belatedly undertaken such a visit (no doubt

engaging in the surreptitious conversations for which he was famous), and had become convinced that Flemming left Ohio Wesleyan with virtually every pocket of money depleted and was in the process of doing the same at Oregon. Davis was adamant that Macalester should not make an offer to Arthur Flemming.

"That just stuck in my craw," said Jackson. He said he was tired of Paul Davis calling every shot at Macalester. He knew that Davis had suggested Arthur in the first place, but the board had interviewed him, run the usual background checks, been impressed with his record in the cabinet of Dwight Eisenhower, and decided he would be an excellent president for Macalester. As chair of the board, Jackson decided it was time to stand up to Davis, and so he told him the board was excited about their choice, and that they were going ahead with their decision. "You see," he concluded, "I have to take responsibility for everything that's happened."

A long silence followed that statement. Then he continued with what was his real message for the day. After reminding me that he'd done everything he could to support the president, he told me, "Arthur Flemming is through at Macalester College. You can in your position as chair of the Advisory Council cooperate with me in trying to make this as smooth for Flemming and the college as possible, or you can marshal campus support and make it as tough as possible. Either way, this will be his last year."

He went on to say that he had put out feelers in Washington to find a suitable position for Flemming, that it would take some time but would allow him to announce his resignation in order to accept a new position. A graceful end would surely be in Flemming's best interests and would also, Jackson thought, be best for the college. His hope was that I could silence calls from the campus for firing the president.

Jackson then gave me three reasons for wanting the transition to be as smooth as possible. We need our donors to have faith in the college. We must continue to attract students. And when Flemming has left, we will need to attract a new president. None of these things will be made easier by a contentious firing of our current president. I remembered his reasoning years later when I was chair of the board in a church where the pastor, nearing retirement, had stayed a little too long. I repeated Mr. Jackson's reasoning in making the case that nothing was to be gained by forcing the retirement by a year or so.

The faculty had by that time broken into highly partisan camps. There was a self-styled "conservative caucus" that, for some reason, drew most of its members from the science division. The sciences at Macalester are housed on the south end of the campus, separated by a playing field and an outdoor plaza from the rest of the campus, including the administration buildings. Certain members of that division were fond of standing in the field and explaining that Macalester consisted of liberal arts (with a wave of the hand to the north) and (facing south) the sciences. These people didn't just want the president gone; they were for a public humiliation, and I found that I had taken on a big job to keep them from votes of no confidence or other moves they hoped would hasten his departure in ignominy.

Of course there emerged a counter caucus, bent on saving a president they greatly admired and (correctly) assumed to be in trouble. My efforts to forestall action by the conservative caucus required that I meet with them on occasion, and that fact did not raise my credibility with the new caucus. Soon we had a women's caucus and a caucus of untenured faculty who had good reason to worry that in the impending financial crunch, they would be the ones crunched.

As the campus community slowly came to grips with the idea that Flemming's days as president were numbered, it was natural to look to Lou Garvin as the obvious person to lead the college, perhaps even to be the next president. He was, after all, the one the trustees had selected in 1963 to lead the ascent to national recognition, and under his direction all had been going well until Flemming arrived. Also, to most of us, Garvin had done one other thing that spoke to his wisdom. He had hired us.

All this being the case, the campus was startled when Garvin announced his intention to retire when Flemming left.

Shocked, and feeling that the college was rudderless, the faculty decided to take on much of the administrative control of the college. For this task, it formed a so-called Super Committee by merging its principal policy committee, the Advisory Council, and the Personnel Committee. As chair of the Advisory Council when this action was taken, I emerged as chair of the Super Committee.

Faculties are notorious for thinking they could run the college better than the administrators. It might help dilute some of that confidence if every decade or so faculty members were forced to take on a plethora of administrative functions: setting financial priorities, resolving disputes within and between departments, deciding which departments get to add a faculty position, etc.

To all these routine problems, our financial strain, exacerbated by Wallace's withdrawal of support, added the problem of reducing the size of the faculty. I had no trouble persuading the Super Committee that this task should be the work of a new committee, which of course came to be known as the Cut Committee. The trouble came in finding anyone to serve. I was fortunate when the faculty elected Joe Konhauser, chair of the Mathematics Department, to chair the Cut Committee.

Should reductions be made by invoking the old rule, "last in, first out?" That would mean trimming departments that had in the recent past been successful in convincing colleagues and administrators that among competing departments, they had the greatest need. Was this a rare opportunity to dismiss a few faculty members who were not working out? This would in most cases run afoul of tenure rules. It was a soul-searching process. I think we avoided a lot of bitterness because the cutting was guided entirely by reluctant faculty members who fully understood our dire financial situation. In the face of such difficulties, twelve positions (about one tenth of the faculty) were cut.

Even at such a time, I got to see in action some of the altruism that one finds in an academic community. A recently tenured member of the faculty asked to have a meeting with Konhauser and me. He told us that as a still-single young man, he could better afford to lose his job than some of the other young people who were in jeopardy. Furthermore, he was encouraged by his tenure review to be confident about his prospects of finding a position in another college. He wanted to be assured that if he resigned, that would be counted as one of the reductions that had to be made. In the circumstances, his resignation was accepted, thereby losing exactly the kind of person you would most like to retain.

It is notable that in this critical period in the life of the college, the two key committees were both chaired by members of the Mathematics Department. It reflects the reputation the department had and has enjoyed during my entire career. I have always attributed the harmony the department has had within its ranks, and with the rest of the college, to Ezra Camp, who was chair of the department during the transformation that took place in the early 60s. It is worth a digression here to describe what I learned from Ezra.

When the decision was made to improve the college's academic reputation, most departments were forced to dismiss treasured colleagues, either because they did not hold the Ph.D. or because they were teaching subjects being dropped from the curriculum. Ezra Camp, however, had the Mathematics Department well-positioned for changes for which he had longed. He knew the positions he wanted to fill when circumstances allowed the addition of more faculty members. Naturally, he was among the first allowed to start hiring. It pays to have your ducks in a row—and paddling in the direction you want to go.

When Camp considered candidates, mathematical competence and classroom excellence were of course high on his list, but collegiality was no less important. He expected people to be genial, supportive of colleagues, and quick to take on a task they saw needed to be done, in the college at large as well as in the department. New people sensed this spirit, sought to fit in, and looked for the same qualities when they were later involved in hiring.

I am aware of great research mathematicians who, despite a cantankerous or pompous personality, made important contributions to mathematics. Research universities must find ways to accommodate them. I am also aware that mathematicians teaching at the undergraduate level are expected to engage in research. In my view, however, the purpose of the research done by faculty members at a liberal arts college is much broader. It models research for its undergraduates; it stimulates the teacher with the excitement of learning something new (even if only to him or her); it keeps the curriculum current as the faculty strives to fill in gaps and to keep up with new developments in the field.

There surely are examples of teachers at liberal arts colleges who continue to make important contributions to new developments in their field, and they surely deserve to be encouraged; but they should be revered for their contributions to the department, not tolerated because of their outstanding research. There is no room to put up with a personality ill-suited to the harmony that is so important to the effective functioning of a small department.

It was my good fortune during 50 years at Macalester to be in a department in which colleagues have been active as writers of articles in journals, writers of textbooks, and leaders in professional societies at both the regional and national level—and in which department members have been genial friends who contribute in multiple ways to the entire college.

When the turmoil was finally over and it had been announced that Arthur Flemming was leaving Macalester to accept a position as director of the Federal Agency on Aging, I got my reward, one that I was able to share with my wife. On their last Sunday in St. Paul, Arthur and Bernice Fleming invited Dolores and me to have dinner with them at the president's house.

I thought I might at long last learn if promises had been made to Arthur that were not kept, if he had been counting on federal aid that did not materialize, etc. I should have known better. Recrimination was not a part of his make-up. He did say that he thought I might be the last person in St. Paul on speaking terms with both him and the chair of the Board of Trustees.

It was many years before the college got around to putting Flemming's picture on the wall in the administration building with the other former presidents. Several photos were hung that day, and with the exception of Flemming, everyone so honored was present to make a few remarks. Flemming was unable to come, not because he was then 91, but because he was on the West Coast making a speech. I was asked to make a few remarks on his behalf. I still have a copy of the page from which I read.

> Macalester's drive to national recognition as a liberal arts college began in the early 60s, and by 1968 it seemed a logical step that we should bring to the campus as president a nationally recognized figure. Arthur Flemming was deemed to be the ideal candidate, and he came; he came with a vision. His vision was that a liberal arts education should be available to minorities that were commonly shut out of such an opportunity.
>
> His vision overreached his resources. His troubles were compounded by a nation divided over an unpopular war, a nation perplexed over the rebellion of its young people, the return of Hubert Humphrey to this campus (he came a little later), the withdrawal of support that he was counting on, and his own involvements.
>
> There are a number of people in this room who played key roles in helping the college through this period, and we are forever in their debt. Difficult though it was, it's clear that during this period Arthur Flemming brought the college to share his vision. It's seen in our many graduates of color; it's seen in the persistence of the effort through all the years that have passed since; it's seen in today's commitment to multiculturalism as a distinctive of the institution.
>
> How in such troubled circumstances did he leave such an impact? His convictions were deep; they were genuine. He

had a great ability to articulate. He had unrelenting energy in the pursuit of his goals. On the last Sunday that he spent in St. Paul. he invited Dolores and me to join him for dinner, and Bernice confided to Dolores that committee meetings seemed to do for Arthur what golf does for most men.

It has already been said that he is 91, but it's not his age that prevented him from being here. It's because he has commitments in San Francisco. He writes as follows,

"I regret that an engagement in San Francisco prevents my being present on campus. If I were there I would be delighted to have the opportunity of expressing to President Gavin my deep gratitude for the leadership that he has provided over the years. I appreciate very much having my portrait join the portraits of all the presidents. Please give all of those present on Thursday my greetings and my best wishes. I will never forget the opportunities I had to participate in the life of Macalester. They were stimulating and rewarding experiences. Macalester is a leader among liberal arts colleges in this country and is making a very distinct contribution to the life of our nation."

I did admire his ideals and his ability to articulate a vision. I learned a great deal about administration from him, and from the stories he loved to tell about his years working under President Eisenhower. It was a great privilege to know him. He also illustrated, however, that a leader must pay attention to money, lest even supporters abandon ship as they see it headed for the financial rocks. I memorized as a youth in Sunday School that "Where there is no vision, the people perish." It is also true that where no people are, the vision perishes.

Humphrey Returns

In 1968, the same year that Flemming came to Macalester, Hubert Humphrey lost a bitterly contested election for the presidency. In a post-election interview, he said he had been talking for a good many years, so perhaps it was time to go back to campus and listen for a while.

I had learned by that time, of course, that Humphrey had taught political science at Macalester in the early 1940s. When he ran for the presidency in 1968, I had seen in a display cabinet in Old Main a page from an old yearbook. A caption at the bottom of the page said (as close as I can remember), "Political Science Professor Hubert Humphrey announced that he was taking a leave of absence to get some practical experience by running for Mayor of Minneapolis. Here he is shown with Walter Mondale, student coordinator of his campaign."

I wondered when I read in the paper that he was going "back to campus" if it really meant that he was coming back to Macalester. That is exactly what it meant.

Wisely, instead of having him teach a course or two that would give only students in his classes a chance to meet him, it was decided that he would come as a guest lecturer to any class to which he was invited.

Hubert Humphrey

When I heard that he accepted an invitation to speak in an art appreciation course, I wondered what he would have to contribute in that setting. I asked the professor of the course. It was, he said, an excellent presentation on the role of government in funding public art. He told me that Humphrey had come to his office several days ahead of time to ask questions about the course and borrow a copy of the text being used.

According to my colleague, Humphrey appeared hesitant and uncertain when he appeared in his office a few minutes before the class, so much so that he wondered how this idea was going to work out. That doubt lingered as they walked to the class, but when Humphrey got in front of the class, he sprang to life: animated, informed about channels through which the federal government supported art, and witty during the time he left for student questions.

Being Humphrey, of course, he got involved in a lot more than visiting classes. There was the time, for instance, when a neighborhood apartment owner rented an apartment to a White student after having refused to rent that same apartment to a Black student. When the incident came to light, it appeared for a while that there might be violence in the streets.

If I ever knew how, I have forgotten now, but apparently a group from the campus, working with the city housing authority, got the landlord to back down.

An increasingly raucous crowd was assembling on the campus lawn when news of the resolution got to campus. By the time I joined the crowd, Humphrey was on the steps of the union, first letting the crowd know that the matter had been settled, then congratulating them on demonstrating their support for the student in a peaceful way while a campus delegation worked through the proper officials to bring about a peaceful resolution.

I wondered how long the crowd would have remained peaceful if the matter had not been so quickly resolved, but that didn't deter Humphrey. He was intent on drawing a lesson for everyone in that crowd on how things should be handled, and it turned out that he had one more objective in mind.

The Flemming era was still fresh in the minds of the Twin Cities media, and this event had all the earmarks of another example of Macalester as a troubled, highly politicized campus ready to boil over at any provocation. They were there, cameras ready.

Humphrey directed a rhetorical flourish to them. "I want to

see pictures on TV tonight and in the paper tomorrow of these young people, peacefully demonstrating and bringing about a just outcome. No windows got broken; no noses got bloodied. This too is news—good news!"

I'm sorry that I don't recall what coverage came out of the event.

Humphrey had not been on campus too long before an advisee of mine told me that he was organizing a symposium at which Humphrey had agreed to speak about his role in handling the Vietnam War. I (naively) thought it would be nice to give Humphrey a chance to present his views, since students the country over were sure that he had been complicit in supporting a war for which there could be no defense.

I was disabused of the organizers' intentions when, alighting from my bus the morning after the symposium, I ran into that student. I asked how things had gone the night before. The student (who was Black, as were all the organizers of the event) was jubilant. He said students had been able to nail Humphrey on his racist attitudes, his failure in a long career to get meaningful civil rights legislation passed, his willingness to send disproportionate numbers of Black young men to Vietnam—on he went.

As fortune would have it, I hadn't gone much farther on my way across campus when I encountered Humphrey. I told him I heard that he had a pretty rough night. He was still sputtering. "Those young kids have no idea of what it has cost me to champion civil rights. I was taking brickbats for my support of civil rights at Democratic conventions when they were still kicking slats out of their cribs. This damn job is harder than being vice president of the United States."

I thought as I walked on my way that he probably had hoped for something a little more constructive when he'd said he was going back to the campus to listen for a while. Nevertheless, he did take aggressive steps to visit with people. For example, he sent a memo to the faculty saying he would like to schedule a series of lunches with two or three faculty members at a time. Those willing to join him were to call his secretary. It was an opportunity I did not want to miss; I actually got to go to two such lunches.

One was dominated by questions from a colleague who seemed to know a lot about foreign affairs. He asked about a military base we were maintaining on some Pacific island I never heard of; his questions sounded critical. I've forgotten other details of that conversation, but I do remember being surprised that Humphrey knew so much about that island and that his answers seemed to surprise my colleague as well.

I remember the second meeting much better, perhaps because I better understood the issue, but probably because the subject got Humphrey riled up. The discussion revolved around Humphrey's support of decisions by a committee he was on; in fact, I think he chaired it. He was being criticized by conservative newspapers around the country because the committee had approved numerous loans to minority-owned businesses, some of which had subsequently gone out of business. I recall his voice rising, his face beginning to flush. I can't recall his exact words, but the gist of it went like this:

"They treat me like I'm a simpleton, like I don't know that these loans are risky, like I don't know that commercial banks wouldn't make them. Of course they wouldn't, and they shouldn't. The people we're trying to help need experience, and they can't get any because banks won't help them get started. It's not the function of banks to take chances with inexperienced businesses. That's exactly why the government needs to help them. How else are they ever going to get some experience?"

From that outburst he went back to ruminating about his critics. It was not that people disagreed with him, he avowed, that aggravated him. It was that they treated him as if he was mindless in the solutions he proposed.

"I'll tell you something that will surprise you," he said. "One of my best friends in the Senate is Barry Goldwater." He was certainly right; he surprised me.

He went on to explain their relationship. He claimed that their respect and friendship for each other stemmed from the fact that they generally agreed in their identification of the same problems. "Our disagreement comes in how we think the problems should be solved." He based his respect for Goldwater on the fact that "he doesn't content himself, as so many do, with just criticizing those of us who are trying to solve problems. He proposes solutions. If we disagree on what to do, we nevertheless understand that we are both trying, that we are motivated by the same objective."

I've taken liberties with my use of quotation marks, but I do remember leaving lunch that day thinking that I should always remind myself when I have a disagreement with someone to focus on the point of disagreement; don't allow yourself to begin questioning the motives or the character of the person just because you disagree.

More Table Talk

The Macalester dining room was the site of many discussions. There were several good reasons for me to stay on campus for the evening meal on Wednesdays. It was possible to arrange my schedule so that I could work in my study at home on Thursdays, the time that enabled me to write six books and take on other projects in the mathematical community. But since Fridays were quiz days in my classes, Thursdays were days when students were most likely to be seeking help with the past week's homework. I tried to address this problem not only by inviting phone calls to my home but by being in my office on Wednesday evenings.

It worked out well for another reason. Dolores went to choir practice at the church on Wednesday evenings. After practice, she'd pick me up at the office and we'd enjoy a Wednesday "date night" at a favorite ice cream parlor. Regular dates with your spouse are a very good idea.

Conversations with students over dinner are much different from those held over a steel desk in an office. I made it a point over the semester to have dinner with each of my advisees. On occasion I ate with the officers of the IVCF group. My habit was well known, so occasionally a student would stop in my office Wednesday afternoon to make an appointment for dinner that evening.

One student I remember well in this regard was Dan Ghura, an international student from Mauritius. Dan had great curiosity about the Christian faith. He would sometimes think for a week about one of our conversations and be around to set up another dinner the following week. I learned quite a bit about the faith by looking things up after a dinner with Dan, who was a Muslim.

Dan Ghura

Dan majored in economics, went on to get his Ph.D. in economics, and took a position with the World Bank in Washington, D.C. He maintained correspondence with me for years as he rose in the ranks of the bank. Once when I was walking along the mall in Washington, a big limousine pulled over to the curb, and out stepped Dan. I subsequently learned that he headed a division in the bank that numbered several hundred people who routinely travelled the world.

Not so long ago, our Economics Department invited him back as a distinguished lecturer. He told the chair of the department that when he came to campus, he wanted to have dinner with me. Those are the kind of students someone in my business cherishes.

My Introduction to the National Science Foundation

Near the end of my second year at Macalester, Ezra Camp, chair of my department, told me he had obtained a National Science Foundation (NSF) grant that would support six students in a summer research program. Explaining that he thought I would enjoy working with Dale Varberg from Hamline University, he hoped that we would jointly supervise the program.

Having written above about Ezra's expectations when he hired someone new for the department, this is the place to say that once in the department, a new person was supported in every way possible. There were conversations too numerous to recall that offered hints on classroom management, textbooks to consider, meetings to attend. You were pointed in directions that somehow fit your interests and abilities.

In thinking that I might enjoy working with Dale Varberg, he certainly thought right. He knew that Dale and I were both analysts, that we were both supportive of the IVCF chapters on our respective campuses, and that we seemed to enjoy talking to one another when we met at sectional meetings of the MAA. He might have suspected that we would become friends. He couldn't have known the extent of the collaborations that would develop, but he was the catalyst.

The six students with whom we worked that first summer were excellent students. By the time the summer was over, each one had chosen a function that exhibited a nonintuitive property of interest to analysts and had written a paper proving their peculiarities. The papers were bound and placed in the libraries of associated colleges, where they proved to be popular references.

Given the success of our program, it was natural that we propose to NSF that a similar program be funded the next summer. Camp thought that it would be a good experience for me to submit the next proposal. It was. I described in great detail an ambitious program, again for six students.

My proposal was rejected. Reviewers commented favorably

on the program but felt that the funds I had requested were insufficient to support all that I proposed to do. It was a mistake I never repeated.

The proposal I submitted the next year focused on convex functions. Convexity is a subject with a long history in numerous branches of mathematics: geometry, optimization, analysis, and more. A region of the plane is said to be convex if, given any two points in the region, their mid-point is also in the region. A similar definition defines a convex solid in space. Roughly speaking, a convex function of one variable is a function having a graph that holds water.

It is remarkable what can be proved about convex functions. As students combed through references, it occurred to Varberg and me that a great deal was known about convex functions, but the information was widely scattered throughout the mathematical literature. As the summer came to a conclusion, we began to think that a book about convex functions would be a useful addition to mathematical libraries.

The reigning expert on all facets of convexity at the time was Professor Victor Klee from the University of Washington in Seattle. We invited him to Macalester to show him the material that we, with the help of our students, had assembled. He was impressed, encouraged the idea of a book, and when informed that we both had sabbaticals coming up the next year, he invited us to come to Seattle, where we could make use of the extensive files he had accumulated over the years.

With this segue, I pause to describe the value of sabbatical leaves. It is a common

Victor Klee

courtesy observed in academia for schools, particularly research universities, to provide office space, library privileges, and free access to classes and seminars to faculty members on leave from their home institutions. Relieved of classroom teaching, committee responsibilities, and community involvements, the visiting scholar can focus on research, writing, or studying new branches of his or her discipline. Faculty members return to their home institution, perhaps having completed work on some topic they were working on over a period of years, perhaps having made new contacts in their area of specialty, and certainly having an updated view of new topics emerging in their field.

That is an idealized summary of what a sabbatical can mean to someone expected to keep abreast of ever-changing understandings of the world around us. It's certainly not realized by every person granted a sabbatical, and it's harder to realize if one's circumstances prevent a physical change in environment. In my years as a provost, I always encouraged getting away from campus responsibilities, campus politics, even from home routines to focus on whatever was envisioned as the sabbatical's purpose.

Our sabbatical experiences were certainly a boon for Dale Varberg and me. We decided that our children were at an age when they could appreciate the wonders of the national parks on a drive from Minnesota to Seattle. A joint cross-country camping trip was planned. It was the first step in a long process that developed valuable ties between our wives, our children, and our understanding of each other.

Sabbatical in Seattle

There was an initial hiccup when, just before we were to leave, Klee told us he had accepted an invitation to spend the coming year at an IBM research facility in New York. But it turned out to be a great benefit to us. He arranged for me to occupy his office in his absence and for Dale to be just across the hall. It gave us unlimited access to the three walls of file cabinets in his office.

It's not much of an exaggeration to say that in those files one could find histories of most of the papers written on the subject of convexity in the past several decades. Just as we had done with our idea for a book, someone would get an idea and send it to Klee for his comment. He would respond with suggestions, perhaps thereby initiating several exchanges before a finished paper would appear in a journal somewhere.

Klee's family did not accompany him to New York, so he returned at regular intervals. He always made time on these visits home to confer with us, answer questions, and read whatever we had written since his last visit. It could not have worked any better for us.

There were other benefits to being in the department. Klee's presence over the years had attracted other mathematicians with interest in convexity. Branco Grunbaum was a world expert on convexity as it appeared in geometry. Terry Rockefeller was a young mathematician building a reputation in convex analysis, and attending his classes greatly expanded our view of what should be included in an introductory text on convex functions. There was a weekly seminar on convexity that brought experts from around the world, and also made us aware of research going on by graduate students studying in the department.

Dale and I had an unusual working style as coauthors. We did not adopt the usual division of labor in which we each wrote certain chapters. We each wrote our own version of each section, then worked side by side to arrive at a final version—a version in which neither of us could point to a sentence and say, "I wrote that." Later, after years of writing together, we were invited to participate in a panel at the University of Minnesota for young coauthors. When someone asked if our style didn't result in numerous arguments, Dale said, "I can't recall that we ever had an argument, but sometimes we got to talking quite loudly."

It was at this conference where we told of our families camping together on the outer banks of North Carolina. One night, after everyone else had retired, Dale and I stayed up, using the light of a lantern in a screen house set up over a picnic table to work on a problem that had both of us stumped. It was quite late when, defeated, we retired to our respective tents.

A huge storm erupted later that night, blowing over the Roberts tent and giving us a soaking. The screen house also blew over, and being as wet as I could be anyhow, I put it back up and made it more secure. The next morning, I chided Dale a bit about not coming out to help me. He responded by telling me that the storm awakened him, but while lying in his sleeping bag, he had a new idea regrading our problem, and while I'd been working on the tents, he was able to solve the problem.

The story caused a wag in the audience to stand up and say, "That story shows that when you guys work on a problem, you can be in tents."

Getting a publisher for our intended book was not a problem. Because of my calculus book, I knew the editor at Academic Press, and unlike that one, an introductory text, our intended book on convex functions would fit quite naturally in their well-known Pure and Applied Mathematics series. The fact that it had the endorsement of Victor Klee sealed its acceptance.

One problem remained. The hospitality extended to us as visitors at the University of Washington did not extend to providing a typist for our manuscript. This being the days before scientific word processors were available on desktop computers, we considered renting an electric typewriter equipped to include familiar mathematical symbols. Neither of us was a skilled typist, however, and the intended book would still require inserting many symbols not included on available typewriters.

Recalling the training I received in the drafting room at the Commonwealth Edison Company as a budding engineer, I suggested to the editorial staff at Academic Press that I could handprint the manuscript. They assured me that no print shop would work from handwritten pages, but I submitted some sample work anyway.

To everyone's surprise, their printers agreed that they could work from such copy if it was all as neat as the samples I submitted. Thus, I took on the job of hand-lettering the entire book. I had 605 pages of meticulously lettered pages when I finished. I kept a copy for myself. It is the closest I have ever come to producing something that, in my mind at least, is a work of art. It still occupies a prominent spot on a shelf in my study.

Another Book

Even as I immersed myself in writing *Convex Functions,* a project of a very different character was forming in my mind. I was aware that my understanding of Christian faith had been challenged in multiple ways through four years of college, five years of graduate school, and six years of teaching in a liberal arts college.

- David Carley had made me realize that along with my Christian faith, I had in my youth embraced many economic, political, and social views that needed to be reconsidered. Subsequent reconsideration had been sporadic.

- The faculty Bible study in which I participated in my early years at Macalester had certainly made me aware that there were people who knew their Bible very well but understood much of what they read in ways different from what had been taught to me in my youth. I wanted to understand how people in different Christian traditions understood the common assertion that the Bible is the Word of God.

- Arthur Flemming based many of his actions on his belief that humans, created in the image of God, were basically good. He challenged me again and again to think about how my view of humans as basically sinful affected my thinking.

• A Curtis Akenson sermon reminded us that reports of possible personal failings of Martin Luther King in no way excused us from hearing his clear call for just treatment of Black Americans. I was reminded that I needed to come to grips with the fact that most of the Christians I knew, starting with the rioters in Cicero and continuing with me, were a long way back in the drive for civil rights then raging across the country.

• My church community was equating attitudes toward the Vietnam War with what it meant to be a Christian. It was a source of real distress, as I found that my support of protesting students on the Macalester campus was alienating me from friends in our church.

It seemed that the time had come to try to clarify my own understanding of Christian faith. Moreover, from lectures I'd been giving about deductive thinking, it was clear that I knew the place to start. I would begin by identifying my initial assumptions.

A few of my Christian friends thought it odd to say that my faith would rest foursquare on assumptions. I told them that not only was this the only way to build a coherent system of thought but that it followed the Biblical pattern. The Bible does not start with arguments trying to prove the existence of God; it starts with the grand assumption, "In the beginning, God . . . ." If you don't accept (assume) the existence of God, the rest of the book won't make sense.

When Moses asked who he should say sent him, the answer was, "I am." And to those who missed the message of the Old Testament, the New Testament states it plainly:

Without faith [assumptions] it is impossible to please Him, for he who comes to God must believe that He is, and that He is a rewarder of those who diligently seek Him. (Hebrews 11:6)

As I thought about how I might try to sort things out, I was reminded of Descartes' "rules for the mind" that had come up in a reading in the Man and His World course. Descartes decided as a young man that he wanted to develop a set of beliefs and guides for living, not based on what others told him but "to study my own self, and to employ all my abilities to try to choose the right path." I thought that he set forth a purpose identical to what I had in mind when he wrote almost 400 years ago,

> I did not wish to imitate the skeptics, who doubted only for the sake of doubting and intended to remain always irresolute: on the contrary, my whole purpose was to achieve greater certainty and to reject the loose earth and sand in favor of rock and clay.

Drawing an analogy with a man intending to build himself a new house, Descartes began by describing some rules he would observe while rebuilding his set of beliefs. After reading them through several times, I reformulated them as I thought they would apply to my purposes.

First, he advised that one should, while holding one's own belief system in abeyance, live as closely as conscience would allow in the intellectual house built for you by those who trained you as a youth. This would free you from the continual distractions that would come if those closest to you began to feel that they must argue and correct your new habits. To me, this meant that though I saw little connection between Christian faith and many of the rules of our fundamentalist church, I would avoid many hassles if I continued to eschew things which, by that time, held little attraction for me anyhow.

His second recommendation was to be sure, when examining the rules by which you would live, to seek principles to provide guidance, not rationales to provide justification for things already decided. That recommendation brought to mind an experience I had while a teaching assistant at the University of Wisconsin.

A student, raised in a fundamentalist home, came to my house after midnight and awakened me, ostensibly to raise questions about the rules given to the Israelites in the Old Testament. Was it not likely, for instance, that prohibitions against eating pork were intended not for religious reasons but for reasons of health, since lack of refrigeration in those days would have made trichinosis a real hazard. If so, he wondered, would it not make sense to set the rule aside today?

I allowed that it was an interesting question but not one you would expect to drive a student to your door after midnight. After an hour or so of discussion, the real question came to light. Might prohibitions of premarital intercourse have been a sensible rule for avoiding unwanted pregnancies, venereal disease, etc.—not a religious injunction? If so, wouldn't the availability of condoms similarly negate this as a religious issue? The question had come to him earlier that evening after an encounter with a young lady out on a pier on Lake Mendota. He was not in a position to consider the question dispassionately.

In his third recommendation, Descartes dealt with the possibility that while he expected to come to clear decisions on many questions, there would certainly be some questions about which it was hard to make a decision. For such situations, he drew an analogy with a person lost in the woods.

Such a person, he said, should draw on everything he or she ever learned about determining directions: how moss grows on trees, the position of the sun or the stars, etc. One should then decide on a direction to go and resolutely stay with that decision. Unlike the person who walks in one direction for a while, then in another, and then another, the person who stays the course will eventually come out somewhere. So, Descartes reasoned, when a decision is less than certain, one's best strategy is to consider alternatives as carefully as possible, make a clear choice, and then follow it as resolutely as you would follow the decisions you deem to be clear.

I began to develop notes for a book that I would eventually title *Assumptions and Faith*. I saw little difference between identifying something as an assumption or as something you take on faith. I see a great difference between saying you have decided to take something on faith and saying that you know it to be so.

This is not the place to summarize the arguments of that book. Suffice to say that I found writing that book very helpful to my own thinking. I do find myself sometimes at odds with earnest speakers, particularly at funerals, who assert that as Christian believers we know something to be so. I say to myself (but never to those who seem quite satisfied with the proclamation), "No. We assume that to be the case." Identifying my assumptions was consistent with my understanding of logic, and it seemed to me consistent with the Christian Scriptures as well.

Another Church Experience

Having written quite a bit about our church experience in Madison and the Twin Cities, it may be appropriate to comment here about the church we attended in Bellevue. It was our first experience with a mainline denominational church and left us thinking we may have more sympathy for Macalester's Presbyterian heritage than we realized. The preaching was good, a gifted young tenor frequently provided special music, and a highlight of the service each Sunday was a reading from the Psalms by a man whose brogue marked him as an import direct from Scotland. There was also a Sunday School class on church history, taught by a history professor from the University of Washington, that by itself would have made the church a good choice.

There was one contrasting experience, however, that stands out in memory almost 50 years later. We were invited to a social event that included about 20 adults our age, and somehow the subject turned to the "new math" that was then running its course in many of the nation's schools. "New math," with an emphasis on sets, truth tables, alternate number bases, and some basic axioms of algebra, was an innovation that educators hoped would take some of the mystery and rote manipulation out of mathematics. It befuddled parents who tried to help their kids with homework, and came under fire for all the reasons that generally emerge when something new is introduced in the schools.

It happened that night that we had in our midst a self-proclaimed expert who, lacking neither volume nor confidence, explained that the entire effort was a communist conspiracy designed to weaken the ability of young Americans to do useful mathematics. The effort was led, he said, by a pinko professor at the University of Wisconsin, the same place that had played a key role in introducing Social Security and other socialist programs in our country.

Aware of my standing as a guest in a circle of friends, I held my peace as long as I could, but not so long as my wife would have wished. Eventually I acknowledged that the current leader of the movement was from Wisconsin, Creighton Buck by name. I admitted that he had been my major professor but disputed the description of his pinko leanings, pointing out that he was generally thought of by his friends as rather conservative. He did not initiate new math, I said, but inherited leadership of the movement when, as an active member the Mathematics Association of America (MAA), he took on chairmanship of the Committee on the Undergraduate Program in Mathematics.

There would be little point in trying to recreate the ensuing conversation, even if I could remember it. Suffice to say that nothing I knew about mathematics, the MAA, or the people involved mattered. I do remember thinking on the way home of two quotations that have, over the years, come back to me in a variety of contexts. The first I read in an account of Jefferson's frustration with a colleague when the Declaration of Independence was being debated. The other I heard on multiple occasions from Curtis Akenson.

> Jefferson: To refute him was easy; to silence him, impossible.
> Akenson: Nothing is so vexing as a person who is certain of what ain't so.

The Sabbatical in Retrospect

Dale and I worked hard during the week, but weekends were another story. As our wives got to know each other and found that they had many common interests, they planned joint activities for our families every weekend. We camped in the mountains, hiked along the beaches, spent a weekend in the Olympic rain forest during the rainy season, saw young women clad in two piece bathing suits skiing on a sunny day in the mountains, and saw old fishermen clad in the rain gear of their trade as they arrived at wharves with the catch of the day.

That first sabbatical was a successful experience by any

measure. *Convex Functions* appeared in 1973. It received favorable reviews in all the mathematical journals, and letters from workers in the field were gratifying. The fact that it was volume 57 in a respected scholarly series guaranteed it would be purchased by libraries all over the world. I have succumbed to vanity and looked for it on library shelves when I've had opportunity to travel, and have found copies in England, Germany, Hungary, Israel, Korea, Malaysia, and Scotland. A list of about 25 suggestions for student investigation made it a valuable teaching tool for a number of years at Macalester.

Assumptions and Faith did not, of course, meet with such wide acceptance when it appeared in 1974. As soon as I got a copy, I took it to a colleague, Jerry Weiss. Jerry was an atheist, and students had learned that he and I provided lively entertainment when they invited us to debate on various subjects in dormitories or the chapel. The day after I gave him the book, while I was sitting in my office helping a student with his homework, Jerry stuck his head in my door and said, "Wayne, I stayed up half the night reading your book, and you are just as crazy as I thought you were."

With that, Jerry was gone. The student was nonplussed, unsure of what to say or do.

I said to him, "Professor Weiss is a wonderful scholar who reads widely and seems never to forget anything he has read. He is a formidable opponent in debate with a quick wit that I greatly admire. I would say he is an excellent teacher except that I think he has come to exactly the wrong conclusion on many of the major questions of life."

I have always been glad for the time I had in Seattle, in consultation with Dale Varberg, to work through my Christian faith. *Assumptions and Faith* has been the basis for discussions with many students and not a few members of churches I've attended.

Undoubtedly the greatest benefit of the sabbatical was the friendship Dolores and I developed with the Varberg family. Dale and I wrote papers and another book together, and discussed with each other the books we wrote independently. We arranged to spend two other sabbaticals together, and we often turned annual mathematics meetings into little trips accompanied by our wives, who became each other's best friend. When they got to college age, our sons bicycled through Europe together, and when we got to the age where we could afford it, Dale and I, with our wives, included some of the revered mathematical centers in our own trip to Europe. Our cooperation on numerous projects was surely a benefit to both Hamline and Macalester.

Dale Varberg and Wayne Roberts outside the Mathematics Institute at the University of Gottingen

V. Settling In

*It is always better to think of
a solution to new conditions
rather than complain about
changes beyond your control.*

A Changed Outlook

The climate when I returned from Seattle was much different from when I left. The Twin Cities newspapers that had been carrying stories of our drive to academic excellence had switched to describing what they saw as the results on campus of Arthur Flemming's permissiveness. We were the school that abandoned our Presbyterian heritage to become the center of sin, sex, and drugs in the upper Midwest. It was proving easier to recruit students from the far reaches of the country than from the upper Midwest, where our troubles were so well-publicized.

A new president, Jim Robinson, was in place, having come from the top administrative job at Ohio State University in Columbus. When I met him, I asked why he would leave a position at a major university to come to Macalester College. He told me that running Ohio State was like driving a freight train. The momentum just pushed you along the tracks set before you. "I wanted to come to a place where something would happen when I turned the wheel."

The idea of having some control was mostly an illusion. Saddled with accumulated debt, circumstances forced upon him one unpopular cut after another. Mr. Wallace did not resume his giving. A struggling institution has great difficulty attracting new supporters in the best of times, and these were not the best of times. Anti-war demonstrations and civil rights activism on campuses were alienating the nation from its institutions of higher learning.

In addition to the issues on campuses across the country, we had our own. We still had on campus a sizable group of Black students recruited under Flemming's EEO program. They understandably felt that the promises of financial support made to them when they came to Macalester should be kept, even in a time of slashing budgets. Racial tension added to our troubles.

It took less than three years for Jim Robinson to decide that it was better to be at a school forcing you down the rigid tracks in front of you than to be at one that seemed to be running off the rails. He announced he was leaving to assume the presidency of the University of West Florida. Any hint of progress in dealing with our problems had to be put on hold while we began another presidential search.

That search eventually brought John Davis to our attention. He was then superintendent of the Minneapolis schools, a most unlikely place for a liberal arts college to look for a president. While considering the job, he visited my office and (among other things) asked if the faculty would hold against him the fact that his Ph.D. was in education. By the time he asked that question, his warmth and earnestness had completely won me over. I told him that if he was savvy enough to know the prejudice that many liberal arts faculty members have toward education departments, I was sure he would have no trouble dealing with it. We couldn't have known it then, but years later, an issue of Macalester's alumni magazine would have a picture of Davis on its cover with the caption, "The Man Who Saved the College."

John Davis

The caption was right, but when Davis arrived in 1975, we were drifting perilously close to the financial rocks. It would take a number of years before Davis could right the ship. In the meantime, the excitement of being an institution on its way up had been replaced by what I might call a maintenance mentality: Can we keep from sinking?

A Holding Pattern

We began the 1972-73 academic year with six full-time faculty members in the Math Department. All of us had been hired by Ezra Camp, who had retired in 1969. Three of the six had been hired in 1968, and in those days of great expectations, no one would have guessed that the next tenure-track hire in the department would take place in 1982, and that hire was forced by the relentless pressure to obtain a computer scientist. We were not able to hire another mathematician until 1990.

Camp left the department well-balanced, able to keep up with a rapidly changing field in spite of not hiring another full-time mathematician for 21 years. The six of us covered the sub-fields of classical applications to physics and astronomy, algebra, real analysis, statistics, geometry, recreational problem solving, and number theory. Two of us were producing text books; one was editor of a national journal; we had one who regularly published significant research; and one, Alan Kirch, who regularly attended workshops and summer institutes to keep abreast of developments in the then-emerging field of computer science.

Among us, our interests covered most of what constituted a well-rounded mathematics curriculum. When developments in computing brought finite mathematics to a place of central importance, we combined our talents to introduce a new course to undergird the computing courses Kirch was teaching.

Anyone who goes to conferences designed for chairs of small departments hears the suggestion that one way to keep the department's faculty from getting isolated from research in their field is to hire a number of people in the same branch (analysis, algebra, topology, etc.) of mathematics. They should all be able to teach any undergraduate math course, and having specialties in the same area gives them people close at hand with whom to talk and collaborate. It is an especially attractive idea for people who want to see every faculty member involved in current research, and I have seen it work in a few cases around the country.

I have already argued that it is not reasonable to expect cutting-edge research from every member of a department in a small liberal arts college. No one will be surprised, therefore, to find me an advocate of a department such as we had, where the spread of faculty expertise gave students the opportunity to be exposed to the rich diversity that exists in mathematics. There is also reason to question the claim that anyone with a Ph.D. in mathematics should be able to teach any math course in the undergraduate curriculum.

I'e heard very convincing arguments that statistics, for example, should be taught by someone trained as a statistician, not by a mathematician. A mathematician is sure to lay emphasis on the algebraic skills used in statistics, and to skip the all-important topics of collecting unbiased data, deciding on the size of the sample to be used, choosing an appropriate estimation procedure, and more. The idea that anyone who knows college-level algebra can do an adequate job teaching statistics is easy to refute. In time we came to understand that the same was true of teaching computer science.

Finally, it's only when individual faculty members have allegiance to the good of the department rather than to their own specialty that they jump in to re-educate themselves when something new (like computing in our case, or like big data, to bring my examples up to date) comes along.

We would certainly have jumped at the chance to hire new colleagues as computing demanded new courses in our field, but that wasn't an option, given the financial condition of the college. Looking back, however, I realize that we enjoyed those days when it was up to us to keep the department current.

Part of keeping up, and much of our enjoyment, involved attending sectional meetings of the Mathematics Association of

America (MAA) twice a year. Leaving campus after Friday afternoon classes, the six of us would crowd into a car for a two- or three-hour drive to whichever campus was hosting the meetings. Conversation in the car would often include group appraisals of strengths and weaknesses of students majoring in our department, and sometimes resulted in developing a coordinated plan for the benefit of a particular student. Stories of what was changing in our various sub-disciplines also stimulated cross-fertilization in our courses.

Talk would continue over a late Friday night pizza when we arrived at the site of the weekend meetings. We invariably wound up with Joe Konhauser challenging the group with puzzle problems, of which he had an apparently inexhaustible store. His prowess as a problem solver was undiminished by the prodigious amount of beer he could consume.

Joe Konhauser

Needless to say, the congeniality of the department was an essential ingredient that made all this work. I knew of departments with personalities too much at odds to endure a two-hour ride in the same car. That's really too bad, not only because members of such departments are denied the enjoyment that accompanies working with close friends but because times spent in genial conversation can be a real benefit to the quality of education in a department.

Where conversation on the way to the meetings focused on individual students and the courses that we taught, we usually talked on the way home about what we heard in the different sessions we'd attended. In this way, questions were raised about whether some course in our curriculum should be revised, or whether we needed to add a new course.

Mathematics for the Liberally Educated

One frequent topic of conversation was the role that mathematics should play in a liberal arts education. It was a topic that surfaced every so often in faculty meetings when someone, always from another department, proposed that our graduation requirements surely should include a course in mathematics.

Our department always opposed the suggestion, arguing that such requirements have one of two predictable results. One is that the Mathematics Department becomes the ogre of the college, responsible for holding back some deserving student who could graduate and make wonderful contributions in, say, English literature. The other common outcome is for the Mathematics Department to design a course for math-phobic students that is watered down to the point where it is little more than a rehash of high school math. Students required to take such courses abhor them almost as much as those who are required to teach them.

Like many colleges, we did offer a course that was optional for nonscience students. It was a mish-mash of topics from high school algebra and geometry, together with some baby statistics. After teaching it once, I thought this surely could not be what Plato had in mind when he said that mathematics could purify and illumine the eye of the soul. It got me wondering just what topics should be included in a mathematics course that would make a real contribution to the education of a nonscience major.

The first thing that came to my mind, of course, was the segment on deductive reasoning that I had contributed to Man and His World. It's essential, I think, for an educated person to understand that any deductively organized system of thought must begin with undefined terms and assumptions. It's difficult, however, to grasp the idea that rigorous thinking involves the use of undefined terms and assertions that one cannot hope to prove. That is why, in my presentation in Man and His World, I began with assertions about pokes and lokes, words that would not stir up any preconceived ideas in the minds of my audience.

That may (or may not) have worked when our intention was to think about thinking. Leaving basic terms undefined or beginning with assumptions we don't try to prove is a much more difficult sell when trying to develop a logical basis for a political system, a religious faith, or a theory of economics. Mathematics is a wonderful place to underscore the essential components of deductive thinking, and I felt that this important idea would meet Plato's expectation that mathematics could re-illumine the eye of the soul.

I next thought of my reactions to a book, *How to Solve It*, by a famous mathematician, George Polya. Polya would pose a problem, discuss different ideas that might come to mind in an effort to solve it, and ultimately present a solution. He would then review the ideas that didn't work as well as the one that did, and from this review, he would distill those methods that had been tried. These ideas were accumulated in a list he called problem-solving heuristics.

Polya was thinking of mathematical problems when he wrote this enormously popular book, but it occurred to me that the heuristics he offered could be applicable to many problems that we grapple with in all phases of our lives. I thought one could use simpler problems to illustrate the same heuristics, summarize the heuristics in a list, and with each heuristic give a description of how it might be used in thinking about a nonmathematical problem.

Developing a collection of problems useful to my purpose took time. The puzzles Konhauser proposed in pizza parlors over the years were certainly a helpful start. My goal was to lead to a list of heuristics that might be useful to anyone, long after the problems that motivated them were forgotten.

When I described my ideas to Dale Varberg, he was soon contributing ideas of his own in response to what became our guiding question: What should a nonscientist who graduates from a liberal arts college know about mathematics? It was only natural that in time a book would emerge. We settled on four themes to include in our proposed answer. Thinking that a well-educated person should be able to name more than Euclid or Newton when asked to name an influential mathematician, we picked a notable mathematician to associate with each of our themes, and explained why he or she had been chosen.

I. Solving Problems. This consisted of the ideas described above. Of course we chose George Polya as our representative mathematician.

II. Finding Order. We described procedures for systematic counting and emphasized that there are laws associated with probability. We described ways to organize data, and the usefulness of algorithms, hinting at how computers are programmed. Leonard Euler, a mathematician whose collected works will fill about 75 volumes when completed, was our choice of a mathematician who could see order where others did not.

III. Reasoning and Modeling. Beginning with the material I had once developed to teach the rudiments of deductive reasoning, we went on to describe how systems developed with undefined terms and assumptions could prove useful in understanding the physical world. We aimed to develop an understanding of Einstein's observation that "All that we create is false," and Einstein was our choice of a mathematician who used theoretical constructs to understand the universe around us.

IV. Abstracting from the Familiar. Arithmetic on the clock, where 5+9=2 was used as one example of a number system abstracted from the familiar counting numbers. There are others, and in this section we tried to identify the rules used in ordinary arithmetic that, in the abstract, lead to other useful algebraic concepts. The natural choice to represent this work was Emmy Noether. Introducing her provided a place to emphasize the folly once indulged in by mathematics, as in other disciplines, of putting artificial barriers in the way of women.

We thought that *Faces of Mathematics* was a clever double entendre title for a book associating the faces of four mathematicians with four facets of our subject. We also felt that if the topics we selected replaced a rehash of beginning algebra, there would be a much better chance of realizing Plato's goal of using mathematics as a means of illuminating young minds. The book was published in 1978 and enjoyed enough commercial success to merit three editions.

The idea of incorporating linear algebra into a calculus book had been developed while I was still in graduate school, and I had time to write the book because a grant to the college enabled me to teach only half time in my first year. The initial ideas for the book on convex functions emerged from the NSF-sponsored summer institutes that Dale Varberg and I conducted, but the administrative burden I carried during the Flemming era would have prohibited writing the convex function book if it had not been for the sabbatical in Seattle. It was the almost total lack of administrative duty during the six academic years from 1972-73 through 1977-78 that enabled me to devote time to writing *Faces*.

My only significant administrative duty during my second six years was to write the report required for Macalester's accreditation review. This assignment came as a consequence of the load I carried during Flemming's last two years, and it was primarily discharged during the summer of 1975.

Accreditation

Colleges are reviewed on a 10-year cycle by their accrediting agency. It's important to colleges, of course, to be accredited, so colleges make serious preparation for this visit. Typically, they set up numerous ad hoc committees to report on the rigor of the academic program, the adequacy of the facilities (from the dorms to the science laboratories, from the gymnasium to the library), the financial management and stability of the college, and even some follow-up with graduates.

As luck (or bad luck) would have it, Macalester was due for such a visit just as we were in the presidential transition from Robinson to Davis. Moreover, we'd had three different deans of the faculty in the decade to be covered, including one change near the end of Robinson's tenure. In discussions to which I was not privy, the administration decided to bypass the usual appointment of committees. They asked me to prepare the required self-study of the college. Feeling that I did know a lot about the decade from 1965- 66 through 1974-75, sensing that I would learn a lot more, and pleased to get support for summer work, I agreed to the task.

I was flooded with reports: reports from each academic department covering the last ten years; reports from the Admissions Department (number of applications, number accepted, demographic description of each year's entering class); reports from the Development Office; a report from the Athletic Department detailing our brief hold on the national record for consecutive football games lost by an NCAA Division III school; financial reports; and much more.

This was the decade during which Macalester implemented its drive to nationally recognized excellence. It was fascinating to compare the planning documents from the early 60s with what transpired. It was interesting to read Garvin's strategy. I knew, of course, that he had made regular visits to top graduate schools in his effort to find promising young professors for the long haul. I hadn't realized that while on these visits he also sought to bring senior faculty to Macalester for short visits. While visiting, they lectured and offered advice, but perhaps more importantly they were made aware of the transformations underway at Macalester. It was a great way to spread the word of our ambitions in a hurry.

I also spent days poring over financial records. I learned about the High Winds Fund established by Mr. Wallace and named after his estate in the East. It had been his observation that many prestigious schools in the East found themselves in increasingly decaying neighborhoods. The idea of the High Winds Fund was to create an organization separate from Macalester, dedicated to maintaining its neighborhood.

If a house within a defined neighborhood of the college was put on the market, it was evaluated. If it was well-maintained, the policy was to let market forces prevail. But if the house needed repairs or updating, the organization bought it. Using Macalester tradesmen where possible, repairs and upgrades were made before selling it. Since renovations done this way often stretched over a year or two, the house would be a rental property while the work took place. Rents, coupled with price increases due to improvements and natural inflation, enabled the organization to do very well while maintaining a neighborhood of attractive housing.

I actually enjoyed writing the self-study. One of my idiosyncrasies is that I enjoy the challenge of bringing order out of chaos, and chaos is what I had when everybody dropped a report on me at semester's end. Organizing the material over the summer was made more enjoyable because I did not have a committee making continual changes as I went along.

I enjoyed reading the plans for the great leap forward that were made before I arrived in 1965. I enjoyed reading the different points of view people had about the past 10 years, but especially about the Flemming era. I enjoyed most of all the opportunity I had when school resumed to address the faculty the afternoon of the day the self-study was released to them.

It was a jovial crowd. They were pleased to have it recognized that they'd been the constant in maintaining a stable academic program over a 10-year period in which there had been three presidents, with a fourth about to start that fall, even more provosts, and numerous other changes in the top administration.

I called to their attention that in this same period, the second-level staff (administrative assistants, supervisors of admissions, the registrar's office, etc.) had remained unusually stable, and I got a big laugh when I followed that observation with the comment, "When one thinks about the work these people have done while top administrators came and went, one suspects that . . . well, never mind what one suspects." I did think the faculty was justified in feeling good when our self-study was praised for its candor by the evaluation team that recommended our continued accreditation.

That would be the end of the story on accreditation except for a matter related to the High Winds Fund. In my report, I noted that the system worked as planned. Its management had been questioned only once, when the fund bought some houses and then demolished them to provide land for a new college building. This had potential to become a source of disagreement when Mr. Wallace called a recess in his giving to the college. It also introduced me to the fact that colleges have lawyers to whom they must turn on occasion.

Soon after my report was published, I was told of an appointment set up for me by Bruce Kiernat, an attorney used by

Macalester. Unfamiliar with the ways of high-flying attorneys, I assembled the materials on which I based my report and appeared at his office, expecting to show him the basis for what I'd written. I was surprised when I arrived to be met by a secretary who had a statement, supposedly prepared by me, disavowing what I had written, saying that I'd misinterpreted some documents. I was asked to sign it. I objected, and offered to show Mr Kiernat the documents on which I had relied.

I was told that he was too busy to see me, so I left—without signing my confession to confusion. As I noted in discussing life in Miss Tucker's calculus class, there is a wonderful peace of mind that accompanies honesty.

I have come across Mr. Kiernat's name a few times since then. The last time I saw it was in a newspaper article describing some action, not involving Macalester, that threatened to land him in the penitentiary.

Two more activities in the department, undertaken during my second six years at Macalester, must be described as prelude to my second sabbatical.

My Introduction to Mathematics Competitions

My faithful attendance at section meetings of the MAA made me a candidate for assuming a responsibility for the MAA when I returned to Minnesota in 1973. The sectional officers asked if I would serve as Minnesota coordinator of the American High School Mathematics Examination (AHSME).

AHSME started as a regional competition in New York shortly after WW II. It grew slowly until 1957, when the MAA and the Society of Actuaries took it over and made it into a national exam with a goal of identifying the nation's best young mathematical talent. By 1972, over 350,000 students from Canada and the United States were taking the exam each year, and in 1972, the top scoring 100 students were invited to participate in the first USA Mathematical Olympiad.

The practice in Minnesota was that the MAA section would provide a coordinator one year, and the Minnesota Society of Actuaries would do so the next. The coordinator was to see that all high schools received an invitation and some follow-up encouragement to participate, collect registration fees, count out and mail exams ordered by each school, assemble results, and report state winners to the national MAA office.

So prestigious had the exam grown that some years before I was invited to take over, there had been an instance of egregious cheating in a small town in Minnesota. A teacher at that high school reasoned that if his students did extremely well on this exam, recognition of his prowess as a teacher would surely follow. The practice in those days was that answers as well as questions were sent to the supervising teacher in each participating school. The teacher was to grade the multiple-choice exams and report the scores. It was therefore a simple thing for him to alter a few choices here and there to achieve the desired results.

He was right about drawing attention. An inquisitive Minneapolis reporter noticed the results. He went to see what they were doing in this small town that resulted in their students doing so much better than those in the city schools. He soon discovered the reason for their uncommon success.

Minnesota then devised its own system of grading. Exams and duplicate answer sheets were sent in the initial mailing to schools so that student responses were recorded on an original and a carbon copy. The carbon copy of each student paper, postmarked on the day of the exam, was mailed to a cooperating actuarial office. Answer keys were then mailed out so that teachers could grade the exams from their school and send the paper of the top-scoring student to the actuarial office.

Volunteer actuaries then sifted through the carbon sheets from a school to find the copy for the top-scoring student, and verified the score. When I was asked to take over, there were about 700 participating schools in the state, and over 14,000 answer sheets were being sent to the office for checking. I was told that it was getting harder each year to get an insurance company to volunteer the services of its actuaries. I believed it.

This extra effort in Minnesota had an unexpected consequence that attracted national attention. The actuaries who rechecked the winning paper submitted by each school discovered that teachers who reported grades made an error on almost a third of the papers submitted. This was understandable, even if embarrassing. Problems on the exam were partitioned into four categories of difficulty, and were assigned point values of 1, 2, 3, or 4 accordingly. If there was no answer, 0 points were awarded, but if a wrong answer was given to a question worth n points, then n points were deducted.

Other objections were developing to using this grading system on a notoriously tough exam. The chief one was that teachers felt it was demoralizing to the many students who wound up with negative scores. Minnesota's reports of widespread errors in grading simply added to the pressure to simplify the system.

When the complexity of the Minnesota system was explained to me, I reasoned that we should be able to simplify things in an age when computers were appearing on the scene. I also reasoned that it would take more than one year to work the kinks out of computerizing the operation, so I said I would take on the responsibility if I could have the job for several years. No one rose to complain, and, as it turned out, I kept the job for the next 20 or so years until the national office (drawing heavily on our experiences in Minnesota) developed a system for scoring exams from across the country on one central computer.

Our first year was memorable. This was still in the days when computers worked by reading decks of punched cards. With the help of my colleague Allan Kirch (still our department's computer expert), we devised a card on which students could encode their name and then punch out small rectangles (called chads) to indicate their choice of an answer. We then ran these cards (about 14,000 of them) through Macalester's card reader, and had the computer calculate a grade for each.

The instant problem was that kids didn't punch out the chads cleanly. Hanging chads frequently caused the computer to misread what was intended, and chads that dropped off the cards blew through the reader like autumn leaves, with color produced by the operator who had to periodically stop proceedings to rake out the confetti.

We wound up having to visually inspect each card as they came in and poke out the hanging chads before we could run a deck. It turned out that Florida used punch cards for a national election that year, and the whole nation had to wait on Florida (even in those days) while they struggled with hanging chads. We were more sympathetic than most of the nation.

Things got better as scanners were developed to read pages on which bubbles were filled in with a dark pencil, but these were in use for several years before Macalester got a scanner. We were obligated to take our sheets to be scanned during night hours at the computer center at General Mills.

At this point, I shall digress a bit. I have in the preceding paragraphs made reference to what we did. In places the reference is to Alan Kirch, on whom I relied heavily for all manner of help related to use of the computer. For everything else, I was greatly helped by a Macalester student, Karla Ballman.

In my first years of teaching, I always declined the help of a student assistant. Colleagues used assistants to grade homework, record grades, etc. As explained elsewhere, I did not collect homework, preferring to give quizzes every Friday and grade them myself. I felt that in this way I became much better acquainted with each student and saw clearly when some idea needed to be reviewed in class.

It was the monumental workload imposed by the AHSME that forced me, in my 8th year on the faculty, to ask for student help. Karla was enrolled in my first-year calculus course, where I noted her work habits and requested her as an assistant. She's the one who taught me just how helpful a student assistant could be.

Karla was the one who counted out and mailed the 14,000

exams, opened envelopes and filed punched cards when they came back, helped clean chads from the card reader, and later nursed the scanner through reading the 8 ½ x 11 sheets that, in those early days, occasionally turned sideways as they left the feed tray, folded themselves around rollers, and generally misbehaved. She worked in my office for four years, and that turned out to be just the beginning of a long professional relationship. Her name recurs in chapters to come.

About 50 years have gone by since we first worked together. There is much in the news as I write about the MeToo movement that has women coming forward from all walks of life to describe ways men took advantage of them in one way or another. It seems worth saying that when men make a woman around them feel uncomfortable or debased, it not only affects her life but almost surely disrupts what could otherwise be a long and fruitful relationship.

There is no way I could have anticipated, when Karla was a student, that I would know her through a long and successful career, but I have every reason in looking back to be pleased that we worked with mutual respect and good humor in those early days of long hours, sometimes late into the evening. Not everything was to go as we would have wished in the years to come, but we did not have to deal with awkward memories from the past.

The most interesting thing I learned as I got into the routines of Minnesota's AHSME coordinator was not about the developing computing machinery but about the scores of the top students in our region. For administrative purposes, the U.S. and Canada were partitioned into 10 regions, Minnesota being in a region consisting of the Dakotas, Iowa, and parts of both Wisconsin and Manitoba, Canada. The surprise was that the top-scoring students in our region would not have received honorable mention had they been in any other of the 9 regions. I found by checking that this had been consistently true for many years past.

This was surprising, not only to me but to people with whom

I shared this information. Some, knowing that Minnesota's spending per student in its precollege educational programs compared favorably with other states, were convinced that my data were wrong. The vice president of Sperry Univac, the company that had for many years sponsored a lunch and tour of its facilities for the top-scoring students from around Minnesota, was very surprised. As I shall subsequently relate, he responded in very substantial ways.

I Get Some Lessons in Applied Mathematics

The other significant activity in which I engaged during this six-year period was the continuation of the NSF-sponsored summer undergraduate research program that had first brought Dale Varberg and me together. Naturally, when we returned from Seattle with the *Convex Functions* book full of topics suitable for undergraduate research, we wanted to use them. Since we were building on the results of previous support, it was easy to get support for the first summer after we were back. That happy state of affairs might have lasted two summers. It wasn't too long, however, before things changed drastically.

These were the years of Jimmy Carter's presidency, and the nation was faced with soaring gasoline prices and great concern about looming energy shortages. In this context, NSF announced that any request for research support would have to address the nation's energy problem. The guidelines were written to make it clear that only schools with major engineering schools would be in a position to apply.

I joined colleagues from liberal arts colleges around the country to protest the decision. We noted that undergraduate research was primarily a training experience, that it would be short-sighted to cut funding to schools that trained a substantial number of the undergraduate students who went on to study science in graduate schools. This proved futile, of course; you can't fight city hall and you certainly can't fight NSF. We went without funding that year.

It is always better to think of a solution to new conditions rather than complain about changes beyond your control. Given a year to think about it, I did devise an alternative program.

I had, after all, come to Macalester because it was located in a major city. Why, I wondered, couldn't we develop research experiences for students in cooperation with Honeywell, 3M, Sperry Univac, Control Data, Cray Research, and many lesser-known research companies that had their headquarters in our area?

It turned out to be easy to find scientists and engineers who would like to teach a student, and in talking to them, we decided that a common theme of operations research could be used to give the program reasonable cohesiveness. We decided that during the first two weeks of the summer, mornings would be used to teach a course describing the field of operations research. Afternoons would be used for representatives from cooperating companies to describe a research project or two under way at their place of employment. Students then listed in order of preference three projects to which they would like to be assigned.

Students were assigned to a project for the next 8 weeks. On Monday through Thursday, they went to the site of the cooperating company or agency. On Fridays, students and their supervisors came to campus for a seminar to explain their projects, describe progress over the past week, and share ideas.

NSF acknowledged that it was a good idea, but they were reluctant to provide stipends to students who were working at private companies. We argued that the companies were providing professional supervision and the time of the supervisor who would be coming to campus one day a week. Moreover, the arrangement would allow us to insist that students not be assigned to data entry or some other menial job where, while undeniably doing something useful for the company, they would not be learning much mathematics.

We strengthened our proposal in one other way. Macalester belonged to the Associated Colleges of the Midwest: Beloit, Carleton, Coe, Colorado, Cornell, Grinnell, Knox, Lake Forest,

Lawrence, Macalester, Monmouth, Ripon, and St. Olaf. We were the only college situated close enough to industrial and governmental research labs to make such a proposal as ours work. It was easy to secure the cooperation of the associated colleges in applying for the grant, understanding that we would consider applications of students from all the schools.

Other negotiations were necessary. I had to replace Dale Varberg with Alan Kirch from our faculty as a co-supervisor because virtually every project involved computers. We had major problems working out details with personnel offices of the organizations involved, addressing such issues as whether their insurers would cover nonemployees on the premises, access of students to proprietary information, and more. Eventually, however, we got our funding, so perhaps it was not quite fair when I said above that you can't fight NSF. The fact is that NSF has been flexible and has been a great asset to this country.

The theme of operations research agreed upon by representatives of the cooperating organizations is a broad field. Roughly speaking, it draws upon mathematics to improve decision making or operating methods in managing complex systems. It emerged as a discipline during WW II and grew rapidly after the war. The breadth of the field is suggested by just a few of the issues we addressed over the summers that we ran our program:

- The 3M Company makes Scotch Tape by coating a transparent tape as it is pulled through a machine. The process must be monitored to be sure the viscosity of the coating stays consistent: too thin, and the tape is not sticky enough; too thick, and the machine gums up. The speed of the tape and the monotony of the process render human observers useless. The output of high-resolution cameras trained on the moving tape makes a perfect coating, when it is wet, look like the surface of the moon. The goal is to teach a computer to process camera pictures and recognize when things are running normally, and when adjustments are needed.

- A medical research lab wanted to test the hypothesis that breast cancer could be detected by temperature variations in cancerous tissue. Thousands of heat-sensitive photographs were available, coded as to which were from women with cancer. The challenge was to have a computer pick out the pictures taken of women with cancer. (So far as I know, this never worked. Some ideas don't.)

- The Federal Reserve Bank was in those days (circa 1975) trying to develop computers that could read and process checks exhibiting all the variation in handwriting that humans employ.

- The Metropolitan Transit Authority had three bus barns located throughout the Twin Cities. A fourth was to be built. Several sites were available throughout the metro area. Hundreds of buses make thousands of trips in and out of the barns each week. Where should the new barn be located so as to minimize the so-called deadhead miles the buses traverse getting to and from their various routes? And which buses go to which barns?

- Why does it happen that buses leaving one end of the line at 20-minute intervals sometimes wind up bunched together as they approach the other end? What instructions should be given to drivers when they realize they are getting bunched? The challenge was to create a computer simulation that would enable schedule makers to try various ways to tweak the system.

The first three examples, besides having occurred in the program's first year, had another thing in common. All three involved what is called pattern recognition. When I realized this, I looked for an expert in getting a computer programmed to identify certain patterns in a picture. It took some hunting. I finally found someone in the school of forestry at the University of Minnesota. He was working at identifying areas of diseased trees from aerial photographs. His lecture to the group on one of our Friday morning meetings was of as much interest to the supervisors as it was to the students.

NSF was quick to see the value of our program. In 1977 *Change Magazine* cited our program as one of the nation's most 25 innovative programs in economics, mathematics, and philosophy. Beneficial as it was to the participants, it may have been more beneficial to me.

I realized as we got deeper into the program each summer that my training in mathematics had been highly theoretical, that I knew very little about applications, especially modern applications of mathematics. I was learning a great deal as I moved about the Twin Cities looking for organizations with which we could work.

I was also coming to realize how little I knew about operations research, an emerging field in mathematical studies. That was true for my colleagues in the department as well, and as previously noted, we were as a group trying to fill gaps in our program as we saw them. These were the considerations that led me to go to the operations research department at MIT for my second sabbatical.

Finally, it was in developing this program that I came to know a good many leaders of the mathematical research that was going on in industrial, medical, and governmental organizations in the Twin Cities. Many of them were surprised to find that students in a liberal arts college were interested and even eager to participate in applied science. And though I certainly did not realize it at the time, I would, upon returning from my sabbatical, be very grateful for all the contacts I had made among the nonacademic mathematicians in our state.

A Sabbatical Year at MIT

Our first lesson in Boston concerned housing. Having been warned that the rent we could get for our house in St. Paul would not pay the rent on a house in Cambridge or even in the nearby Boston area, we ran an ad in the *Boston Globe* describing our needs. Only one answer described a house in our price range. It was an old family summer home located on the ocean front in Manchester, a small town north of Boston. The house was not used in the winter, they said. It was described as being about an hour's drive from the MIT campus (which we found out was true on Sunday mornings), but convenient to the B & M commuter railroad.

The long commute, I reasoned, would be forbidding if I were making a career move. But for one year, during which I could arrange my schedule to go to campus on Monday, Wednesday, and Friday, the experience of living on the ocean front seemed irresistible, and the price was in our range. We rented it, sight unseen.

When seen, it was a sight. The house had an obvious tilt from the outside that manifested itself on the inside, where doors that had remained rectangular over the years didn't fit into frames that had faithfully tilted with the house. Not only would doors not close but they wouldn't sit in an almost-closed position, the tilt being so pronounced as to cause them to drift open. At my wife's insistence, before unloading anything from our car, I drove to the nearby town to buy tools necessary to fix the bathroom door so that it could be shut. Firmly.

There were other problems: grimy floors from sand and dust blowing through doors, some windows that wouldn't open, others that wouldn't quite shut, and clear evidence that the owners came to the beach house to enjoy the beach, not to clean and paint the house. Most of those problems were fixable, however, and except for the outrageous bill for heating this summer shelter during the winter, we soon came to love our house.

It was actually on a cove, separated from the beach by a narrow stone road. We came to appreciate the art of the men pulling lobster traps just yards from the picture window in our kitchen. I wrote in our Christmas letter that year that living so close to the beach, we saw those who love the sun by day, and those who love each other by night. We learned to regulate the times of our walks by the tide tables, and we enjoyed from second-story windows the waves that an occasional storm produced.

Academic Life

At the operations research center at MIT, I was treated with all the courtesy and provided with all the support one could imagine. I was given a desk in the main office, guaranteeing that I would see all members of the department on a regular basis. In the first term, I attended a course entitled Finite Optimization.

By explaining just a bit of what is meant by finite optimization, I can once again buttress my argument for the usefulness of sabbaticals, and at the same time respond to people who wonder how there can possibly be anything new to learn in mathematics.

Optimization is, of course, a process for finding the best way to do something. In mathematics, it often involves finding the value of a variable that gives the best possible result. An example is in order. Figure A and Figure B each show a cone inscribed in a sphere of radius 1. The cone in Figure A is drawn to look as if the radius of the base of the cone is $r = 1/4$; in Figure B, it is drawn as if $r = 1/2$. Clearly, the volume of the cone in Figure B is larger than the one in Figure A.

It is equally clear that any choice of r between 0 and 1 yields a cone; our choices for r are infinite in number. The optimization problem asks for the value of r that gives the largest possible volume for the inscribed cone. It's a question for which the calculus is perfectly suited.

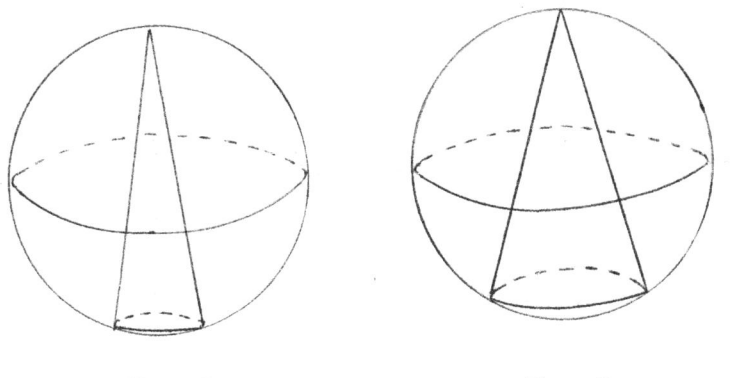

Figure A   **Figure B**

Any student in a calculus class (we speak hopefully here) should know how to determine that the biggest volume for a cone is given by

$$r = \frac{2\sqrt{2}}{3} \approx .943$$

For many problems, the methods of calculus will point to two or three values that might be optimum. In such cases, one can simply try each possibility to see which one gives a value that is biggest (or smallest, if that's what is desired). When this happens, mathematicians feel that the work is done.

Mathematicians, thinking in this context, are likely to say, "When finding the optimal value is reduced to choosing between two or three possibilities, the problem is solved." That is certainly the way I was brought up, mathematically speaking. I learned in the Finite Optimization class at MIT that they occasionally used this phrase in derision.

Of course I should have known better. The problem of locating a new bus barn that we encountered in the undergraduate research program puts to rest forever the idea that a problem is solved when one only has to choose among a finite number of possibilities. In that case, one can begin by picking one of the several sites under consideration. Then for each of the hundreds of routes, and for each of the four barns (the three existing barns plus the new one under consideration), calculate the deadhead distance (the distance a bus must travel from the barn to the beginning of the route, and then the distance back to the barn from the end of the route). On the basis of these calculations, decide which routes are to be serviced from which barns. Finally, determine the total number of deadhead miles to be covered if that site is chosen for the new barn. Then do the same calculation for each of the other sites under consideration.

The number of calculations is, to be sure, finite. So, unfortunately, are the life spans of those who do the calculating, and the sheer number of calculations to be made seems forbidding, even with a computer.

There are many practical problems for which optimization would involve considering a mere finite number of possibilities, that mere number being so large as to preclude anyone from attempting it. Why was it that I (and so many students over many generations) got through years of formal training in mathematics without realizing that finite optimization is a most difficult area? It may be that some students did confront the difficulties inherent in finite optimization, but most of us did not. The problem was passed over, I suspect, because there were no techniques such as the calculus that could be used to solve them. We tend to direct our attention to problems we'd have some idea how to solve. Certainly the advent of computing machinery made these problems more tractable, but in many cases the finite number of possibilities is too large for even a computer to try all the possibilities.

I did learn a variety of techniques that are helpful in certain problems having "only" a finite number of possible solutions. More important, I learned to see such problems in the world around me, to point them out to students and not say stupid things about them. Finite optimization became an area from which a number of student honors papers were drawn at Macalester in future years.

In my second term at MIT, I took a course that focused in large part on another problem I had encountered in our summer research program. It arises in any city having a number of traffic signals on a heavily traveled thoroughfare. The problem, when not addressed by traffic engineers, irritates every driver. Why can't they fix these lights so that if I move along at a constant speed, each one turns green as I approach it?

Drivers know that it can be done because on occasion they experience it. It's more of a trick than they might imagine, however, because there is typically a grid of streets; getting a couple of north-south streets correctly regulated will clash with getting the east-west streets similarly regulated. Considering a car moving around a block reveals the problem. It was in the context of this problem that I was introduced to the idea of integer programing. I never mastered much of it, but I did understand why it was needed for the traffic light problem. I learned enough to develop a talk that I titled "Eliminating Red Light Districts."

I had by this time developed enough of a reputation as a writer to be invited by a publisher to write a textbook for a standard linear algebra course. I signed a contract, and the writing occupied me on the days that I stayed in Manchester rather than riding the train to campus.

It was a bruising experience. For the first (and last) time, I had an editor who was himself a mathematician. Each chapter sent to him came back with suggestions for another approach, a different proof, etc. Many of his suggestions were good, and I wound up writing, rewriting, and then rewriting again. When I finally finished the book that I never would have started without his encouragement, his publishing house wrote to tell me that they had decided to withdraw from publishing mathematics texts.

I never knew whether they really wanted out of mathematics, or he simply decided he didn't like what I'd produced. In either case, with a contract in hand, I thought they owed me something for producing a book they requested. They pointed out that the contract said they would publish the book after I produced a manuscript acceptable to their editorial staff.

Incensed, I wrote to the editor with whom I had worked at Academic Press to ask if he had any advice for me. He was very kind, but in the end his advice was clear. Publishers cannot promise to publish a book until they have in hand a manuscript they are convinced will sell. However the contract looked to me, he assured me that it had been drafted by lawyers with the interests of the publisher in mind. His advice was to get over it and then set about finding another publisher. It was good advice; it was all a good lesson. I didn't like it.

Some new mathematics learned, an interesting talk ready to use when invited to give guest lectures, a book manuscript ready to circulate to publishers: a good if rather standard list of accomplishments for a sabbatical leave. But one more thing happened on this leave that had a major impact on the rest of my career.

I Learn about Math Leagues

After we settled into our house on Boston's North Shore, it occurred to me that we were living fairly close to Hamilton-Wenham High School, a name familiar to me because it frequently appeared on the list of high-scoring teams in the AHSME examination. I decided to visit.

Having lived in the Chicago area as a youth and in the Twin Cities of Minneapolis-St. Paul as an adult, my first impression of Hamilton-Wenham as I pulled into its parking lot in the fall of 1978 was that it was a surprisingly small school. Indeed, I learned from administrators that they felt the school was too small to offer an enriched mathematics program, so, for example, they offered no advanced placement calculus course. They also told me that on Boston's North Shore, they suffered financially from their inability to pass a school bond issue in a community where so many families sent their children to private schools.

The obvious question to ask was, "How does a small school, pinched for funds and offering a bare-bones mathematics program, manage to do so well on the AHSME as to come to the attention of someone living in the Midwest?"

The answer was quick: "We are very active in a math league."

I had never heard of a math league, but the idea intrigued me. I learned that math leagues had grown like Topsy up and down the East Coast after World War II. Before I returned to Minnesota, I had visited competitions (they called them meets) in several leagues that operated in Massachusetts.

The easiest way to describe a math meet is by comparison with a track meet. There are typically four or five events scheduled, but instead of a hundred yard dash, a pole vault, and a shot put, the events might be story problems, quadrilaterals, trigonometric equations, and conic sections. As in a track meet, so in a math meet, students don't enter all events but prepare only for the events they will enter.

Students in a particular event are given a list of questions dealing with the topic for that event, and they get points for each problem they solve within the allotted time. The rules specify how many team members can enter an event, and the team's score in the event is simply the total of the points earned by its members.

Unlike track meets, the events change from one meet to another, so if four topics are covered in a meet, then twenty topics can be covered in a series of five meets in a year. Another variation of a math meet is that it typically ends with a team event in which all members meet together in a room. They are given a list of questions, most of which focus on topics of the individual events of the day. Team members may cooperate in any way they wish, but at the end of the allotted time, they turn in just one list of answers. Here the team score is the sum of the points allotted for each correct answer.

From talking to experienced teachers (who were called "coaches" by the students), I distilled a list of guidelines that I thought should be used if we were to start a math league in Minnesota. They are worth repeating as a context for further things that I wish to say about math leagues.

1. Have schools come to a common site for meets, as opposed to having teams taking exams at their home schools and reporting results to a central office. There is great value to bringing together the best mathematics students from several schools. They find there are other students who actually enjoy mathematics, and seeing how others work at it challenges them.

2. Design your rules so that a school that happens to have a little Isaac Newton does not immediately get far ahead of the competition. Don't, for example, let any one student participate in every event, and don't weight the hardest questions (the ones that only little Isaac is likely to get) with a lot of points. Make the rules so that an exceptionally talented student who really gets interested in the competition sees that the way to help his or her team win is to recruit other able students and help them develop their talents.

3. Let a team bring alternates, students whom the coach did not enter as a team member in any event that day. Let alternates choose events to enter, selecting as many events as they could enter if on the team. Alternates who earn points get to add them to their individual season total, even though their points don't count toward the team's total for that day. It also gives the alternates a chance to show their coach the error of not having put them on the team that day.

4. See that coaches from unsuccessful schools feel encouraged by the other coaches; try to help such schools become competitive.

5. Do all you can to be sure that coaches are paid extra for their work. Administrators don't take seriously any activity in their school that doesn't cost anything.

Family Life

I have argued that sabbaticals provide a great benefit to both an academician and to the home institution. They also provide some wonderful opportunities for a family to come together in ways not so likely to happen at home, where everyone has their own friends, activities, and obligations.

Having begun my account of our year in Boston with a description of the deficiencies of our house, I'll end by saying how much we came to love life on Kettle Cove. Following essential repairs to the bathroom door already described, I made a number of minor repairs to doors, latches, window casings, loose trim, etc. Dolores washed all the silver adhered to the drawer with dried jelly, and went on to apply a much-needed coat of paint to the kitchen cabinets. In time, our cat had the mice at bay, and we washed the windows that provided a view of the cove. We all came to enjoy watching the lobster men at work, walking the beach at low tide to see what had been washed up, and driving up to Gloucester to enjoy the catch of the day for dinner.

After we had been there six weeks or so, the owner stopped by to see how we were doing. He walked in, looked around a bit, and said, "My God, we should have rented to you people years ago." When I showed him a candle-lighted lantern that I'd found in a shed and cleaned up, he told me I could keep it. Forty years later, it sits on a table in the entryway of our house in Minnesota, a reminder of our year living in a beach house.

Maxim #1: Always try to leave a place a little better than you found it.

We'd heard that we would find New Englanders a bit "standoffish," but that was not our experience. Neighbors were congenial. On the day of the biggest storm of that year, I got a call about 4 a.m. from a neighbor on the hill behind us. "Mr. Roberts, is your car down there?" When I answered affirmatively, she said, "The water is already high, the tide is coming in, and it's being blown by a real gale. You get out there right now and get your car up here in our yard." It was good advice. Large rocks, too heavy for me to lift, were soon being tossed into our front yard. The local paper ran a picture of our house surrounded by water the next day.

As spring came, we suggested to a group we had gotten to know at the North Shore Community Church that they come to our place for a cookout on the beach. We were surprised to discover that almost everyone present could instantly produce from a wallet or purse a tide chart that they deemed indispensable for planning something on the beach. We also learned to boil fresh lobster in vats of water scooped from the ocean.

Maxim #2: He that hath friends must show himself friendly. (Proverbs 18:24)

We were sorry to leave it all behind, but the kids were looking forward to getting back to their own school, Dolores was beginning to feel the isolation of life, even in the beauty of the cove, and I was looking forward to introducing a math league in Minnesota,

Maxim #3: It's always good to have something to which you look forward.

VI. A Math League for Minnesota

*Relationships worth having are worth
intentional efforts to maintain.*

A Special Program for Special Students

As I compared myself to the top students that I observed in my mathematics classes during my formal education, two things were quite clear to me. First, there always seemed to be a few in any class who caught on to new ideas more quickly, worked more accurately, and did a little better than I did on classroom tests. Second, I could maintain a spot near the top of the class with consistent study and with very good work on papers assigned to do at home.

I recall occasions in high school when graded tests and papers were returned that some guy would say something like, "You're lucky, Roberts; you get this stuff." And I was lucky. I came from a stable home where loving parents instilled a good work ethic in me, I had good teachers, and I had a mind that generally saw the logic of what was explained to me. I don't think that in those days I was properly thankful for all those things. What I remember is that I wanted to say (but of course never did), "Part of my luck comes from doing homework at night when you're out cruising for chicks." (To use the phrase they used to describe their evenings).

I've already described the effort it took for me to stay in the game in graduate school. I've often said to students who expressed dismay over how much effort they had to put into their homework, "I understand; I stand before you as an example of an overachiever."

In short, my idea was that there are people who seem to have a real knack for mathematics, but sooner or later, as they get deeper into the discipline, everyone comes to a point when they must add hard work to their innate talent. Nothing had ever prompted me to ask if students with interest and talent in mathematics should receive special training along the way.

It wasn't until I began comparing the top scores earned on the American High School Mathematics Examination (AHSME) that it occurred to me that certain parts of the country, and certain schools with names I was beginning to recognize, were consistently doing more for their mathematically talented students than was being done elsewhere—in Minnesota, for example. My exposure to and then involvement in math leagues got me thinking about what should be done for academically gifted young students of mathematics.

I have now been involved in trying to answer that question for 40 years. In this chapter, I try to describe what I think I've learned; and as I reflect on the conclusions that I have drawn, it seems to me that much of what I've concluded would apply to programs for academically gifted high school students in most disciplines. That's my reason for writing so much on the topic.

Getting Started

I found, when I returned to Macalester after my year in Boston, that things had not turned around for the college as quickly as we all hoped when John Davis assumed the presidency. He, and the college he served, remained proud of our much-publicized effort to make a liberal arts education accessible to minority students. The underfunded EEO program he inherited, however, was a part of the financial problem, exacerbated by Mr. Wallace's diminished support. As Vietnam War protests and civil rights activism continued to disrupt campuses across the country, colleges lost much of their hold on the respect of the American people. It seemed harder than ever for Davis to deal with the local perception that Macalester had become the center of drugs, sexual revolution, and racial agitation in the upper Midwest.

It was a propitious time for me to suggest to Davis that I use Macalester as the base from which to start a Minnesota State High School Mathematics League. He would have been supportive of anything that would raise Macalester's standing in the eyes of local observers, and as the former superintendent of Minneapolis schools, he was immediately supportive of the college doing something for secondary mathematics education in Minnesota.

He knew Ross Taylor, mathematics coordinator for Minneapolis schools, and knew Jack Nichols, a vice president at Unisys, the company that had long sponsored the awards luncheon for Minnesota's top scorers on the American High School Mathematics Examination (AHSME). He offered to host a luncheon at which I could document the need to improve instruction for our top mathematics students and explain the concept of a mathematics league. To his list of invitees, I added Chuck Lund, the mathematics coordinator of St. Paul schools, and mathematics teachers from two schools in each of the two districts.

This group was quick to see from the statistics I presented that the best AHSME scores being attained in Minnesota were consistently lower than the top scores in other regions of the country. The idea of a math league challenging our best students had instant appeal. Based on what I'd seen in Massachusetts, I suggested a season of five meets, each having four individual events and one team event. I said I liked the idea that the first individual event cover a topic normally taught in 9th grade, the second covering a topic from 10th grade, etc. The group was amazingly amenable.

Jack Nichols asked how much I thought it would cost to get a league started. I said I didn't like asking secondary teachers to take on another task with no extra compensation, that we would need to run a bus to bring teams to a common site, and that we wanted to have refreshments at each meet. The teachers present agreed that an annual stipend of $1,000 for coaching seemed reasonable, and Jack Nichols wrote out a check for $5,000 on the spot. With great aspirations, we decided to call our creation the Minnesota State High School Mathematics League (henceforth in this chapter, the League).

I agreed to write questions for five meets so that we could start in 1980. It was the last time I offered to write the questions with no compensation. Four questions for each event, four events and a team event of six questions at each meet came to 22 questions per meet. For five meets, it was a month's work by the time I had them printed up and ready to distribute.

As a result of having coordinated the AHSME exam for several years, I had gotten to know, in many schools throughout the state, a teacher who was interested in identifying and working with kids talented in mathematics. I drew on this information when selecting the four teachers to come to our initial luncheon, but even so I underestimated the zeal and energy of the people with whom I was working. When the original four teams (and I) arrived at Edison High School in Minneapolis for our first meet, we were met by the school pep band and a group of cheerleaders who had written cheers for the occasion. I had never stopped to think how many words rhyme with pi.

We like to win
At Edison High.
Let the figuring begin,
We'll eat your pi.

The League was launched with great enthusiasm.

As we neared the end of that first season, one coach got a call from the librarian at his school. "What," she asked, "was being done differently in the Mathematics Department this year?" He asked what prompted her inquiry. She explained that shortly after the Russians launched Sputnik in 1957, the district had provided extra funds to put some mathematics books in the library. She had dutifully purchased a number of math books, but since students in mathematics classes rely entirely on their texts for problems and explanations, no one ever checked them out. "But this year, several students have been checking them out regularly."

We didn't anticipate parental endorsement, but we got several notes that said something along the lines of, "My kid isn't into athletics and really didn't get involved in extra activities in school until the Math League came along. It's awakened a new interest in school for him/her. We appreciate it."

Cautious Expansion

The coordinators in the two districts were impressed after the first year, and saw that teams were formed at all 13 of the schools in the Twin Cities for the 1981-82 season. Also, since I had Macalester's backing, I went to the development office to see what ideas they might have for raising money to support expansion beyond the Twin Cities. They introduced me to the Blandin Foundation, formed with paper mill money and dedicated to improving educational opportunities in the northern part of the state where they operated. With their financial help, we also started in 1981-82 a division of eight schools on Minnesota's Iron Range.

Word of mouth made it easy in 1982-83 to add a third division of schools from the northern suburbs of the Twin Cities, with the definition stretched enough to include one school from Duluth. Duluth East was eager enough to participate that they agreed to make the 150-mile drive down to five meets. Their enthusiasm dictated that a division of schools in the Duluth area had to be added in 1983-84, making us a League with four divisions in our fourth year.

The eagerness of schools to join the League was certainly an encouragement, but there was another. We were surprised at how rapidly Minnesota's results on the national exams improved. For the first time in years, we had a couple of students from Minnesota qualify for the second round of MAA tests designed to identify the country's best secondary mathematics talent.

When people commented on what a good idea the League was proving to be, my standard answer was that we hadn't done anything novel, that everything we were doing was copied from what I saw on the East Coast. There was, however, one way in which that wasn't true. Leagues there had grown up regionally. Eight or ten schools in a region would decide to start a league, and when they had their meets, they all came to the same site. Our variation was to have one league cover the state, with new groups in geographic proximity forming a new division of the League.

We enjoyed some great economies. One set of exams was used in meets all over the state. One appeal to a foundation for funds could be made on behalf of all the divisions. Inevitably, since they were all taking the same exam, competitions developed among teams and individuals in different divisions. More advantages were to emerge.

There were also attendant problems that made me glad for the advice to start small. Using the same test at different locations, we needed experience in getting tests distributed, held securely until test day, and given at the same time so as to thwart communication that might take place between students if tests were taken at different times at different sites. We had to learn how to cope with the fact that a snowstorm might prevent holding a meet in one part of the state while meets went on elsewhere. Common scoring rules had to be agreed upon. Students wanted electronic procedures to quickly disseminate results so they could know, during a meet, the results of schools and individual leaders in other divisions with whom they were in competition for statewide leadership.

By the end of our fourth season, we felt we were ready to expand in a way that would lend credibility to our claim to be a state league. With the major help of a grant from the Minnesota Department of Education, we planned a two-week residential conference at Macalester for the summer of 1984. The first week was for any teacher who expressed an interest in starting a math team at his or her school. During the second week, each participant was to bring along two students who agreed to help organize a team at their school. At the end of the second week, we were joined by the teacher/coaches already active in the League.

I asked Joe Konhauser, the problem-solving guru of our faculty, to conduct sessions each morning of the first week on problem-solving heuristics, being sure to include many classic puzzle problems, and giving references to helpful books of problems.

For afternoon sessions, I invited Bryan Sullivan, a successful coach I met while in the Boston area, to describe techniques he used in coaching his teams. Of the many topics he covered, one was talked about for years afterwards. He emphasized that success in mathematics doesn't just come to people lucky enough to have been born with the right genes, that it also requires work. To make his point, he brought along a recording of an interview with the most outstanding student (whom he called a mathlete) in his Massachusetts League the previous season.

Sullivan: So, how much time would you estimate that you spend on mathematics homework each night?

Student: Well, I find math class pretty easy, so I usually get my work done in class.

Sullivan: What about all those problem-solving techniques you seem to know about? Where do you learn about them?

Student: Oh, that comes from reading books about problem solving, collections of problems that have been used in competitions, problem sections in journals, etc.

Sullivan: Evidently I asked the wrong question. How much time do you spend working at problem solving?

Student: About three hours a night.

Sullivan: Wow. Isn't that extreme? What do your friends think of that?

Student: Well, I have a friend who hopes to go to college on a football scholarship. I got to watching him. He gets up early and runs three miles every morning. By the time he warms up, runs, and showers, he's devoted more than an hour to conditioning before he heads for school. Then after school there's a two-hour practice. And sometimes he goes back to school after supper to watch films of next week's opponent. I figure he easily puts in three hours a day to get good at what he does, so why shouldn't I put in the same time to get good at what I do?

We used that recording in many subsequent workshops for both teachers and students.

During the second week, when the students were present, we

formed teams of two coaches and their four students. The coaches worked together in the morning preparing their team for a meet. In the afternoon we ran a simulated meet: four individual events and a team event. In five days, we simulated an entire season of five meets. The coaches, working as partners, got ideas from each other about how to coach, and I got ideas from all of them by eavesdropping.

On Saturday, when our already participating coaches had arrived, some very useful interaction took place between those who had some experience with coaching and those who had just completed the institute I have described. Perhaps the most important thing was the development of an esprit de corps among the teachers. They began to think of themselves as founders of a new enterprise in Minnesota. We ended the conference by attending a dinner theatre, the cost of that event borne by the 3M Company.

Guidelines for Development

The conversations in which I was involved during that conference, coming on top of four seasons of competition, taught me several things that were to guide me as the League expanded across the state.

1. Students who have interest and talent in mathematics still need encouragement, guidance, and a willingness to work if they are truly to excel.

When seeking funds from government or foundations to get the League started, I often heard that bright kids doing well in school will make out just fine; it's kids with math phobia that we need to help. The eyes of people I hoped would help fund the League glazed over when I used statistics to demonstrate that our best kids weren't doing just fine when compared with AHSME results from other states. And in truth, it is difficult to argue with someone who wants to direct all available aid to those who are struggling.

I finally hit on a response that resulted in better understanding.

"Why," I would ask, "do we spend so much money in this state on bantam hockey programs? The kids in those programs are clearly athletic and have parents who will encourage them; they'll do just fine. Why don't we concentrate on kids that can't skate?" People in Minnesota do understand that kids, even athletic kids, aren't likely to make their high school hockey team if they don't get started in bantam hockey.

In time, as Minnesota scores improved and top scorers in the Math League began to garner scholarships at top colleges and universities, it got easier to make my point. We need to pay attention to young people with exceptional talent if they are to realize their potential.

2. Competition, even in academic work, is a great motivator for most kids.

Not everyone is drawn to competition, and we surely need to be alert to helping noncompetitive spirits. It was surprising to me, however, to see how quickly we began hearing from schools whose students wanted to form a team to compete with a team they heard about at a rival school.

3. Young people, like all people, like to be recognized for what they can do well.

Coaches quickly caught on to the extrinsic motivators used so successfully by their school's athletic departments. T-shirts for team members, articles about team members placed in school and community newspapers, signs and announcements of upcoming events, even the awarding of letters in some schools: All these things worked. As a League, we provided trophies to top-scoring individuals and teams. And we had more to learn.

4. Teachers, when called upon to work with quick-witted students, are sometimes intimidated and always appreciate suggestions for teaching them.

The teachers most likely to step forward to work as coaches were often the youngest members of their faculties, eager to be recognized by their administrations and not yet encumbered with other responsibilities like coaching sports, advising clubs, teaching driver education, or any of the myriad ancillary activities that vie for a teacher's time. Unfortunately, these are the teachers most worried about not knowing the answer to a student's questions, the ones most likely to be intimidated by students who can see through a problem or perform mathematical operations faster than they can.

I learned very quickly that one of my roles was to help teachers get over the idea that they must be the most nimble-minded person in the classroom. I was helped by the fact that I could be honest in self-deprecation, assuring them that I had to learn at Macalester to teach students who thought more quickly than I did. I emphasized that they were not in a race with students to see who could solve a problem most quickly. Their role was to point students to good sources, warn them of places where they are likely to have trouble, have a store of problems worth working on because they will illuminate key ideas, help students place what they are learning into a broad context, etc. The thinking I had done about mathematical heuristics, what to do when you don't know what to do, proved helpful.

5. One needs to take seriously the critics who question the value of competition and rewarding those who can think quickly on timed examinations.

I had not been long in promoting the League before I ran into critics who reasonably questioned my focus on improving results on timed tests. Was there any evidence that kids who got good at solving puzzle problems on a timed test will go on to become engineers and scientists? Might not there be people who do not do well under the pressure of a timed test but who excel at solving a problem that they can ponder?

The first question has a good answer. Nura Turner did a study for the MAA that followed the careers of students who had excelled at the AHSME exams in high school. She found that these students went on to careers in science and engineering at a much higher rate than those in the general population. And for my own part, I go back to the idea that problem-solving heuristics, learned to solve mathematical problems, can be useful in other types of problem solving as well.

The second question hit me more personally. In my own training, especially in graduate school, I had never been in the quick-witted group who anticipated the next step in an argument, or quickly spotted errors the instructor might make on the board. I frequently learned what went on in class hours later while pouring over my notes in a library carrel.

There are reasons, however, that I believed (and still believe) in mathematical competitions. It's widely understood that runners, swimmers, and other athletes that participate in individual competitions will do better if there are several people in the race capable of pushing each other to their limits. Similarly, students will push themselves harder if immersed in the company of other students who take initiative to read widely, who challenge themselves by attempting problems they find in books or journals, who join in conversation with other students who love mathematics. Coming to meets in a Math League competition brings students into exactly this kind of setting.

Of course there will be excellent mathematicians who prefer to work alone. I would not argue that all future mathematicians will emerge from mathematical competitions. The evidence is overwhelming, however, that mathematical competitions draw people into the discipline who might otherwise have gone on to something else.

Summer Conferences Become Part of the Program

The idea of holding a long-weekend summer conference for coaches proved popular and became a regular part of the League program. At these conferences, we distributed materials useful for team practices, invited speakers who were successful teacher/coaches in other leagues around the country, and spent time talking about ways to tweak our rules and procedures.

The conference, including room and board on the Macalester

campus, was free to participants and their spouses. Spouses, especially those from outstate areas, used free time to shop or enjoy the Cities, and of course they liked the plays, dinners, and other events arranged for Saturday nights. More than once, we heard teacher/coaches say that their spouses encouraged them to continue to work with the League because they liked coming to the summer conference.

As the League grew and stabilized operations, schools paid a fee to participate, and the League became financially self-sufficient, operating without foundation support. However, we continued to obtain outside support for the Saturday night entertainment at our conferences. I didn't want to wake up some morning and see a headline in the paper saying that money from school budgets was being used to entertain teachers and their spouses.

It was in raising this money, principally from Minnesota's high-tech companies, that I made wonderful use of the contacts I had developed while running industry-related undergraduate research programs. These companies felt they had a vested interest in supporting a program for strong mathematics students. They gladly accepted invitations to send a representative to talk to coaches at our conferences, and they often sent a company official to join the Saturday night event for which they were paying. We always urged them to say a word of appreciation to the coaches for the extra work they put in to develop the kind of talent needed by high-tech industries, and of course we made sure that such expressions were scheduled so the spouses would hear them.

In time, the president of the Minnesota High Technology Council (MHTC) came to think of the League as an organization that MHTC should foster. For some years, he took on the responsibility of finding a company to sponsor our Saturday night social event.

Adding Schools and Programs

Our first summer institute had the planned effect on our size. We had finished the 1983-84 season with 43 schools formed into 4 divisions. We began the 1984-85 season with 84 schools formed into 10 divisions. It also had an unplanned consequence. The coach from Hibbing, a school that was dominating competition in the Iron Range Division, made it clear that his kids wanted a face-to-face competition with schools from the Twin Cities. The result was that a season-ending state tournament was planned for the 1984-85 season. It started a feature of the League that has persisted ever since.

The original plan was to invite the top-scoring team from each division to participate in a meet that was typical of meets held during the regular season. Soon, however, we added an event to which top individuals during the regular season, regardless of their team affiliation, were invited. Our closing ceremony included trophies for top individuals as well as top teams.

As a League, we soon recognized that a state tournament provided us with a natural opportunity to recognize students who worked at mathematics. We sent articles about the tournament, the teams, and some of our more colorful students to the state's largest newspapers, as well as local newspapers in areas from which participating teams came. We went so far as to hire a professional publicist. With her encouragement, we designed an event that might attract TV coverage.

We called it a Math Bowl. We published qualifying standards that brought our top 10 students together on the stage. A problem was posed, and to keep action going while contestants worked, a step-by-step solution was projected on a screen where the audience (and hopefully a TV camera or two) could see it, but the contestants could not. When time was called, 30 to 90 seconds depending on the problem, each contestant held up an answer card. Contestants with correct answers got a point. A winner was declared after 10 questions, with extra questions ready in case of a tie.

It would give me great pleasure to report that this effort proved effective in attracting media attention. Alas, they prefer stories about pie-eating contests or cats returning home after a month's absence. Recalling failed efforts to attract publicity for students who excel at mathematics does bring to mind a favorite story, however.

Larry Hartman, the principal of a large urban high school, took a lively interest in the League. He was instrumental in getting me on programs to promote the League at conferences for principals; he served on the League board; he wrote helpful letters of support when we applied to foundations for support. One disappointment, however, was that the math team from his high school went for years without coming out on top of their division.

When his team finally won a tournament berth by coming in first in their tough urban division, an ecstatic Hartman called St. Paul's *Pioneer Press* to ask if they would run a picture of the team in its neighborhood section. The response was lackadaisical: It was a busy day; they were short on photographers . . . . Larry correctly concluded that his request would be ignored.

As it happened, later that day, workmen removing ceiling tiles to make repairs in a hallway of his school hit a pocket of insulation that rained asbestos dust onto the floor. Before they got the mess cleaned up, the paper had a photographer on the scene to record the terrible dangers to which school children were exposed.

Hartman was incensed when he called the paper a second time. He told the editor, "I'll give you one more chance. If you send a photographer, I'll personally stand on a stepladder and shake asbestos on the heads of the team."

Despite failing one intended goal, the Math Bowl proved popular with students, and we had stumbled into one more activity that became an annual League event. And once in a while, on slow news days, the event does merit some attention in the papers or on TV.

We made a final addition to the League's annual program in the summer of 1987. Just as students throughout our state had set up a clamor for a statewide competition, so participants in established leagues around the country wanted a sort of super meet, in effect a national tournament. The result was the American Regions Math League (ARML). It attracted teams from nationally known technical schools (Stuyvesant in New York, North Carolina School of Science and Mathematics, etc.) and teams made up of all-stars selected from math leagues around the country.

The ARML competition had been described to me by enthusiasts when I was first learning about math leagues. It was a single meet, held at Penn State over the Memorial Day weekend, since by then the university students were gone, making the dorms available. Teams entered either of two tiers, A or B. I was told that a large percentage of students obtaining the highest AHSME scores in the nation regularly showed up in the A tier at this event.

As our improved AHSME scores in Minnesota began to attract national attention, my acquaintances in the Boston area put increasing pressure on us to bring a Minnesota team of all-stars to ARML. We decided, after our seventh season of operation, to take the plunge.

Uncertain of whether we were ready for such fast company, we decided to treat our first year as a learning experience. We would take two teams, Maroon and Gold (the colors of the University of Minnesota). The Gold team would be made up of our best students, who were repeatedly told that they were trailblazers, that they were being coached by people who had never been to an ARML meet, and that they should be proud of having been selected, no matter where they finished in the standings. The Maroon team would contain only underclassmen being groomed for the next year. Not suffering from overconfidence, we entered both teams in Tier B.

The ARML competition is set up for teams of 15 members. We sent letters to the parents of the 30 students we wanted to fill out our teams, stressing the honor their son or daughter had earned. We admitted that this initial trip was a learning experience for all of us, and then spelled out the commitment we expected of each student. Anyone agreeing to be on the team should plan to attend training sessions, 9 a.m. to 3 p.m., at Macalester on the three Saturdays preceding the Memorial Day weekend. Moreover, while the League could supplement the cost of airfare, room, and board for two days, and lunch on the three Saturdays, each student would be responsible for raising $350.

We had no idea how parents would respond to this. Those driving a student from outside the metro area would be giving up three Saturdays in May, a tough decision for Minnesotans anxious to emerge from wherever they burrow for our winters. And while we did all we could to encourage schools and even businesses from a student's locale to help with the cost, $350 can look forbidding.

All 30 of the invited students accepted. All were present at 9 a.m. for the first practice, some having gotten up for a three- or four-hour ride to the Twin Cities. Parents were effusive in thanking us for the opportunity being given to their children, and we learned that friendships formed among these kids continued for years afterwards, even as they scattered to colleges and universities across the country.

Parents respond well when they feel that the educational system is providing a special opportunity for their kids.

I accompanied the first team to Pennsylvania. It sowed in my mind the idea that mathematical prowess is somehow related to good behavior. After we had been on the plane for an hour or so, a stewardess came to ask me if I was with that big group of kids. When I admitted that it was so, she said, "They're the best group of teenagers I've ever had on a flight. They're sitting back there working on math problems."

We had to fly to Pittsburgh, from where the group had to be taken ten at a time on a small commuter flight to State College. I wondered how things would go when I'd be separated from several groups for several hours. I need not have worried. When I arrived at State College with the third group, I found that the early arrivals had set up a chess tournament. Multiple games were underway throughout the small terminal.

I recalled that at one of our state tournaments, a reporter who covered the event stood with me looking through a balcony window at the students who were in the cafeteria below us, waiting for their event to be announced. The reporter was impressed. "Look," he said to me, "the kids are all sitting around tables, talking, laughing, and working on problems." No one was running around, throwing wads of paper, or otherwise engaged in favorite teenage pastimes.

As good as memories of good behavior are, they don't compare with memories of the euphoria the kids felt about their performance in the first ARML meet in which a Minnesota team competed. Of the 26 teams entered in Tier B, our Gold team finished in 3rd place, the Maroon in 6th. ARML rules dictated that on the basis of finishing in the top 4, our Gold team had to enter Tier A the next year.

Our young mathletes showed that their 1987 performance was no fluke. At the 1988 tournament, the Maroon was 4th out of 31 teams in Tier B. The Gold team finished 6th out of 28 teams in Tier A, good enough to bring home a traveling trophy awarded each year to the team showing the most improvement over the previous year.

Rudy Perpich was governor of Minnesota at the time. He was very conscious of the impact of high-tech companies on the state's economy, and thoroughly convinced of the importance of good math and science programs in schools. He had taken an interest in our League, and when he heard

Rudy Perpich

about the trophy coming to Minnesota, he hosted the 30 kids and their coach at a reception in the Capitol rotunda.

I enjoyed getting a plaque commemorating my work in starting the League. He seemed to enjoy meeting my wife at the reception, putting his arm around her and singing "How I love the kisses of Dolores." It's always nice when a man can enjoy his work.

I had met Perpich when I was looking for state money to start the League, but the reception at the Capitol was the beginning of an opportunity to work with him for years to come. He knew that several states had started schools of science and mathematics for their most promising high school science students, and he thought Minnesota should follow suit. He appointed me to a committee set up to explore the idea.

The committee, after visiting several states that had schools he thought of as models, unanimously recommended against forming such a school in Minnesota. Why? Our reasons were spelled out in a lengthy report but can be summarized thusly:

- The top students in any class set the standards on tests, making clear what can be expected. They're the ones who will interrupt in class if a concept has not been made clear, who will notice a mistake made at the board, and who provide leadership when the class is formed into small groups to work on a problem or grade each other's homework. A class from which the top one or two students have been removed will be a very different class.

  What is true in the mathematics classroom is true in a much larger sense. Students who are leaders in their classes are very often leaders in the school. To consistently take such students out of a school diminishes the school.

- If a school is not prepared to teach its best students, the solution is not to send those students elsewhere to be taught. The proper remedy is to improve the school. Many a school has improved its program in response to pressure from parents when they realize that their child is capable of more than is being offered there.

There is a national program, Math Counts, that tries to identify and encourage middle school kids who show promise in mathematics. More than once I've received a call from a high school principal who had been approached by parents whose child did very well in Math Counts. What, they wanted to know, does the high school have to offer by way of special attention for their mathematically talented kid? That's when the principal decides that the high school should be involved in the Math League.

• Finally, for a school that is to serve the entire state, the cost of building an academic building and dormitories is only the beginning. There is the continuing cost, not only of a faculty but also the staff required to provide room, board, and 24-hour supervision of young teenagers. Would the state accept such costs into the foreseeable future, or would we in time have a state school serving only those kids from families able to afford substantial tuition?

A Summer Mathematics Institute

The governor was disappointed, but reluctantly accepted the verdict. He followed that up, however, by asking me if the state should be doing something for young people who showed great potential in the sciences. After discussing the question with the Math League board, we offered him this idea. Mathematics is the language of all science. Why not run a residential six-week summer math institute that would have the following characteristics?

• Students would not apply; they would be invited from across the state on the basis of teacher recommendations.

- The program would be free to participants. It would be held on a college campus.

- Curriculum would aim at enrichment, not acceleration.

- Recognized master teachers would be selected from across the state, and paid generously enough to make them want to come.

The goal would be to first invite a student who had a distinguished first year in high school, a student with talent and interest in mathematics as authenticated by a teacher. A student who did well would be invited back following 10th grade, again after grade 11. It would be entirely residential, the expectation being that there would be programming into the evening hours. The economic status of the family would not matter.

Holding the institute on a college campus obviously required no capital investment, and modern classrooms and computer labs would be available. College students, always looking for summer employment, would be available to work as lab assistants and dorm supervisors.

There are plenty of mathematical topics that are accessible to secondary students but not covered in the secondary curriculum. We wanted to be sure we didn't create problems for high schools by sending back students who had already studied what their home school planned to teach them the next year.

There would be no tenure problems. Teachers who worked out well would be invited back; others would not. (After the first year, we included two young teachers just coming out of training, giving them a chance to work with master teachers. That's a stark contrast to the common practice of assigning beginning teachers to remedial classes, the very toughest to handle.)

Governor Perpich embraced the idea and did what he could to funnel some state money into running what was intended to be a prototype. I also got funding from the National Science Foundation, companies from the MHTC, and from the treasury of the

Math League, which was by then building up some surplus.

The easiest college campus for me to use was Macalester, of course, but I deliberately did not teach in the institute. Indeed, I stayed off campus most of the time, wanting to demonstrate exactly what we had in mind—a program run entirely by master secondary teachers. Even the dean of the program, Kathy Trier, was a high school teacher, drawn from the ranks of the Math League coaches. We ran the institute for four summers, 1990 through 1993.

It was an unqualified success in every way. When I did drop in a few evenings to see how things were going, I would find groups of kids sprawled out on the floors throughout the science building, working on projects. The kids ate it up, and the program really ran all day and into the evening hours. At the closing ceremony, when Kathy was introduced, there was a sustained standing ovation—this for the person who was, among other things, the enforcer of rules for kids living together in dorms for a part of their summer.

Each student's school was informed that its returning student(s) had completed a project of his or her choosing, and had been rehearsed in making an oral presentation. We hoped they would be given an appropriate opportunity to make such a presentation in their school. Best of all, this was a time when increasingly sophisticated hand calculators were making their way onto the market. We presented each participant with such a calculator to use at the institute and then take back to their schools. We heard from teachers across the state who greatly appreciated having a student in the room thoroughly familiar with the latest in calculators.

I do believe that if Perpich had been elected to one more term, he would have gotten the Legislature to adopt funds to make the Summer Math Institute a permanent part of the state's educational enterprise. Unfortunately, from my point of view, he was defeated. I could not raise funds to keep the experiment going on a continuing basis, so a great idea was "temporarily" shelved. As I write, it has been shelved for 26 years, and I am now on the shelf beside it.

The institute does have a lasting legacy, however. As Perpich pushed a variety of programs to build Minnesota's technology base, a group of concerned citizens became alarmed that the arts were being ignored. They began a model residential school of the arts. It was designed to run during the school year, the model Perpich originally envisioned for a school of science. More politically astute than me, they got their school funded by the Legislature, and Minnesota has for many years now had a Perpich School for the Arts. It is a constant reminder to me that my political skills are not all that they might be.

A Stable Part of Minnesota Education

By the time we made our entry into ARML competition, the League was financing itself by charging an annual fee to each participating school. We set a fee that provided

- One month's summer pay to me for writing exams for the season to come.
- Compensation for a proofreader.
- The cost of getting the exams printed and distributed to the various sites on time.
- Overnight lodging for teams travelling more than 50 miles to the state tournament.
- Costs (trophies, a stipend for the coordinator, publicity, a closing dinner) of running the tournament.

ARML costs were partially subsidized on the grounds that the ARML experience benefited a very small percentage of students in the League. ARML participants still raised a substantial part of the cost of that program. Finally, we were able to make the summer conference free for coaches and their spouses (later understood to be for coaches and their significant others).

Somewhere along the line, we incorporated the League as a nonprofit corporation under the laws of Minnesota. The League board elected its officers, and management of League business was accomplished at an annual board meeting.

Significant Help

I once read that the key to good administration is to surround yourself with competent people and then stay out of their way. I can't take credit for surrounding myself with competent people in managing the League. It simply happened that as I started to build it, I had the good fortune to be surrounded by people who had exactly the competencies I would ultimately realize I needed. I believe I can take credit for staying out of their way.

A case in point was Stan Hill, an actuary whose involvement in Minnesota math competitions went back to the days when managing the AHSME was a joint project of the MAA and the Society of Actuaries. When I started the League, Stan stayed on to manage our funds, and after we incorporated, he stayed on for years as our treasurer. Our year-end financial reports were professional masterpieces.

In the League's early days, when we were in sore need of funds at year's end, Stan would help out with a donation. Then as grants began to come in, Stan managed them. Whenever he saw a chance to squirrel away funds left over from a grant or at the end of a fiscal year, he invested them wisely. This went on for perhaps 20 years. In the last weeks of his life, he called me to his home to tell me that since he doubted he could manage the League's investments any longer, he had decided to close the League's brokerage account and have me place the money in the League's checking account until a new treasurer could take over and advise the board. He then handed me a check for a bit over $90,000.

In the same way, I inherited an administrative assistant, without whose skills the League would never have grown as it did. When I started, it was natural that the administrative work was handled by the secretary of the Macalester Mathematics Department, Kathy Grundhoefer. As the League grew, however, the workload became too great, and Kathy resigned from the department to focus entirely on League activities. A new desk was set up for her in the departmental office. Her salary, plus reimbursement to the college for identifiable League expenses (a computer, supplies, postage, etc.), became one more expense covered by fees paid by participating schools.

With Kathy serving just the League, we were able to devote more effort to expanding to all areas of the state. Kathy would identify an area and set up a lunch or a dinner, to which we would invite the principal and a math teacher from each of the target schools. I would explain the purpose of the League, its mode of operation, and the benefits that accrued to member schools; she would have applications for interested schools to complete. This procedure continued for years until we had close to 200 schools participating, pretty much justifying our claim to be a state League.

Kathy had a winning personality and was blessed with a marvelous memory for names and personal tidbits, an area in which I am woefully weak. I came to rely on having her at my side at all manner of League events. When a coach (what was his name again?) approached, she would say something like, "Well if isn't Al Stanley, the king of fishermen from Moose Lake. How's it working out to be coaching your own son on your math team?" With such prompts, I could slide into the conversation.

We both began to realize as we traveled and were so often seen together that people might begin to wonder about our obvious pleasure in being together. We began to talk about the need to maintain, in appearance as well as in fact, a clear sense of propriety. We made sure that our spouses got to know each other, and when possible, we got them to accompany us to League events, where they would chat with each other while Kathy and I were mingling with the math teachers in the room. With conscious efforts of this sort, we were able to maintain our happy marriages and achieve our professional objectives.

Relationships worth having are worth intentional efforts to maintain.

As already mentioned, the first group to listen to my proposal for a Minnesota math League included Jack Nichols, a vice president at Unisys, who laid on the table a check for $5,000 to get us going. The quickness of that response surprised me. The bigger and far more important surprise came in the form of continuing generous support from Univac for more than 25 years. Foundations and philanthropists typically see it as their role to provide startup funds for a new idea, expecting that if the idea proves beneficial, others will see that and find a way to provide sustaining support.

The League did in fact follow that pattern, sustaining itself within just a few years on the membership fees of participating schools. At the same time, however, as befits a dynamic organization, new ideas were continually being proposed: a statewide season-ending tournament, participation in a national tournament, a summer math institute, and more. And for reasons already explained, I insisted that the social event accompanying each year's summer conference for coaches be sponsored by an outside organization. For all of these reasons, we were grateful for continuing support from Unisys.

There was more! Unisys stayed involved in League affairs through the indefatigable work of Judy Cognetta, who was employed in their public relations office. In this capacity, she was involved with a great many civic events in the Twin Cities. She took a particular interest in the Math League and brought to us a wealth of experience in developing a public image. She was particularly supportive of the idea of a summer institute, channeled very substantial support into the effort, and occasionally dropped in to see the institute in operation.

She also dropped in on League meets, chose from the events listed above to make an appearance, and was always ready to meet with League officers to give counsel when a new venture was being considered. She was a friend of the League, and became a trusted advisor and friend to Kathy Grundhoeffer and to me, one more person who gave me reason to feel surrounded by extraordinary help.

I have tried never to talk about the success of the League as measured by national examinations without mentioning that in 1980, the League's first year, the University of Minnesota started a program for secondary students who were showing strong mathematical prowess in their high schools. Known as UMTYMP (University of Minnesota Talented Youth in Mathematics Program), it made it possible for students to finish a three-semester calculus sequence while they were still in high school. It was directed by Professor Harvey Keynes of the U of M's Mathematics Department.

The start of these two programs in the same year was a coincidence. Harvey and I didn't know each other when we started our respective programs. They were in many ways very different. Students in UMTYMP attended a class in the late afternoon or evening taught at the university by adjunct faculty. Those who completed a course received college credit and advanced standing wherever they chose to go to college. Students who participated in the Math League continued to attend the regular mathematics courses in their high school, and they received no extra credits.

Both programs were catering to the same mathematically talented students, of course, and many participated in both, attending courses at the university and practicing with the math team at their high school. The higher scores being attained by Minnesota students on national exams were earned by a mix of students, some from UMTYMP, some from the League, some from both. Harvey and I worked at coordinating our programs, taking care not to schedule events at the same time, discussing options for students in both programs, and sometimes relying on the same teacher/coach for help. No attempt was ever made to gauge the contributions of each program to improved scores.

Someone unfamiliar with the situation might think that

Harvey had a great advantage in attracting students, since in UMTYMP they earned college credit, while in the League they did not. It didn't work that way. Schools anywhere in the state could participate in the League, but they had to be within reasonable driving distance of a university campus, either in the Twin Cities or in Duluth (with a few more sites added as time went on) to participate in UMTYMP. Students involved in sports, music, or other after-school activities had a hard time commuting between campuses to take courses, and some who could commute simply didn't want to.

There was another factor that worked in favor of the League for talented young mathematicians. Most high school teachers preferred to see their best students participate in the League. There were several reasons for this.

Teachers look forward to those occasions when an unusually interested and talented student shows up in a class. It does nothing for that teacher's morale to have someone identify the talented student, and in effect say, "I'll take that one; you stay here and teach the rest." The League runs conferences and workshops to improve a teacher's ability in dealing with top students. It naturally gets favored over simply moving the student to someone else's class.

A talented student who gets enthused about the school's math team soon realizes that the rules are such that it takes more than one student to score enough points for a team to win. That student is soon a chief aid to the coach in recruiting other students who might be able to help, and then in coaching those new recruits.

Participation on the math team makes you a leader in your school; taking a course at the university draws you away from your school. We all like to identify with the most prestigious organization of which we are a part, and very often the kid who starts taking courses at the university is drawn to attend athletic events at the U and wants to participate in other activities there. His or her leadership is often lost entirely at the high school.

The League also had a natural advantage in that it played to everyone's desire to be recognized for what they are good at. In the League, a student might get to the state tournament; he or she might win a trophy as a high scorer in the division, or even appear in front of peers in the Math Bowl. And there is the possibility of being selected for the ARML team, a sure path to recognition in your home community. In all of these situations, efforts were made, and sometimes succeeded, in getting media attention.

In summary, after 1980, there were two outstanding programs for Minnesota students with interest and talent in mathematics to consider. One provided acceleration, teaching college material to high school students. The other provided enrichment, trying to deepen problem-solving skills and introducing topics often not covered in a standard high school curriculum. Students could participate in one or both programs.

Four Guiding Principles

In 1991, I was invited to describe the League philosophy for an article in the *Journal of the Minnesota Academy of Science*. I built the article around four principles that had become guidelines for me when thinking about the mathematical education of gifted students.

1. A program for mathematically gifted high school students should, if well conceived, serve to lift the school's entire mathematics program.
2. Programs that simultaneously stimulate gifted students and their teachers are to be preferred over programs aimed only at students.
3. Students with exceptional ability need to see themselves in the context of similarly talented young people.
4. Programs should be affordable and available to students wherever they live in the state.

Though it gets ahead of my personal story, I'll conclude my

account of Math League activities by saying here what I've said in many places. By the time I was fully retired from my professional life, I had enjoyed most of the activities associated with academic life: classroom teaching, writing texts and monographs, some leadership opportunities in my national professional association, academic administration, and more. None of them gave me quite so much personal satisfaction as my 30-year involvement with the Math League.

The objective of seeing Minnesota regularly represented in national programs designed for mathematically gifted students has been achieved. It was particularly gratifying to see our team take first place in Tier A of the 1997 ARML meet.

A steady stream of letters from secondary teachers, student mathletes (many of them now teachers of mathematics), and parents have told what the League has meant to them. I was able, when I retired, to turn over a thriving, financially sound organization to a new director in whom I had great confidence. At the time of this writing, the League continues under the leadership of its third director, Tom Young, who served as a coach while I was still the director. He has added still more activities to the League program. It gives me great satisfaction to realize that in his hands, the League more than ever provides an important component in the education of academically gifted students of mathematics in Minnesota.

VII. The Middle-Aged Professor

Sometimes economic necessity forces upon you
some good things you would not have thought of
in more opulent times.

One More MIT Story

One joy of teaching is to have former students keep in touch as they build a successful career, at least in part building on what was learned in your classroom.

When discussing the workload that came with coordinating the AHSME in Minnesota, I paid tribute to Karla Ballman for teaching me how useful a good student assistant can be. She was my assistant for all of her four years at Macalester. After graduation she decided to build on her mathematics major by becoming an actuary.

She was one of those students who stayed in touch after graduation, so it was not long after I returned from my year at MIT that we had lunch together. She told me she was doing well on the series of tests one must pass to become a certified actuary, and that she was particularly enjoying her study of operations research (OR), the topic of her next test.

Then she confessed that while she was making good progress on the actuarial exams, she was not finding her work as an actuary very interesting. In fact, she said, her recent studies had her thinking of forgetting about actuarial work and entering graduate school at the University of Minnesota to get a degree in OR.

I had the temerity to ask her if she was in love or if there was some other reason to stay in the Twin Cities. The answer was no. I then told her that when I'd decided to use a sabbatical to study OR, a little investigation convinced me that the best department of OR was at MIT. I asked her why she didn't apply there. In that respect, it turned out, she was like me when I first considered graduate school: Just go to the nearest school. She brightened up at the thought of MIT. "I'd love to go to there."

It was mid-summer, way past the time to apply for that fall, but I told her that having just come from MIT, I knew the chairman and would contact him to see if she could still get in. To make a long story short, a student they had accepted for the fall term had just written to say his plans had changed, so he would not be accepting the fellowship they had conferred. By late summer, Karla had the fellowship and was on her way to MIT.

That story, by itself, wouldn't merit telling here, except that it's part of a still longer story to which I shall return again. And again.

When I returned to campus from MIT, John Davis was starting his fourth year as Macalester's president. He was still finding it tough going. In describing his supportive role in helping me start Minnesota's Math League, I said that upon my return from the MIT sabbatical, I found him eager to support anything that would raise Macalester's standing in the eyes of local observers. It takes much more time to restore a reputation than it does to damage it.

Macalester's treasurer during those hectic years, Paul Aslanian, was a handball partner of mine. Through his participation with the National Association of College and University Business Officers (NACUBO), he had become a booster of the idea that the college should always be in the first year of a five-year plan. That is, there should be a five-year plan that is annually updated in light of changing conditions. The process, as NACUBO described it, called for establishing an administrative committee to both develop and then monitor the plan. It also called for having a member of the faculty on this committee. Paul asked me if I'd be willing to serve in this capacity, and I agreed.

Working with John Davis

It was in my new role as faculty associate for planning that I got my chance to know John Davis. To introduce me to the task he faced, he began by describing his introduction to DeWitt Wallace shortly after he became Macalester's president. Ushered into Wallace's office in New York, the first question put to him was, "Do you understand the importance of the bottom line?" He claimed that he told Wallace that checking the bottom line was the first thing he did every morning. That was probably pretty close to the truth. The outcome of that meeting was a promise that the college would in the years to come finish every year with a balanced budget. It was a promise he kept, but not easily.

To get better acquainted and make me aware of the faculty-related problems that had to be resolved, he suggested that we meet for a couple of Saturday mornings. That somehow morphed into a pattern where we met every Saturday morning during the year to come. Once again I was to have the opportunity of working with a remarkable man.

On paper, it would appear that John did not have many of the strengths one might expect to find in a college president. He was not a polished public speaker. He was not and never pretended to be a scholar. He was not good with numbers and would sometimes ask me two or three times in one session, "How much are we trying to cut from this line?" But his great strength was his transparent honesty, sincerity, and warmth, his way of conveying respect, even gratitude, to everyone with whom he spoke.

Our Saturday morning sessions usually ran for about two hours. They always ended in the same way. Though the chair I sat on was closer to the door than his, he always managed to get between me and the door as I rose to leave. His purpose was to thank me, not in generalities but in specifics that related to whatever had been the topic of the day. And though I quickly got over it just outside the door, he always managed to make me feel for just a moment that, "Gee, maybe he couldn't run this place without me." My experience was pretty much the norm for everyone who met with him.

I don't mean to leave the impression that John got by on charm alone. There were hard decisions that had to be made: programs to be cut, positions that had to be terminated, disappointed students that had to be dealt with. He did not duck these responsibilities, but he was able to discharge them in a way that left the community feeling certain they were made of necessity, reluctantly, and in the long-term interests of the college. He also had a wonderful knack for moving people from a position where he thought they were ineffective to one where he could often convince them that they were better able to help the college.

The ascendency of the college was not one smooth ride upward. There were certainly bumps in the road, which I'll illustrate by recounting an incident that occurred during our January interim term in 1981.

Jerry's Awful Course

Jerry Weiss, mentioned previously as a colleague with whom I often debated, decided that during our January term he would offer a course on pornography. That might have passed with nothing more than a few letters from irritated parents, but Jerry undeniably had a talent for attracting attention. He somehow managed to get the *Wall Street Journal* and other newspapers around the country to write stories about his proposed course; and lest a college offering credit for a course in pornography didn't get enough attention, he got himself quoted in follow-up articles saying that he was teaching a course in pornography because he liked pornography.

The last time I checked, the college archives still had a good-sized cardboard box full of letters selected from the deluge that poured into the president's office from parents, trustees, editorial writers, and freelance guardians of public morals. It unquestionably brought national recognition to the college, but not the kind toward which John Davis had been working.

As was often the case, I saw in Jerry's action an opportunity for our Macalester Christian Fellowship. I called the student leaders together and suggested that since Jerry's course was sure to be in the national spotlight for the month of January, the fellowship's weekly meetings should be organized around the theme, A Christian View of Sex and the Body. I thought that suggestion was consistent with the idea of Harvey Cox, previously quoted, who said that Christians should "live in the same world with everyone else."

That theme turned out to be a good suggestion. It might have been less well-advised for me to offer myself as the coordinator for such a series, but time for planning was short, and I did have some reasons for thinking I might be able to do a creditable job. I had by that time led dozens of dormitory discussions on the viability of Christian faith, and it doesn't matter where such discussions start; with college students, they always end up on sex.

I had a real advantage in such discussions. I knew what the Bible had to say on the subject. The students were operating under the assumption that Christian teaching on the subject could be summarized with one word: don't.

I liked to begin with Genesis, where it's explained that a man is expected to leave his mother and father to be united to his wife, and the two shall become one flesh. And lest there be any doubt about how they are to become one flesh, I pointed out that Paul quoted this passage to explain that a man who links himself to a harlot has become one flesh with her. No further elaboration was necessary.

I always added that there is to be enjoyment in this union: "Let her breasts satisfy thee at all times, and be thou ravished with her love." (Proverbs 5:18-19, NEB) We moved on to the Song of Solomon, hardly a paragon of sexual restraint, and by the time we worked our way to Paul's reminders that married partners are not to regard their bodies as their own but to use them to satisfy the desires of their partners, we had pretty well put down the idea that the Bible is squeamish about sex.

Even students who had some church background were usually surprised to read these Biblical texts, but their surprise was understandable. These passages are seldom covered in the Sunday School curriculum.

I won't try to recreate discussions I initiated about the Old Testament phrase, "He knew her," but I did use this phrase to argue that I knew my wife and she knew me in ways that we held to be unique. No one knows either of us so well as we know each other. Naked people reveal more than body parts.

Sooner or later, it would dawn on the group that I was saying I had never had sex with anyone except the woman I married. Most groups of young people these days find (or pretend to find) this astonishing. It often prompts some young man (almost always a male in this case), feeling more worldly wise than me at this point, to ask something like, "Since there is such a variety of sexual expression, and since people react so differently, don't you feel that you've missed out on a lot of experiences by limiting yourself to just one woman?"

Experience has taught me not to try answering this with more Biblical texts. It works much better to respond with a question of my own. "You've posed a good question. After I answer it, will you answer a question from me?" Agreement was inevitably forthcoming, after which I would say in all sincerity, "Yes, I'm sure I've missed out on a lot."

Then I'd tell them that my wife and I dated for more than three years while I was in college, and that she is well aware of how we both struggled to preserve sexual intercourse for something that would be special after marriage. And since having achieved that together, she has never doubted that it is just as important to me to keep that part of our relationship something that will always bind us together in a unique way, that I will not destroy that uniqueness by getting sexually involved with another woman. The result, I go on, "is that I have freedom that very few men have to form deep and lasting friendships with other women."

Then I come to my question. "Wouldn't you agree that having given up a variety of experiences, I have also gained something in enjoying the complete confidence of my wife?" Sometimes they agree.

The first of our January sessions drew a much larger crowd than we usually had at our meetings, a crowd that included most of Jerry's class. As usual, the Biblical texts recognizing the joys of sex surprised and somewhat confused many in attendance, but the repartee nevertheless became spirited. There was a lot of laughter.

With time to think over the first week, the group had more

and better questions the second week, and again I thought things were going quite well—until the very end. A young man stood up and read a question so well stated that I wondered if it might have been the work of several collaborators. As well as I can reconstruct it, it went like this:

> Why is it that if I look at a nude woman pictured in the centerfold of *Playboy*, I'm a voyeur, or at least a lowbrow willing to exploit women, but if I contemplate a painting of a nude female at the Minneapolis Museum of Art, I'm a connoisseur of fine art?

I told him I had no idea how to answer that, but I would think about it and try to give an answer next week.

As it happened, Dolores and I were leaving the next day for San Francisco, where I'd be attending the annual meetings of the combined mathematical organizations. I was, as usual, caught up in a round of lectures, committee meetings, and sessions devoted to current research, but as opportunity presented itself, I did ask friends and colleagues how they would answer the question. I got some wise-guy answers suggesting that we buy some of the pornographic publications so abundant on San Francisco street corners and study them for clues, but by the end of the week I was headed home with no better idea of how to answer the question than when I first heard it.

We had a late flight and got home near midnight, so I was surprised when the phone rang shortly after we got in. It was John Davis. He asked if it was true that I was doing something tomorrow night related to "Jerry's awful course."

After I told him what our Christian Fellowship was doing, he apologized for calling so late, and then explained that he'd been calling throughout the evening. "I thought you would want to know that the NBC Today crew is going to be on campus tomorrow to do a show on our pornography course, and they plan to be at your session tomorrow night."

He went on to explain his own plans for the morrow. He began by reminding me that Nixon once appointed a committee that was to answer three questions: What constitutes pornography? Does it really have any effect on the behavior of people who look at it? If so, what can we do about it? With this background, he went on to say, "There are some serious questions one can ask, and there's no question that academic freedom guarantees Jerry's right to offer this course, but I have no interest in trying to explain these things in a three-minute clip on national television."

With tongue in cheek, he told me that it had occurred to him that he had a number of calls he had to make on people off campus, so he would be unavailable the next day. As usual, he thanked me profusely for what I was doing and told me he'd like a report the next night on how things went.

The question I'd promised to answer loomed much larger. Desperate, even though it was by then about 1 a.m., I decided to call a woman I knew who taught art at Bethel College, a nearby school closely associated with a Baptist denomination. She was gracious once she understood my dilemma, and we talked for close to an hour, but from all of that, I only remember one exchange from the conversation.

She said at one point that serious art should fill an observer with awe, perhaps bringing to mind the spirit if not the words of the psalmist who was overcome with the thought that he had been "fearfully and wonderfully made." I remember that she laughed heartily when I responded with the observation that I had seen pictures of some of the models in *Playboy*, and they seemed to be quite wonderfully made.

I have forgotten more than just that conversation. I have no recollection of how I stumbled through an answer the next night in front of the cameras. I'm sure I tried to confess, without seeming to be a Philistine in an art gallery, that I really couldn't see much difference.

John was on the phone shortly after I got home from my opportunity to appear with the Today cast. "Did they really show up?" he asked. I told him that it was an experience unlike anything I'd ever faced, that I had walked into a standing room only classroom ablaze with klieg lights and several TV cameras trained on a desk adorned with three or four microphones. As quickly as I set the scene, John said, "I hope you strode quickly to the desk, looked straight into the cameras, and said, 'Thou preparest a table before me in the presence of my enemies.'"

When I told my wife how quickly that line had come to John and added that I really wished I had thought of it, she said, "That's why John is president of the college and you're one of the faculty members."

There are people who will argue that the nature of the job is such that a college president will, over time, come to be disliked or at least held in chary suspension by the faculty. John Davis was proof that it doesn't have to be so. Macalester's faculty was well aware that the college was in serious trouble when John took over, and they came to trust his judgment about what had to be done.

There was widespread campus dismay when he announced, after 10 years on the job, that he felt it was time for him to step aside. In characteristic fashion, he explained that his task was to restore the college's financial condition, that he felt that had been accomplished, and that it was now time for someone better qualified than he to provide academic leadership. It was a sad but grateful faculty that gathered for his farewell.

John and I maintained a friendship after he left Macalester. He was always an interesting person with whom to have lunch. Shortly after he left, the highly regarded Children's Theatre of Minneapolis was rocked by the scandal of having one of its directors exposed as a pedophile. He was convicted of molesting young boys, and there were accusations that others at the theatre had covered up for him. John was called out of his short retirement to head that organization through some turbulent years.

From there he was called to the University of Minnesota campus at Mankato to deal with another school that had gotten into deep trouble. For an encore, he took over and saved the

St. Paul Chamber Orchestra when that organization, the nation's only full-time chamber orchestra, seemed destined to go bankrupt.

For all these experiences, the pornography course loomed large to the end. I visited him in a nursing home just a few days before he died. He was sometimes lucid, sometimes not, and always slurred of speech. I tried to recall some of the experiences about which we could now laugh, and in that context, he muttered something about "Jerry's awful course."

Signs of Improvement

Bumps in the road or not, John made steady progress in drawing supporters, including DeWitt Wallace, back to the goal of having Macalester recognized for its strength as an educational institution. We felt the change coming over the college in our department. In 1981, we were finally able to hire an established computer scientist, Michael Schneider, and in 1982 we added another, Richard Molnar.

The long period during which Allan Kirch worked to give us a presence in the emerging field of computer science, in retrospect, had benefits we never anticipated. The program he developed naturally resided in the Mathematics Department, and he was more than happy to gradually shift his primary load back to mathematics when two trained computer scientists finally joined us. It was natural that as the computer people were hired, they were housed in our department.

As it turned out, it was a long time before we were able to retain a third full-time computer scientist, and by then the program was fully integrated into the department. Before any real momentum for separating the programs could develop, we were hiring young mathematicians so fully conversant with computers that they reveled in being part of a combined department. The natural thing to do at that point was to change our name to the Department of Mathematics and Computer Science.

With the pattern established, the same integration took place when the department greatly augmented its offerings in statistics. As I write today, the college has a Department of Mathematics, Statistics, and Computer Science. One of the last young people hired told me that he chose Macalester from among several colleges that made him an offer because he didn't have to decide whether he wanted to be in a department of mathematics or computer science.

Sometimes economic necessity forces upon you some good things you would not have thought of in more opulent times.

I've already indicated that the principal activity in which I engaged upon my return from MIT was developing the Math League. There were other things, of course, things more typical of the life of a middle-aged professor.

As soon as I settled into routines back at Macalester, I circulated to several publishers the manuscript for the linear algebra book that I brought back from MIT. That troublesome manuscript finally rewarded me with some satisfaction when it became the object of competition among several publishers who wanted to add it to their list. It was published in 1982, the same year in which a second edition of *Faces of Mathematics* appeared.

Faces by that time was serving as the text for a course that I titled The Spirit of Mathematics. The course had become a favorite for nonscience majors as a way to fulfill one of the required courses in the science division.

The use of tantalizing puzzle problems to engage student interest proved popular—too popular. It led me to an idea that proved to be one of the bigger mistakes of my career.

As the Civil Rights Movement gained momentum in the country, every mathematics department was confronting the same question: How can we attract Black students to succeed in mathematics?

I thought I might have an answer. Why not use puzzle problems as an attraction? From my book, from years of creating problems for the high school Math League, and from my association with Joe Konhauser, I could surely pull together a collection of problems of interest to high schoolers who liked sports and games. If carefully sequenced, such puzzles do lead in natural ways to number sense, and ultimately to both algebra and geometry.

I developed a course around this idea. In my mind, it would serve as a summer course to attract students not ordinarily interested in mathematics. Added inducements would include holding the course on a beautiful campus in air-conditioned rooms, providing free lunch, and the chance to earn a small stipend in lieu of what might be earned at a summer job.

The course would give me a chance to establish a relationship with students. I would invite some accomplished Black scientists I'd gotten to know through the industry-related programs I used to run during summers. Most important, the course might convince these students that mathematics is an important stepping stone to a career, something they could learn that is actually useful. They might be persuaded to register for a follow-up course offering the same inducements and a chance to learn some basic mathematics.

I submitted a proposal to NSF, asking for support for the two-summer sequence I envisioned. It received enthusiastic endorsement from the review panel and was funded. That was the last good thing that happened.

My first problem was getting the attention of my intended audience. It was a mistake to think that I had entrée into high schools because of teachers I met through the national contest and the League. The teachers I knew were not in predominately Black schools I needed to reach; and in schools with a more balanced ethnic makeup, the teachers I knew were working with the most talented math students in the school. They didn't have rapport with the Black students I was trying to reach. Written descriptions of the program, sent to school officials I did not know, got very little attention.

As summer vacation drew near, I began visiting target schools. While in the neighborhoods, I would stop and talk with groups of kids I encountered on the streets. My reception was exactly what you would expect. When it became clear to me that the size of my intended class was going to be much smaller than anticipated, I decided I could use some of the funds to provide direct bus service from designated pickup spots. That helped—a little bit.

I was completely disabused of my idea that the kids I attracted would be interested in the puzzles I'd created. I pulled Joe Konhauser into my program, hoping that with his enthusiasm and wonderful sense of humor, he might have success where I was experiencing failure. No such luck. Attendance began to dwindle. It was a long, long summer.

As the first summer of my intended program was coming to a merciful end, I called the program officer at NSF to describe what was happening and to tell him that we would certainly not be holding the classes projected for the following summer.

He tried to offer encouragement. He suggested that the next summer we try again to run the first-year phase, using the intervening year to try other approaches to attracting an audience. He also explained that in the NSF accounting system, funds had already been committed to a second year.

My discouragement was palpable. I told him in no uncertain terms that I could not face another summer like the one just experienced. I remember his final response: "I suppose that in the long history of our republic, someone has sent money back to Washington, but I'm sure I will have a hard time finding a precedent."

It is good these many years later to be able to say that I am not under the illusion that all my ideas were good.

The Ombudsman Committee

As I reflect on the period between my second and third sabbaticals, an activity I considered something of a lark at the time turned out to be influential in setting the agenda for the last part of my career. It came about because I'd met R. D. Anderson when he was a consulting editor for the company that published *Faces of Mathematics*.

Anderson was a widely known mathematician, first because he was often mentioned as a student of the famous R. L. Moore, also because he did some distinguished work as a mathematician, and principally because he was an affable gentleman frequently elected to high-visibility posts in mathematical organizations. He had been called upon enough times as a consultant to troubled mathematics departments around the country that he decided the Mathematical Association of America should have a committee that would act as an ombudsman. He took it upon himself to form such a committee, and he invited me to be part of it.

R. D. Anderson

It was a wonderful experience. It gave me an opportunity to see what can go wrong in a department, and always to come home more grateful for the colleagues with whom I worked. More important to my own future, however, it gave me an opportunity to meet and work with the other people that Anderson chose for his committee. It is worth mentioning some of the problems we encountered.

The committee came into being just as handheld calculators capable of symbolic manipulation were coming on the market. Some teachers felt that such calculators would be a great teaching tool. Others, including members of some of the most prestigious departments in the country, were dead set against the use of such devices. They were quite certain that in using them, students would miss learning some essential skills of the discipline.

Knowing this, and being an enthusiastic booster of using available technology, Anderson made it a habit, whenever we visited a school, to give a lecture advocating the value of technology. Being R. D. Anderson, his lectures always drew a crowd, and he always tried to make the medicine go down by sweetening it with his famous sense of humor.

He was giving such a lecture when we visited the University of Tennessee on a humid day that seemed to promise a storm. Anderson was just getting started, reminding his audience that every mathematician once knew how to use an algorithm similar to long division to find the square root of a number. It was a skill rendered obsolete when virtually every textbook began including tables of square roots. He chided his audience a bit, saying that in a room full of successful working mathematicians, there were probably very few who could use that algorithm without spending at least a few minutes trying to recall how it worked.

He then added an off-hand remark, saying that with the advent of calculators, the time might soon come when we wouldn't have to teach long division. Just as he said that, as if on cue, a tremendous flash of lightning struck a beautiful old tree just outside the window, splitting it in half and bringing a huge limb crashing to the ground. The bolt of lightning caused an eerie flash in the room. Anderson calmly walked to the window, looked at the remains of the tree, and casting a glance heavenward, said, "Okay, we'll continue to teach long division."

Another visit took us to a Big Ten university where the School of Business had declared war on the Mathematics Department because so many business students were failing calculus. Our committee met with representatives from the two groups. We asked early in the conversation why the business students were required to take calculus. We asked because we knew it was common practice in many programs to require calculus as a filter, weeding out students unable to pass the course, a sign of a quality program. The probable answer was that calculus was required because it was required in other business schools with which they competed.

That last answer is not acceptable to say out loud in a meeting with outsiders, of course, and we didn't get it. Instead, the business representatives outlined a list of things they hoped their students would learn: simple and compound interest, amortization, annuities, present value, and other financial instruments. When told that none of these useful topics are taught in calculus, it became clear that the business people had a very linear view of mathematics. Reasoning that the things they wanted were arithmetic and algebraic, they felt they would surely be covered in any sequence of courses that got as far as calculus.

The big lesson from the conversation was that the two sides never sat down together to discuss what was wanted and what was being taught. The conclusion was that they would work together to develop a course covering the desired topics. I hope they did.

We also visited a state university in New England where the students had marched on the state capitol to demand that calculus courses be taught by people who could speak comprehensible English. This was the consequence of the department's use of teaching assistants from foreign countries.

The arrangements for that trip sounded wonderful. We were to be housed in rooms on the second floor of a country inn well known in the area for the food served in its dining room on the main floor. The food, it turned out, was excellent. The rooms on the second floor were an afterthought. There were three of them, so the two women on the committee each got a room, and Anderson and I shared the third. The four of us had to make do with one bathroom.

Ann Watkins was one of the women. Some years later, when she had become the third woman ever to be president of the MAA, I told her how when I began my teaching career at Morton Junior College, I used to regard whomever was president of the MAA with what almost amounted to reverence. I said I never expected

I would ever meet a president, much less that she would be someone that I had seen in a bathrobe with curlers in her hair.

We met with some legislators on that trip, along with the chair and several members of the Mathematics Department. I felt that our committee was window dressing, a display trotted out by the department to prove to the legislature that the MAA was aware of this problem; and that if the department was to maintain respect in the mathematics community, the legislature would have to provide more money so that they could decrease reliance on teaching assistants.

There were some visits where we simply played the role of conciliators trying to resolve personal conflicts between people in the Mathematics Department. Unfortunately, it sometimes takes outsiders to get the principals, whether in the same department or not, to sit down and talk

For me, the great benefit of service on the committee was that it made my name better known among people at the MAA office and elsewhere in the larger mathematical community.

It was probably because of that exposure, and perhaps in part to my role in high school math competitions. that I was appointed to the Committee on the Undergraduate Program (CUPM), the committee that Creighton Buck had chaired while I was working under him on my Ph.D. It meant a great deal to me to think that I could follow in his footsteps in this way. It also put me in a position to see that change was going to take place across the nation in the way calculus was being taught. That awareness shaped a great deal of my work in the decade to come.

A Chance to Live Like a Student Again

For the interim term of January, 1986, Macalester obtained a grant for which my life story, or in this case lack of a story, made me an admirable fit. Citing the college's long history in trying to give students an international outlook, the grant was to be used to encourage faculty members who had never been abroad to plan a trip that would enable them to bring an international component into their teaching.

Never having been abroad, I was admirably qualified to apply. I knew that Macalester joined other colleges that had an interim term to provide month-long courses in Europe, so I looked into what was being offered. I was pleased to find a course led by two professors from a sister college titled "The Rise of Modern Science in Europe." It was to start at the Royal Observatory in Greenwich and proceed to points important to scientific development in Oxford, Paris, Munich, and Rome. I applied, proposing that I join this group just like a student. When my proposal was accepted, we decided that Dolores would enroll as one more student. With us, there were about 25 students from a variety of colleges.

We had only been in Greenwich for 20 minutes or so before I became a bit disillusioned with our faculty leaders. Kids were wandering about aimlessly, asking each other what the big deal was about this place, and why was a prominent line drawn through the grass and over sidewalks and pathways?

Being a member of the student group, I knew that readings had been assigned before we left the U.S. that would have answered their questions. But also being a teacher, I knew that most of these kids, having gone home after fall term finals to join in celebration of the holidays, had probably not done the assigned reading. Finally, being an idealist, I expected our faculty leaders to seize the teachable moment, gather the group together, and explain the meaning of the word *latitude*, the importance of the prime meridian, and the accomplishments of Christopher Wren.

None of this happened. Indeed, our faculty leaders were not in sight. I took it upon myself to try explaining the significance of 24 lines of latitude, the necessity of starting somewhere, and the convenience of giving the initial line a name—something like prime meridian. I told them that the legal description of the property on which their house stood back in the States ultimately made reference to this line.

It was a tough sell. I remember a highly skeptical young man who identified himself as from a middle-American state. He thought of turning the prime meridian on an axis through the poles (okay for rough thinking). Did I really mean that someone knew how many degrees one had to turn that meridian so that it would pass through his back yard at home? I told him that was what I meant.

Time and again our leaders missed wonderful teaching opportunities. I was very disappointed when we stood outside of the house where Galileo had been held under house arrest. Surely, I thought, someone will mention Santillana's *The Crime of Galileo*. Shouldn't someone mention that the authorities at the time reasoned that 7 is God's number of completion, that they illustrated this truth by pointing out that humans have 7 openings in their head, and that they therefore refused to look through Galileo's telescope because 7 planets had already been identified. "If I look through that thing and see another planet, I'll be as confused as you are," is a quote attributed to one of Galileo's inquisitors.

What an opportunity to point out that scientific inquiry does depend on our starting assumptions, that for scientific theories to change, it is often necessary to change basic assumptions, and that we surely need to recognize that reasoning by analogy may stimulate ideas but never serves as proof. The failures of our leaders in front of Galileo's house were themselves a crime.

If asked what I learned on that trip, I could list a lot of things. One is that years later, when talking as a provost to a faculty member preparing to lead a group of students abroad, I would have some good questions to ask. Have students been given an appropriate reading list beforehand? How will you insure that they actually do the reading? Do you know sites along the way where you and the students can enter into dialogue? What specific points do you hope to make with these students?

In spite of my disappointments, our faculty leaders did have the trip well organized. We kept to our schedule and got to all the promised places. The students respected such rules as were made to keep harmony while we lived together for a month. By the time we got to Rome, the students knew each other and enjoyed being together.

On a free night in Rome, the young women organized what they called a toga party, and they even invited my wife to join in; she did, and reported having a wonderful time. I went walking through Rome that night with one of our faculty leaders, a priest who had trained in Rome. It was a wonderful tour of a city he knew well. At one point I told him that his collar must make him look hungry, that I was amazed at how often we were propositioned as we walked along. He told me that there were so many priests in Rome that they were not treated any differently than any other man roaming the streets after dark.

A Sabbatical Year in Chapel Hill

In my first two sabbaticals, I'd been able to supplement the half salary that Macalester paid during a full year away by securing grants for promising young faculty. By 1985-86, I was a 51-year-old professor—still promising, but no longer so young. No grant was forthcoming. I chose to go to North Carolina's Research Triangle, thinking I might be able to supplement my salary by teaching at either Duke or the University of North Carolina.

It was UNC that came through, offering me the opportunity to teach a course in each of the two semesters I'd be there. Then, just before we left to go south, I was contacted to ask if I'd be willing to teach a third course because one of their regular faculty had broken a leg in an accident and wouldn't be able teach in the fall semester. It turned out that I made a bit more than the half salary I'd hoped for.

The additional course I was assigned was in discrete mathematics, a course being introduced in most mathematics departments around the country to provide the mathematics needed as a foundation for computer science majors. I reviewed a lot of material I hadn't thought about for quite a while, learned a few new things, and spent more time preparing for class than I'd counted upon.

My writing projects on this sabbatical were minimal. I forced myself through the requisite revision for a second edition of my linear algebra book, but poured my creative energies into an idea that had been percolating in my head ever since listening to those talks Dick Anderson gave making a case for allowing calculators in the calculus classroom. It seemed to me that we should be able to use calculators not only to simplify necessary arithmetic calculations but also to help students better understand calculus concepts. I wanted to write problems so that students, doing calculations that would be overwhelming by hand, could be led to discover things for themselves that often appeared as if by magic in standard courses.

I managed to write about half a dozen such lessons. I was particularly pleased with one that led students to discover that 2.7183 is a number that crops up in numerous problems. Only after they discovered this on their own did I tell them it was such an important number that it had the special name e, and that it was perhaps even more important than 3.1416.

When I returned to Macalester, I got Allan Kirch involved, and he soon produced programs that enabled students to make these same discoveries using computers. Incorporating these computer programs into worksheets set the stage for one of the biggest projects of my life, second only to the Math League. Describing that project will consume much of Chapter 8.

Oh yes, the League. As usual, I had written all the questions for the 1985-86 year in the summer before we left for Chapel Hill. When the season started, however, I was more dependent than ever on Kathy Grundhoefer. She dealt with the operational issues (what to do when snow hits one part of the state on a meet day, etc.), and we resolved over the phone mathematical questions such as, "Should we give credit for an answer of log 100 when it should be simplified to 2?"

It all worked well enough until we got to the day of the state meet at season's end. A question I'd written, used in the final event of the day, could be interpreted in a way that I hadn't intended, indeed had not even thought of. One of the top-scoring students in the state did think of it in this way, however, and of course got an answer that was marked wrong. He protested, but since he had made a much more difficult problem of it, none of the judges on the spot realized that with his interpretation, his answer was right. The *Minneapolis Tribune* carried a story on the tournament and reported someone else to be the state champion.

Only when the young man's coach had time the next morning to digest the unusual interpretation and the answer given did he conclude that a protest was justified. The judges agreed this time, and by noon on the day after the tournament, a new state champion had to be recognized. I readily acknowledged that the real mistake was in how I'd stated the problem. It was Kathy who attended to the sensitive problems of getting the trophies transferred to the right persons, correcting reports in the media, etc.

Does Sweet Tea Make One a Southern Baptist?

It turned out that on this sabbatical, the church we attended was a significant part of the enriching experience. In what we intended to be the first of several church visits around town, we happened into Binkley Baptist Church after we had gotten settled in our house for the year.

Students were just arriving for the fall term during the week of our first visit. The minister addressed himself to them. He spoke with great enthusiasm of the opportunity they had to attend a great university. It was clear as he spoke that he availed himself of many of the activities (lectures, plays, musical events) the university had to offer beyond the classroom, and he encouraged them to do likewise.

In time, he acknowledged that if they were first-year students, they might find that some things they'd been taught in their home church would be challenged. My initial surprise came when he followed that up by telling them not to respond too quickly. It may be, he told them, that some of your ideas need challenging, and in any case, it can never hurt to think seriously about what you believe.

He extended to them a sincere invitation to come to his office to discuss questions they might be confronting. Above all, he implored them to continue the good habit they were initiating that day. "Join us for the support of a congregation, all of whom struggle in one way or another with their faith." No one could have doubted by the time he finished that he loved the university, that he loved interacting with students, and that he loved his work.

In time we learned that Binkley Baptist was started by a group that broke off the First Baptist Church of Chapel Hill. Tension in First Baptist over civil rights had come to a head when the church leadership refused a student request to invite Martin Luther King as a guest speaker. I did not doubt that I could learn a lot about ministry to students from this pastor. We never visited another church in Chapel Hill.

It was probably on our second or third visit when it was announced that the men's fellowship would be having its usual fall kick-off dinner, with coach Dean Smith discussing last year's basketball season and prospects for the year to come. UNC was the national champion in basketball right then, having had the talents of Michael Jordan to carry them to the NCAA title the previous season. The main street along the campus was still painted Carolina blue from the victory parade of last March when we arrived in town.

I assumed that they must have a connection that enabled them to bring Dean Smith to the church each year for this fall event. Smith, after all, had a national reputation as a coach who annually had North Carolina ranked among the top teams in the country. Indeed, they did have a connection. I learned that Smith had been an active member of the church for years. In time, I came to joke that down there in basketball country, having Dean Smith present was like having God in the congregation. The university was building a new basketball emporium while we were there, known about town as the Dean Dome. Donations in honor of Smith came in so fast that twice while building was underway they made upgrades to the plans.

Dean Smith

Of course I went to the men's dinner. It featured not only the promised talk by Smith but also a movie of clips selected from films of last season's games. Someone with an obvious flair for music had matched the spectacular moves of Jordan on the basketball floor to ballet music. It was a work of art that should have been on national TV.

I later met the man who had created the film. He'd been a concert pianist and a teacher in UNC's School of Music until, in an accident, he lost one hand. He was a member at Binkley when this happened, and Dean Smith offered him a job filming UNC basketball games.

The pastor, Bob Seymour, was probably right when he said that everyone in his congregation struggled in one way or another with the faith. He saw to that. I have never heard any minister, and certainly not a Baptist minister, so consistently bring Biblical passages to bear on current controversial subjects.

He tackled head on the country's racial problems and the shameful role that Southern churches had and (according to him) still played. He felt strongly that the Christian church should lead the way in caring for the needy and infirm; he wondered out loud how people who were united in their support for the death penalty could be so adamant against abortion in all cases; he was (in 1985, remember) wanting the church to be accepting of homosexuals, and I can still almost repeat his sermon calling for some sort of gun control in this country.

Rev. Robert Seymour

Seymour's passion for taking his Christian concerns into the community led him to write a regular column in the Chapel Hill newspaper, which carried the column for years after he retired. He was surely a prophetic voice in that community.

I had lunch with Rev. Seymour a number of times. He had great rapport with college students, and there was a lot to learn as he talked about his approach to counseling them. I sometimes challenged him about positions that surely put him at odds with many ministers in the Southern Baptist Convention. His responses were always vigorous and rooted in his understanding of Scripture. When I asked if he ever felt out of place with the Southern Baptists, he told me that he still loved sweet tea.

He liked to say of controversies that arise out of modern technology, "Do you really think the Scriptures are so clear on that point as to justify breaking fellowship with people who want to draw on a little compassion and common sense?"

We developed a good relationship, and when he took to publishing books of old sermons and newspaper columns, he sent me a copy of each one as they came out. It seems appropriate to conclude my appreciative recollection by quoting from the preface to the last book he sent to me. It was written by Dean Smith.

> The day I was named as UNC's head coach, Bob called to congratulate me. At that time, I was serving as chair of our church's Student Affairs Committee, and Bob said, "Now that you're head coach, you have no more Student Affairs Committee meetings to go to: your primary church work is the opportunity afforded by your vocation. Go find a Black basketball player for the university."
>
> That is vintage Bob Seymour. His ministry fostered our congregation's commitment to the principle that "church work" is not what you do inside the church "headquarters," as he calls it, but what you do out in the world in the course of your day-to-day activities. . . .
>
> And students from the university have always loved him. I still remember one coed from a very strict Baptist background who asked Bob, "Can a Christian dance?" With a twinkle in his eye, he said "Some can and some can't."

Once again, even without a newly written book under my arm, I returned to Macalester thinking that my sabbatical had been an enlightening time that left me better prepared to be a contributing member of the Macalester faculty.

VIII. Lessons in Academic Leadership

*It's important to remember that positions
you take can be wrong.
And in academia, you are surrounded
by people who have the freedom and the ability
to show you that you are wrong.*

Venerable Calculus Looks Vulnerable

A national consensus was developing by the time I returned to Macalester in the fall of 1986; something had to be done about the teaching of calculus.

Calls to reform mathematics teaching at all levels have a long history. Someone is always discovering anew that students should be taught to understand, not just perform rote calculations or memorize formulas. Calculus, a tool used in so many client disciplines (physics, chemistry, economics, engineering), has been a particular target of critics with ideas of how it might be better taught.

The impetus for change in 1986 was more pronounced, however. A prominent computer scientist, Tony Ralston, had suggested that as we entered the digital age, perhaps a course in discrete mathematics should replace calculus as the basic course taken by all engineers and scientists.

For generations, calculus has been the culmination toward which high school mathematics built, and at the same time the entry point for higher mathematics. To suggest replacing it? Them's fight'n words.

When defenders rushed to the mathematical barricades, however, the most thoughtful among them were dismayed by what they were called upon to defend. Led by mathematician Ron Douglas, the troops gathered in a 1986 Sloan Foundation-sponsored conference at Tulane University to assess the situation. Their report, *Toward a Lean and Lively Calculus*, was published by the Mathematics Association of America (MAA), and it identified a number of problems they felt would complicate an effort to defend the course:

- An unacceptably high percentage of students who began the study of calculus were not finishing the course with a grade of C or higher.
- Texts were becoming encyclopedic, most running over 800 pages.

- Applications being taught were artificial and archaic.
- The course was being taught as if calculators and computers had not been invented.
- Students learned nothing of the central role that calculus has played in scientific work, how the ideas of calculus came to be discovered, or the names of those who made the discoveries.

A Personal Reaction

I had not been a participant in the conference; neither was I in the vanguard of those seeing a need to make major changes in the way calculus was being taught. The effort I'd made in my first textbook to introduce a new approach to the calculus of several variables was long behind me. My department, like most, would from time to time tire of the textbook in use and switch to a different one, and I would incorporate my own ideas into whatever textbook we next chose. Students reacted well to the traditional course I was teaching, and I was reasonably content. Nevertheless, as I read the problems cited in the report, I found myself largely in agreement with what it said.

Very few Macalester students were failing our calculus course, but we were a selective private college. Statistics from around the country certainly showed that a high percentage of students who entered Calculus I never made it to the end of Calculus II. Everyone knew that certain undergraduate programs (pre-med, pre-law, and business programs being notorious in this regard) required calculus as a way to identify if not "weed out" weaker students. With that intention, it might be expected that there would be a lot of attrition.

Nevertheless, it was certainly true that at many universities, senior faculty were quite content to turn the teaching of calculus over to graduate students and accept high failure rates as an inevitable consequence of enrolling unqualified students in a demanding course. The fault, they figured, was undoubtedly with the poor preparation being provided by high schools. I never forgot the (hopefully extreme) advice given to us as teaching assistants at Wisconsin: "If you think half of them should fail, fail them."

I regarded it as entirely reasonable to be concerned with the high number of students that were not succeeding in calculus, though I thought it probably had more to do with who was advised to take the course than it did with how the course was taught.

I heartily agreed with the second criticism, the size of the texts. I believed, I still believe, that as a student, I had a good course in calculus, in which we used a then-popular text by Clyde Love from the University of Michigan. It covered differential and integral calculus in 421 pages. Texts in the late 1980s were typically running 750 to 850 pages.

I did not come lately to the idea that texts were becoming too large. In my first calculus text, published in 1968, I wrote, "A conscious effort has been made to reverse the trend of calculus texts to be encyclopedic." In the preface to the second edition, I admitted to making a concession to the publisher by including an introductory chapter on analytic geometry, but then concluded that "we have adhered to the principle that conciseness should take precedence over the temptation to say everything you can think of about the subject at hand."

I have an abiding interest in the nature of proof, as is evidenced in much of what I've written in this book, and I understand why Bertrand Russell said that "obviousness is always the enemy of correctness." I still believe, however, that when new material is introduced, it's a great help to appeal to intuition, to make something that is true look as if it's what one would expect. A proof can come in a later course where students can be expected to have an interest in knowing how to deal with examples showing that things can go wrong.

In an introductory calculus course, I think a short presentation that acknowledges but does not dwell on subtleties is much to be preferred over an encyclopedic treatment.

A few paragraphs back, I enjoyed pointing out that my calculus books, running contrary to the trend at the time, were written with brevity as one goal. I can make no such claim about avoiding artificial applications. I included the following:

- A farmer with 200 yards of fencing wishes to maximize the area of a pasture that he [nobody worried about sexism in those days] could enclose if one side of the field is bordered by a [always assumed to be perfectly straight] river. What should be the length of the side parallel to the river?
- A quart of soup is to be sold in a cylindrical can. What should be the ratio of the radius of the can to its height in order to minimize the area, including the top and bottom, of the metal used in making the can?
- Maximize the volume of a box formed by cutting squares out of each corner and folding up the sides of a rectangular piece of cardboard that is 16 inches long, 12 inches wide. [Warning should have been given not to try making a useful box this way].

I've been guilty of them all.

It's easy to make fun of the goofy stuff that authors of calculus books offered as applications. It's not nearly so easy to decide what to do about it. A significant problem in electronics requires a good deal of background about circuits that the average student does not have. To provide it takes a lot of classroom time (and more pages in the text). It asks students to invest time and energy in a subject in which very few (except for budding electrical engineers) have any interest, and it puts most teachers in the position of having to teach something about which they know very little. The same criticisms could be made for almost any nontrivial application one might consider.

The safest way for an author to demonstrate the usefulness of calculus as a tool for optimization is to draw problems from within the confines of mathematics:

A circular cone is to be inscribed in a sphere of radius 1. Find the radius of the base of the cone that will have the largest possible volume. (See the figures on page 151).

In most people's mind, however, that doesn't qualify as a useful application.

For authors of texts who worry about the length of their book, the difficulty of including meaningful applications of calculus seems to be a problem without a solution.

Of the suggestions made by those trying to improve a calculus course, the idea that students should make use of technology was the most controversial. Critics imagined students no longer bothering to learn basic facts because they could be found on a screen. They thought of calculators and computers as tools that would enable students to get answers without having to understand the processes being used. They liked to point out that a student's understanding was not improved because he or she was able to solve problems involving more complicated calculations.

I saw little merit to most objections to technology. Some seemed contrived, like the concern that students would rely on looking up on their computer things that (in the suddenly sanguine memories of the critics) all students once knew. Should we then also prohibit students from using dictionaries, hoping in this way that they would become better at spelling? I thought that if available technology simply led to using exercises requiring more complicated computation, the problem was with the one posing the exercises, not with the one using technology to solve them.

As already mentioned, I had been thinking about ways to use calculators and computers to help students discover things for themselves. That certainly put me in the camp of those who thought that a judicious use of technology could enhance the teaching of calculus. It was an uncomfortable place for me, however. People of that persuasion had moved way beyond me in their mastery of computer algebra systems. They were thankful for the rapid advances in technology. I was thankful for the availability of my colleague, Allan Kirch, who could answer questions I had about existing technology,

The pressure from students to use calculators and computers surely dictated the outcome; technology would be used. The question was whether their teachers would think of ways technology could be used to deepen student understanding.

The last of the expressed concerns, calling for placing calculus in historical and scientific perspective, surprised me. It's not that I disagreed; it was just that no calculus class I ever heard of spent significant time on the history of the ideas or the lives of the people who developed them. Even in the days when I wondered what mathematics had to contribute to a liberal education, it had not occurred to me to include material of this sort in a calculus course.

When I gave thought to it, I came to believe there was more here than just human interest. From the historical development of calculus there are important lessons to be learned about the costs of letting gender or ethnicity affect one's idea of who can succeed in doing mathematics. Instructive stories can be told about what motivated certain discoveries, about sibling rivalry, and about seeing connections that others fail to notice. I agreed that a student who finishes a calculus course should know something about the place of calculus in the development of science.

The effect of the report was to make me realize that I'd been teaching calculus for a long time without thinking about whether I might improve the course. There are people possessed of such self-confidence that they bristle at any suggestion that what they are doing might be improved. I am not one of them. When the National Science Foundation announced a followup conference in Washington to stimulate possible responses. I decided I had a reason to go to one of my favorite cities.

Action and Reaction

There was another good reason for me to attend the conference. I was, as previously noted, serving on the Committee on the Undergraduate Program in Mathematics (CUPM). This long-standing committee of the MAA is charged with monitoring and in some cases trying to influence the teaching of mathematics. It would certainly be involved in any effort to improve the teaching of calculus. Everyone on this committee made a point of being at the conference, and it was from my position on CUPM that I had an opportunity to see the wide variety of responses that were developing around the country.

The most immediate responses came from advocates for making use of technology. Manufacturers of calculators hired mathematicians to help develop instruments with features that would be useful in teaching calculus, and published books explaining how to use them in the classroom. (I contributed a chapter to one such book for Texas Instruments.) Others embraced computers to the extent of wanting to make calculus a laboratory course. A dizzying array of manuals began to appear to this end. There was no agreement on which computer language should be used, however, and nonbelievers argued that students spent more time learning a computer language than learning calculus.

A spate of new textbooks appeared, unavoidably alienating a significant segment of their intended audience by what they omitted, and then partially vitiating these steps toward leanness by adding pages to include meaningful applications.

To keep calculus concerns from pushing all other business off the table, CUPM formed a subcommittee: Calculus Reform and the First Two Years (CRAFTY). I volunteered to serve on the subcommittee, thinking that CRAFTY should try to bring some order out of the chaos. It was soon clear to me that even if we had dictatorial powers, we wouldn't be able to get agreement in our own committee of six on which suggestions should be adopted. I probably expressed too strongly my feeling that CRAFTY should take some leadership. I was soon asked to chair the committee.

That's one way to wind up as chair of a committee: Show some interest in the most time-consuming topic on the table.

As soon as the news circulated that I was to be chair, I got a call from Creighton Buck. He congratulated me, but that was not really the purpose of the call. Drawing on his experience of being chair of CUPM when "new math" was being introduced in the schools, he called to give me fair warning.

He said people will come out of the woodwork with ideas, some good, some bad, some resurrections of ideas abandoned 30 years ago. Every idea for change of any kind will have vocal opponents, he warned, and "as chair of the committee trying to give direction to suggested improvements, you will be blamed for anything that anyone dislikes." The warning brought to mind the experience I described in Chapter 3 when Buck had been roundly criticized as some pinko professor trying to weaken the nation's youth.

The changes taking place during Buck's tenure were directed at public schools, so the criticism he experienced came from parents frustrated by their inability to help their kids with math homework, from school administrators bearing the brunt of parental criticism, and the public press.

Changes in the way calculus was taught did not arouse these groups. Criticism of calculus reform came from some (certainly not all) of the leading mathematicians in research universities. Most of them hadn't taught calculus for years; many wouldn't have known what text was being used in their own schools. They interpreted efforts to improve the number of students who would succeed in a calculus course as a plan to "dumb down" the course and were sure that the introduction of technology would have the same effect.

Without really looking at what was being proposed, many of these critics liked to point out that the traditional course had served them very well, and they believed it would surely serve the next generation just as well. The fact that they had been at the top of their mathematics classes throughout their schooling and would no doubt have done very well under almost any kind of instruction seemed never to occur to them. Most of their criticism seemed unjustified to me, but they were people to whom I looked up as leading lights of my profession, and their criticisms hurt.

There are times when anyone who aspires to leadership must remember Harry Truman's advice: "If you can't stand the heat, get out of the kitchen."

The experience reminded me of a visit that William Sloan Coffin, while chaplain at Yale University, made to Macalester during the Vietnam War era. He was calling for faculty members to include in the curriculum some history of Western involvement in Vietnam. He observed that while college faculty members think of the business community as stuck in their conservative ways, and like to think of themselves as open-minded scholars in constant search of better ways to do things, their resistance to curricular change of any kind belies that self-perception. "At least industry has economic pressure to force change," he quipped. "If Edsel had been a course, faculties would still be teaching it."

I can no longer recall the order of events during my tenure as chair of CRAFTY. I got to visit many experimental programs around the country. I became aware of how many advanced placement calculus courses were being taught in high schools. I know I was confused by the arguments of those wanting to limit technology to handheld calculators versus those wanting calculus to be taught in a computer lab. Departments were dividing into camps, depending on how individuals felt about calculus reform.

It was clear that as a committee of the MAA, an organization seeking to serve all the nation's schools, CRAFTY could not take sides when the members it was to serve were so divided on what, if anything, should be changed. Eventually I decided that our best service would be to produce a wealth of exemplary materials to be freely drawn upon by authors, technology companies producing manuals to go with their products, or classroom teachers wishing to supplement whatever text they were using. The materials I had in mind would be in the public domain, so no one wishing to use them would need to worry about copyright issues. Ideally, the material for a particular application or a short history of an early contributions to calculus would be in a format ready for a classroom teacher to make copies and distribute to a class.

The CRAFTY committee thought such a project might be worthwhile, but they were all in that part of the mathematics community who agreed that current calculus courses indeed had problems that needed to be addressed. Those who were opposed to any major changes were getting more vocal in their criticism, making it an issue as to whether anything should or needed to be changed. The MAA hierarchy decided that to publish the material I suggested would be interpreted as favoring one side of the argument, and they turned it down.

Private Colleges Take on a Public Project

I reluctantly agreed that the MAA should not take on a project about which the membership had strong but very divided opinions, but by that time I was too invested to drop the idea. Having worked years earlier with the 14 Associated Colleges of the Midwest (ACM) in developing a program in undergraduate research, I decided to explore whether that organization might undertake producing the materials I envisioned.

By getting numerous colleges involved, we would have many different teaching styles, many different technologies, and many classes in which to test materials. As I talked about these ideas, faculties in a sister organization, the 12 members of the Great Lakes Colleges Association (GLCA) (Albion, Antioch, Denison, DePauw, Earlham, Hope, Kalamazoo, Kenyon, Oberlin, Ohio Wesleyan, Wabash, Wooster) expressed interest in joining the project. The fact that other people were interested in joining was the first real encouragement to me that the idea might be developed as a successful project.

The next step was to get funding for an undertaking of the

size I envisioned. It was time to make a proposal to NSF. For that I had to get more specific about just what I hoped to produce. From my service on CRAFTY, my travels around the country, and my discussions with representatives from a group that now included 26 colleges, I had ideas for five books that would collectively be known as *Resources for Calculus*.

Five Volumes of Resources for Calculus

I. Provided with leading questions and aids to computation available with modern technology, students can *Learn by Discovery* some mathematical wonders of calculus that traditionally have been introduced by highly theoretical methods. The required leading questions are provided in this volume.

II. The lists of exercises found in traditional calculus texts, intended to illustrate and reinforce a new idea, were often rendered trivial if one had a handheld calculator. New problems, designed to teach these same ideas to a student equipped with a calculator, are provided in *Calculus Problems for a New Century*.

III. To understand significant *Applications of Calculus*, students typically need substantial background information. This volume provides background for a variety of applications, making it possible for an instructor to choose, copy, and distribute material with which he or she is familiar, and for which students in the class have some interest.

IV. An unintended lesson drawn from textbook lists of exercises is that if you can't see how to solve a problem in 10 minutes, move on to the next one. This volume provides *Problems for Student Investigation*, projects on which a student or a group of students are expected to work over an extended period.

V. This volume provides a collection of *Readings for Calculus* from which an instructor can copy and distribute to a class articles giving names and stories important to the development of calculus.

It skips over a great deal of negotiating, both with those who would be producing the material and with the staff at NSF, to say that in 1988, the proposal was funded. Still apprehensive about appearing supportive of the controversial movement to change the teaching of calculus, the MAA was reluctant to be the agent for the project. I therefore turned to Macalester to function in this capacity. I knew that this had grown to be a very ambitious undertaking, but I did not realize that it would be the consuming activity of my life for the next five years.

Getting Started

I began by visiting each of the 26 departments, where I described the project, got a lot of ideas, and looked for five people I would ultimately ask to be editors for the five volumes. These ended up being three from the ACM: Anita Solow (Grinnell), Bob Fraga (Ripon), Phil Straffin (Beloit); and two from the GLCA: Mic Jackson (Earlham), Woody Dudley (DePauw). I also came to realize that I would need two more people in my leadership group.

Mathematics is sequential. Understanding one topic usually depends upon understanding something else first. Editors developing materials would have to have some idea how topics would be sequenced, some sort of syllabus. Developing a syllabus, keeping in mind that it should be lean and flexible enough to be acceptable on 26 campuses, was no small undertaking, requiring someone of great patience and good humor. Andy Sterrett (Denison) brought an easy-going spirit to the job.

Finally, if we were to fully utilize the strength of having 26 colleges involved, we decided that before we selected something to appear in one of the volumes, it should be subjected to testing in several of the participating schools. It was surely a big job for someone, a seventh person we decided, to find "volunteers" to test each submission, collect evaluations, and then give feedback to the respective editors. George Andrews (Oberlin) took on the task.

The addition of Andy Sterrett and George Andrews tipped the balance on the leadership team to three from the ACM and four from the GLCA. That pleased me greatly because I wanted it clear from the beginning that in leading a project involving two consortia, I would not favor the ACM, to which I belonged.

With a seven-person leadership group chosen, the next step was to get them together to meet each other, work out a tentative schedule, and describe ideas for the respective volumes. They felt we should begin with a conference to which we would invite the mathematics faculty from each of the 26 participating schools. This would give the editors a chance to describe ideas they had, hear ideas from those assembled, and recruit writers.

When planning a conference for which there is not an established tradition and a group that habitually attends, thought must be given to how to attract an audience. Location is certainly key. Since most ACM schools are on the west side of Lake Michigan and most GLCA schools are on the east side, a spot at the southern tip of the lake made sense. Meeting on a college campus is attractive because food service is available at a cost considerably below hotel prices, and campuses usually have arrangements with nearby motels and hotels that give price breaks to people coming to events at the college. For all these reasons, Lake Forest College on the north side of Chicago looked attractive.

I must add that in picking Lake Forest, I was also aware that most of the cooperating schools were located in small towns, from which faculty members and their spouses liked to visit Chicago on occasion. Thinking along this line, I scheduled events so that our business would conclude on a Saturday afternoon, allowing time for the group to board chartered buses that got us downtown in time for dinner at a nice restaurant, followed by the evening performance at the Second City Comedy Theatre.

By the time of the conference, each of the five editors had some ideas for articles they would like someone to write. They appealed to the assembled group for authors, and as each editor described ideas for articles, other ideas were suggested by the group.

Anticipating that the effort to develop a syllabus would be contentious, I thought that rather than ask what topics could be deleted from the courses we had been teaching, it might work better to ask what topics absolutely had to be included in any course worthy of being called a calculus course. I invited a non-mathematician, a person skilled in group dynamics, to lead the discussion.

My hopes notwithstanding, it was clear as discussion went on, and on and on, that we were getting close to including most of the topics a large group could think of. This prompted the leader to try posing an altogether different approach.

He pointed out that we all came from small private colleges, each governed by boards that inevitably included members who were graduates of the college. He asked how many in the room knew at least one member of their board whom they had once taught in a calculus class. A surprisingly large number of hands went up. He said, "Graduates invited back to serve on boards are usually wealthy, so I'm going to assume that the board member you know is not a mathematician." That of course got a laugh.

He then asked us to imagine that as we were walking on campus, we saw this nonmathematician board member coming toward us. "Imagine asking this person what he or she remembered from your calculus class. What do you hope the answer might be?"

That question did give a refreshingly new viewpoint as we considered what we should be teaching in our calculus class.

This conference was held in the fall, and the Macalester board met in January, so I decided to try this approach on two members of our board whom I'd had in calculus. It's a digression, but I can't resist relating the experience.

The first one to whom I put the question was Tim Hultquist. He was chairman of our board and an officer in a large Wall Street brokerage. I remembered him well as a good student. When I asked my question, he told me that it was funny that I should ask.

His son had just been home from college over the Christmas break and had told his dad that he was having trouble with calculus. Tim reminded me that I was teaching out of the calculus text I had written when he was a student. He liked it so much, he said, that he had always kept it. He told me that he got it off a shelf in his study, was surprised at how much he remembered, and used it in helping his son. The kid thought the book more understandable than the text he was using, and asked to take it with him when he returned to college.

That was an unexpected and much appreciated boost to my ego.

I next sought out the second board member who had been in my class. I didn't remember her from her student days, but she had introduced herself as a former calculus student of mine when I met her as a new board member. She headed a large insurance company. When I asked my question, she hesitated, then laughed and said, "I'll make you a deal. I won't tell anyone what I remember from your class if you don't tell anyone what grade I got."

That was more what I was afraid might happen. It deflated me back to where I belonged.

Our group's work began in earnest after the Lake Forest conference. We consistently took advantage of the two national meetings organized by the MAA and the American Mathematics Society, one in the summer, the other in January. Depending on the calendar, I would schedule a two-day meeting of the seven project leaders either just before or just after the national meetings, almost always at a nearby college or university.

Colleges and universities are wonderfully cooperative in allowing groups such as ours to meet free of charge in their libraries or other small conference rooms. Since the leaders in the group usually had their way to the national meetings paid by their home institution, this arrangement kept our travel expenses to a minimum.

The nature of the work at these sessions changed, of course, as time went on. At first, each editor would give a report on articles and material being written, and by whom. When there was an idea for an article for which no author had yet been identified, the group as a whole would make suggestions. As time moved on, editors would arrive with the first draft of an article, which the group would then scan and critique. We eventually got to the point where we received reports on what materials were being classroom tested, and then to ideas for using, as much as possible, the same format in each book.

I tried always to schedule breaks during the day: a visit to the host Mathematics Department, a walk through the Art Department or through some special exhibit if there was one on campus. We were fortunate in that Bob Fraga, one of our editors, had debated in college between a major in mathematics or in music so that he could join the ranks of aspiring concert pianists. It was natural, then, that after a day of working together, we'd find a spot on campus where there was a piano, around which we could gather after supper for an impromptu concert. And as my readers will guess by now, I always made sure that we went to a nice restaurant on our last night together.

Like most groups of mathematicians in those days, our group was, with the exception of Anita Solow, entirely male. This often drew attention when we went out to eat. One night, a waitress that appeared to be about college age surveyed the group and then addressed Anita. "How do you manage this?" With no hesitation, Anita said, "Study your calculus really hard." Stories like that became part of the group lore.

In one of our early meetings, an editor described something he was doing that ran contrary to what the group had decided earlier. Restrained reminders from the others of what we had agreed upon were met with resistance. Finally Anita spoke up, and in words shorn of subtlety, told him that we had an agreement and he was to abide by it. The role left for me was to talk to him later to make sure he didn't feel run over by the group.

The incident passed easily, but it set a pattern upon which I came to rely. If discussion of a topic went on too long, if there was disagreement about which author to choose when two were available for an assignment, or if the group couldn't agree on where to have dinner, Anita would step in and end the dithering. The group seemed to appreciate her ability to move us past the time-consuming discussions that sometimes erupt over relatively minor points, and I came to value these interventions that in time made her the de facto leader of discussions.

When I thought the MAA would be the fiscal agent for the project, I assumed they would also publish our collections in their MAA Notes series. This latter assumption was still stuck in my head even after Macalester had become the fiscal agent. It turned out, however, that the committee that selected material to be published in the Notes series balked at the idea of publishing five volumes from the same project.

They finally agreed to publish four of the five, wanting to omit *Volume I, Learning by Discovery*. I was adamant. The editors had worked together as if on one project, the books had been coordinated to look like one set, and I was not going to have one editor's work orphaned. I began to negotiate with commercial publishers until the MAA finally consented to publish all five books.

In the last year of our work together, we got valuable help from two unexpected sources. The first came from Creighton Buck, whom I have previously described as being something like a second father to me. He was retired by then, and having watched our project ever since his warning to me, he offered in that last year to read drafts of all five volumes. The suggestions he produced were greatly appreciated by all the editors.

The other help came from a requirement that NSF imposed. As their investment in the project mounted, they decided they would like an evaluation of how useful these materials were proving to be in the classes where they were being tested. Although George Andrews had been doing exactly that from the beginning, they wanted an opinion from someone outside of our group. In negotiations with them, the name of Kathy Heid from Penn State came up. We welcomed her observations, which were positive, pleasing NSF greatly. More important from my personal view, she proved very helpful to me several years later, as I'll subsequently explain.

Before turning our materials over to the printer, the leadership team set aside a week to meet at Macalester. The plan was for everyone to proofread every volume. Recognizing that one cannot be a critical reader for hours on end, I broke each day into four two-hour segments. Between segments, we walked to a new spot on campus conducive to resuming our reading, or sometimes went somewhere in the larger community, such as going for lunch at the Science Museum of Minnesota. There we could work during the afternoon in the cafeteria, which was deserted after the noon rush. That week ended with an evening cruise on the Mississippi River. A picture of the group as we boarded the ship has ever since graced a wall in my study. Anita stands radiant in the center, as she did throughout the five years.

The five volumes, known as *Resources for Calculus*, were displayed with great fanfare at the national meetings in January, 1993. The MAA director of publications told me that sales of the set made more money for the Association than anything they had ever published; and as a final hurrah, it turned out that when the books were displayed to be purchased as sets or as individual volumes at meetings of mathematicians around the country, it was Volume I that was most often stolen.

Maintaining Cohesive Leadership

Several people with experience in directing long-term projects commented to me when the project was finally finished that

The *Resources for Calculus* editors
Front: Wayne Roberts, Anita Solow, Philip Straffin, Robert Fraga
Back: John Ramsay, Andy Sterrett, George Andrews, Underwood Dudley

it was very unusual for a group of academics to stay together as we did over a five-year stretch. Sabbaticals, new assignments in their home institution, a book of their own that needed revising: It's very common in academia for people, with good reason, to drop out of a project.

I hadn't thought about it at the time, but in looking back, it seems to me that several factors contributed to the leadership team's cohesiveness. To begin with, editors were involved very early in making some key decisions.

Similarity of cover design, common front material, inclusion of the general syllabus, formatting of references and more would make it clear on even casual perusal that the individual volumes were part of a set.

Use of funds would be decided by and transparent to the editors.

Editors would keep each other updated on what topics were being covered in their volumes, and what writers they were using.

The MAA would be our first choice of a publisher, but if the Association refused, I would seek a common publisher of all five volumes.

There would be no compensation to any editor or contributing writer.

With these key decisions made and faithfully followed, the editors felt that they had responsibility, not just for their own volume, but for the project as a whole. At the same time, working within the purpose set out for their individual volumes, each editor had complete control of what material to include, and what writers and/or contributors would be called upon. We had senior editors in the group to whom younger editors could turn for counsel, a nice combination, experience tempering youthful enthusiasm.

I could devote myself to setting times and places for meetings, keeping track of finances, and keeping 26 chairs of departments feel informed and involved. Most important, with Anita keeping the group on schedule and working in accord with agreements, I could focus on maintaining collegiality in the group and, above all, making sure that every time we got together, the group had a good time.

This is a good place to applaud the financial procedures that NSF follows. When a proposal is approved for scientific merit, the proposed budget is scrutinized, and often reduced through negotiation with the project director. Once the budget is approved, the director has great freedom to shift funds between line items as the project unfolds, the only requirement being that the proposed project is completed within budget.

As previously explained, we saved money on travel and by meeting on college campuses when we could. NSF policy then allowed me to use some of the savings to pay for amenities I believe helped to keep the group together over a five-year span. As it turned out, we finished the project with enough grant money left over to send one set of the books to the Mathematics Department of every university, every four-year college, and every two-year college in the country.

When I look back now on the privilege I had of leading this project, I'm struck by how earlier experiences prepared me for the job. The idea of turning to ACM schools built on the experience of getting their support for the summer-industry-related programs I had run in my early years at Macalester, the same programs that gave me my first experiences with NSF.

In building the Math League, I had seen the value of modifying my own ideas after listening to others' suggestions, not always easy to do in the midst of activities you've planned out in your mind. I'd learned to apply for and then manage grants, and had learned many lessons about planning conferences that mixed work with enough fun to make people want to come back. The contacts I'd made with the leaders of the MAA were helpful, and my membership on CUPM proved invaluable.

I certainly never anticipated a project as big as *Resources* turned out to be. For me, the lesson was that if you plunge into worthwhile projects as they come along, it's surprising to see how they prepare you for bigger things. My friend Joe Gallian, working from relatively remote University of Minnesota-Duluth, started his climb to the presidency of the MAA with a series of Undergraduate Research Program grants, the same grants that I had once drawn upon. When president of the MAA, he wrote an article in the MAA Monthly giving advice to young people wanting to get involved in MAA activities. His advice: "Just say yes."

Hitting the Road

The National Science Foundation was pleased at the reception that *Resources* received, and was quick to approve a follow-up grant that would enable me to promote the books around the country. I visited many sectional meetings of the MAA, and in a development I didn't foresee, many colleges invited me to speak at workshops they put on for high school teachers in their area who were teaching advanced placement calculus.

I remember this peripatetic period with real fondness. It was a rare weekend when I wasn't flying somewhere. I got to visit a wonderful cross-section of schools. I made acquaintances with people I stayed in contact with for years afterwards. I enjoyed the repartee that invariably developed around the art of teaching, not only of calculus but of mathematics in general. A lot of humor from those sessions sticks with me yet.

More than once I heard people comment on the irony of having departments that used calculus as a course to filter out weak students complain because the mathematics department was flunking too many of their students. One mathematician marveled that the National Science Foundation, believing that calculus was being taught poorly, was now giving money to fix the problem to the same people that had screwed it up. I learned that I could always get a laugh with the observation that if we had but looked at ourselves, we would have known that it would be easier to be lively than to be lean.

At the Iowa section of the MAA, I was the featured speaker of the morning, just before lunch. Intending to give the usual opportunity to ask questions when I finished, Elgin Johnson, chair of the section, asked, "Is there anything anyone wants to bring up besides their lunch?"

At Wheaton College in Illinois, at a conference for high school teachers, I was to participate in a panel discussion. When I saw the setup on stage, several high school teachers were to be seated on stools in a semicircle around the place where I was to stand. I didn't like standing like the expert in front of questioning high school teachers; I wanted to sit on a stool like the others and asked if they could find another stool.

Bob Brabenec, harried, as is any organizer of a conference, was I think a bit annoyed with this request for a last-minute change on stage, but he sent a student helper to look for another stool. He had begun his welcome to the audience when the student came on stage to hand him the stool. He apologized for the interruption, put the stool in place, and said to the audience, "I have heard of people who like to sing in the shower, but this is the first time I've had to deal with someone who wants to speak from the stool."

I was still chair of CRAFTY during this period, and in this capacity I was asked to conduct several workshops that took a broader look at the goals of the reform effort and the changes taking place. The most memorable of these took place at Daley Community College, an institution serving a mostly Black community in Chicago.

The most memorable part of that conference was that the chairman of the Mathematics Department was about my age. He had grown up about the same distance from Cicero Avenue as I did, he on the east side of the dividing line, I on the west. Each night of that week-long workshop, participants had supper together, after which my host would drive me back to my motel, come in with me, and sit to visit.

We both remembered being told as kids to stay on our side of Cicero Avenue. We both remembered the race riot in Cicero, and other events that got noticed on both sides of the divide. We were able to laugh at some of the things we were told as kids; we cringed at others. It was one more of those unexpected events that contribute to your education in ways never to be forgotten. I remember it as a good week when I saw Cicero from a totally different vantage point.

Association of Christians in Mathematical Sciences

Mentioning Bob Brabenec in the last section provides a nice segue to a new topic. Bob came to Wheaton right after I turned down their invitation, choosing to stay at Macalester early in my career. We communicated quite a bit during his first year or two, always met at the annual meetings, and became good friends.

It was probably after he had been at Wheaton about 10 years when Bob got the idea of bringing together mathematicians who taught at small Christian schools. He thought that perhaps if they got to know each other, they could be of help to one another in such things as recruiting young men and women interested in teaching at Christian schools. He asked me what I thought of the idea.

Bob Brabenec

I did what I could to discourage him. My main argument was that faculty members from small, church-related schools are usually not paid handsomely, and typically have limited funds for travel and professional development. It's easy for people in such circumstances to get isolated from their professional organizations. I wanted to see them use what funds they had for travel to regular professional meetings, not to meetings that would only exacerbate their isolation from the mainstream.

Bob pressed forward in spite of me. In 1977, a fledgling organization met for the first time on the Wheaton campus. Over 100 faculty members from small Christian colleges showed up.

With the grace that is so typical of him, Bob asked me to be the main speaker at this meeting.

I took the assignment seriously, asking the question, "What contributions can a mathematics teacher in a Christian school make to the distinctive purpose of such a school?" I pointed to traits common to all humans, without which we could not do mathematics. We depend, for example, on the fact that what will seem logical to one person will seem logical to another, no matter their race, where they were born, how they were educated, etc. All will find convincing an argument depending on reductio ad absurdum (proof by contradiction), the pigeonhole principle, etc.

As another example, I pointed to the unconscious way in which humans believe the world to be an orderly place. In a science lab, for example, students commonly take readings, say of the length of a rod at different temperatures, and plot them on a graph. They are then asked to draw a curve through the plotted points that shows the likely length of the rod at temperatures for which no reading was taken. Invariably, students will draw as smooth a curve as possible. Suggest a jagged line that goes through the plotted points, but elsewhere darts erratically up and down, and students will laugh. They instinctively agree with Einstein's observation that "without the belief in the inner harmony of our world, there could be no science."

Different reasons can be postulated for this commonality among people, of course, but those who begin with the assumption that there is a Creator God ought not to miss the opportunity to ask how these things came to be, and mathematicians are in an excellent place to do the asking.

I did confess in that talk to my reservations about forming a separate group for Christian mathematicians. I expressed my hope that the organization would become a presence at the annual meetings of the MAA. I suggested that rather than have annual meetings on one of their campuses, they schedule dinner meetings in conjunction with the annual MAA meetings, and have a speaker who would attract mathematicians from secular campuses who have interest in being a Christian presence on their campuses.

Those in attendance greatly enjoyed themselves, and I must say that I did too. I had no idea that there were so many small Christian colleges. Many of those present were in awe of the splendor of the Wheaton campus. Ignoring my advice, they scheduled several more meetings at Wheaton, setting the Memorial Day weekend for their meetings. Bob Brabenec was certainly right in thinking that if there was to be an organization of the type he envisioned, Wheaton was the right place to take leadership, and Bob was the right person to lead it.

It was in 1985, eight years after the original meeting at Wheaton, that a group met to draw up a constitution and elect officers. In January, 1986, the group scheduled their first dinner meeting, in conjunction with the annual meeting of mathematics organizations, held that year in New Orleans. In only a slight variation of an old hymn, they showed themselves willing to "giveth more grace" by inviting me to be their first dinner speaker.

Bob was right and I was wrong about the usefulness of what is now known as the Association for Christians in the Mathematical Sciences (ACMS). Christians should live in the world like everybody else, but it is one of the tenets of the faith that they need to come together for fellowship and encouragement. I have been honored to serve as a board member, as vice president, and as president of the group.

I previously described a conference held at Wheaton for high school teachers of calculus. It did occur to me during the period when I was promoting *Resources for Calculus* that hosting such conferences would be one more way for members of the ACMS to involve themselves in activities of the larger mathematics community. Messiah, Westmont, Dordt, and of course Wheaton scheduled such conferences.

As with many organizations, mathematicians now have many special interest groups that meet at the time of their annual meetings. In a recent program I noticed a listing of meetings of special groups for women, for the untenured, for LGBTQ, and others—and in the list was the Association of Christians in the Mathematical Sciences. Their activities during the meetings include both a dinner and a Sunday morning worship service. Names of members appear in listings of those giving papers in sessions throughout the week, and one member has served as president of the MAA. I am pleased to say that, contrary to my fears, members of the organization "live in the same world as everybody else."

Why do I include this little story in a chapter titled Lessons in Academic Leadership? It's important to remember that positions you take can be wrong. And in academia, you are surrounded by people who have the freedom and the ability to show you that you are wrong.

Public Information Officer

I have always enjoyed writing and can't resist including the story of a short but highly enjoyable period when I had the title of public information officer for the MAA. This cherished title was bestowed on me as the result of a serendipitous event that occurred in 1991.

Our Northwest Section of the MAA had its spring meeting that year on the weekend that began Mathematics Week, an annual public awareness event sponsored by several professional associations of mathematicians. Whether intentionally timed or not, Colman McCarthy, a nationally syndicated *Washington Post* columnist, wrote an article on the Saturday preceding Mathematics Week vigorously suggesting that no good purpose was served by requiring all high school students to take algebra.

By the time our meeting convened that Saturday morning, almost everyone present had read the article. It was agreed that when our business meeting convened after lunch, we should develop some response to be sent to the *Post* and all other newspapers that carried McCarthy's article.

It was an easy article to refute. It contained such sentences as the following:

"Algebra isn't essential to much of anything."

"Algebra has little to do with mathematics."

Not relishing the idea of a room full of sputtering mathematicians collectively trying to write an appropriate response, I spent the lunch hour writing one myself. When it was read at the business meeting, it was immediately endorsed and sent on its way.

We didn't know which papers had carried the McCarthy article, so we sent my response to the MAA office in Washington, suggesting that they determine where it should be sent. They did so, and at the same time decided that henceforth they would call upon me to answer other articles they felt needed answering; thus was I given my title. The McCarthy article and my response are included at the end of this chapter.

Colman McCarthy

This new assignment came as the *Resources for Calculus* volumes were being readied for publishing, so I didn't have time to respond to every opportunity that came along, but there was one other episode that stands out in my mind.

Somehow the MAA staff in Washington came across a problem that had been used in a mathematics competition in Michigan. They thought it a clever problem and wondered, as another Mathematics Week was coming, if I could use it in a press release they planned to send to newspapers around the country. The problem does catch one's interest:

A blind umpire calls balls and strikes at random, meaning that independent of any previous call, the probability that the umpire will call the next pitch a strike is ½. What is the probability that a batter who takes every pitch will be called out on strikes?

I decided to make that the final problem in a series of five articles on baseball and mathematics that newspapers could run during Mathematics Week. Each article contained the solution to the previous day's problem and posed a new one.

The series proved popular, and I was kept busy answering articles from editors as well as readers about the solutions. (The answer to the problem posed above is .656.)

The editor of a large daily on the West Coast was skeptical. He wrote, "According to your calculations, the percentage of times that the batter will be walked is 1- .656 = .344. Since very few hitters have an average of .344, why wouldn't every batter simply wait it out for a walk?"

It's a tough question to answer. The teacher in me says don't ever answer a question in a way that makes the one who asked the question feel foolish. I'm afraid the editor did feel foolish in this case, however. The answer is that, contrary to what many fans seem to think, umpires are not blind. They are not calling balls and strikes randomly, and most major league pitchers can throw a strike more than half the time, especially if they know the batter is never going to swing.

With reluctance, I shall restrain myself from reproducing all the nice little problems about baseball that I used and return to my lessons in academic leadership.

Chair of the Department

There was one other opportunity that fell into my lap in the period from the fall of 1988 to the spring of 1995. It was my turn to serve as chair of the Mathematics Department.

Chairing an academic department is not often described as an opportunity; more often the position is taken as an obligation. Decisions that matter to department members (course assignments, hiring, office assignments) are, in well-run departments, made in departmental meetings. Chairs attend to all the necessary tasks that faculty members are happy to avoid. In small colleges like Macalester, compensation for attending to a myriad of details comes in the form of having your teaching load reduced, usually by one course each year. Most faculty members would rather teach their full load.

Timing made 1988 a significant time, however, to begin service as chair. There were six full-time mathematicians in the department in 1968, one of whom retired in 1983. The other five, with no full-time additions in mathematics, were still carrying the mathematics program in 1988. Three of them were to retire within the next four years, and it would be my responsibility to rebuild the department.

There were a number of factors that made this seem like an opportunity rather than a sentence. Number one in my mind was that during the long comeback period the college had endured, our department had managed to strengthen its reputation. The entire department remained active in our section of the MAA. John Schue and Joe Konhauser had become nationally visible in their specialties. We had gained national recognition as the home of the *Resources in Calculus* project, and we were well known in Minnesota as a leader in providing programs for mathematically gifted secondary students.

As well as things had been going for the department, the position of the college had improved even more dramatically. As John Davis had correctly observed when he chose to leave, college finances had rebounded. Mr. Wallace was, in his latter years, once again donating generously. It was reported when he died that the *Readers Digest* stock he left to the to the college made us for a short period in 1991 the best-endowed liberal arts college in the nation. Once again we could be very competitive in salaries.

As the president to succeed Davis, Bob Gavin moved quickly to resume the drive to academic excellence. A magnificent new library set the tone. It had special significance for us. The science library had been housed in our building, Olin Hall, for many years. When the new library was built, the science library was moved to the main library, leaving a spacious vacated area in the center of our building. Our department got priority because with three new faculty positions in computer science and the need for computer labs, we were the most cramped department in the building. My first privilege as chair was to assign new offices constructed in the space vacated by the old library.

Bob Gavin

The value of the department's reputation was illustrated by the first hire we made. Before we'd even announced a search, I got a phone call one afternoon from Stan Wagon. I was familiar with his name. His wife, Joan Hutchinson, was a well-known mathematician, and I knew they had for a number of years been on the faculty at Smith College, one of the classic Seven Sisters colleges for women in the East.

Stan explained to me that he and Joan had decided to leave Smith to find a place that would accommodate an unusual arrangement. They wanted to hold just one full-time position between them. He said they could afford to live on one salary, they both wanted to continue the contact with students they enjoyed, but they both wanted more time to do research. They had considered a number of schools and decided that they might like to come to Macalester.

With just a few inquiries among friends, I discovered that Joan was considered a national leader in graph theory and was frequently invited to institutes on this topic around the country. Stan was much more a maverick, having made contributions to logic as well as various applied fields. Most interestingly, he was becoming a national expert in the use of new Mathematica software, which was fast becoming the gold standard in computer-aided mathematical research. Indeed, the developers of that software were using Stan as a beta tester to analyze new features before putting them on the market.

Of course I wanted them at Macalester: two established mathematicians, highly regarded teachers, for the price of one. There were obstacles, however. The first was that the college seldom hired mid-career faculty members. When I pointed out to the provost that our department had gotten old together, was retiring together, and that this pattern would repeat if we once again hired all newly minted Ph.D.s, he agreed that it made sense to mix in some mid-career people.

There were more complex problems to be worked out. Macalester (like all other schools I contacted) had no experience with two people holding one tenured position. Would that require two offices for one position? How would tenure rules apply? Do they each get full medical coverage? How will they divide up a five-course teaching load?

By the time we could bring them to Macalester for an interview, our unusual opportunity was well known among the decision makers. Stan and Joan, naturally agreeable people with years of experience on a liberal arts campus, knew how to sell themselves. I can no longer recall if we went ahead with the routines of a search or not. The problems were resolved, and people around campus enjoyed saying that there was a new pair-a-docs in mathematics.

Joan was the first woman to hold a tenure-track position in the department. She was involved in several national programs to encourage young women to consider careers in mathematics, and with more time at Macalester to devote to her research, she continued to build on her reputation in graph theory.

Stan's eclectic interests flourished: astronomy, computer graphics, joining with a young part-time colleague to use a computer to graph solutions to differential equations without first obtaining a solution in the form of a closed mathematical expression. He wrote several books using Mathematica to examine classical problems and started a summer institute that drew mathematicians from all over the nation who wanted to learn how to use Mathematica. One night at a social gathering, he got into conversation with a cardiologist, and in time the two of them published a paper analyzing fluid flow through veins.

When Joe Konhauser died, his wife gave me the collection of problems and various solutions Joe had assembled over a lifetime as an avid problem aficionado. Totally involved in the calculus project, I gave the collection to Stan, who used them (along with materials of his own) to write a book published by the MAA. The cover of the book showed tracks made in soft dirt by a turning bicycle and posed as the title to the book, "Which way did the bicycle go?"

Stan brought a lot of fun to the department. For example, while reading challenge problems in a journal, he came across this question: Suppose a bicycle has square wheels. How should the roadbed be shaped in order to give the rider a smooth ride? He worked out a nice solution and showed it to me.

We got the technician in the physics lab to build such a roadbed that ran the length of a hall in our building. A neighbor

Wayne Roberts rides the famous square-wheeled tricycle.

of mine owned a bicycle shop, and we got him to build a square-wheeled tricycle. Newspapers across the country ran pictures of us riding it; people would come in off the street and ask if they could ride the square-wheeled tricycle. A picture of Stan riding the bike appeared on a U.S. postage stamp.

Enrollments in the department had been exploding. This, together with the social sciences wishing that we would expand our statistics program, resulted in our being authorized to search for an additional position, a person trained in statistics.

Having maintained contact with Karla Ballman at MIT, I knew that work on her thesis had required her to delve into statistics, so I called her to tell her about the new search we were initiating. She applied immediately. When it was clear that the search committee was rating her near the top of our candidate pool, I called her thesis advisor. I wanted to assure myself that I was not letting my long association with her unduly influence my judgment.

He told me that when Karla had been looking for a thesis topic, a request for someone to help with a research project at Massachusetts General Hospital had come to his attention. He said he had been a bit dubious about getting Karla involved because it was clear that it would require a lot of medical knowledge that he didn't have, meaning he wouldn't be able to help her very much.

Long story short: She took it on and plunged into medical books. He said that as the project developed, he accompanied her several times to meetings with researchers at the hospital. He professed to be amazed at how much she had learned about medicine and how easily she fit into conversation with the medical staff. He finished by telling me that he was about to retire, and he thought he had never had a student at MIT with greater potential for research.

We hired Karla Ballman.

In recounting my experience as a new Ph.D. coming to Macalester in 1965, I mentioned that graduate school professors always wanted to send their students to centers of research. That same mindset was still in place in the 1980s, prompting the very able mathematics group at St. Olaf College to address this problem. They obtained a grant enabling them to bring promising young researchers from their graduate school training to St. Olaf, where they could experience two years of teaching on a liberal arts campus.

I had worked closely with colleagues at St. Olaf, and I was well aware of this program. One day I got a call from the chair of their department, who told me they had a young woman in her second year of that program who was clearly the best they'd ever had. They would very much like to offer her a full-time position at St. Olaf, but they were already fully staffed and had no prospects for her. "We would really like to see her go to a good liberal arts college, so we are wondering if you might be able to hire her."

I told him we had no openings right then, but that we had a retirement coming up the following year. He wanted me to talk to her, and arranged for me to meet her at the annual meetings soon coming up. Thus it came about that I was introduced to Karen Saxe in the lobby of a San Francisco hotel. It was a beautiful day, so I suggested that we Minnesota snowbirds visit on a bench at a nearby park. It was quickly clear that she would be a great addition to our staff.

I told her that I could hire her into a temporary position starting next fall; then she could apply as an inside candidate for the tenure-track position that would be open the following year. Alternately, she could wait one year and then apply. I warned her that Macalester procedures would call for a national search, and it was not always an advantage to be applying as an insider, that sometimes an unknown outsider about whom we would only hear very positive things could be very competitive. Without hesitation she told me that she thought she could, after a year at Macalester, emerge on top of a national search.

She was absolutely right, as were the people at St. Olaf who were so impressed with her. She was hired and we benefited from her contributions for more than 20 years before the American Mathematics Society lured her away to be their representative to Congress in Washington. During her first year or two on campus, department members enjoyed introducing her as "a woman that Wayne hired when he met her in a park in San Francisco."

Tom Halverson also came to us with a St. Olaf connection. He had been an undergraduate math major there, then finished his Ph.D. at the University of Wisconsin. He also began in a temporary position at Macalester and continued for several years until a tenure-track opening came up for which he was eminently qualified. In a department full of popular classroom teachers, Tom nevertheless achieved such popularity in his temporary positions that the student newspaper ran a lengthy article extolling his virtues as a teacher.

He was an algebraist who was able to regularly place research articles in the most prestigious algebraic journals. If we had set out to replicate John Schue when he retired, Tom would have been the perfect fit. The one difference was that John's research was a solo effort, typical of his generation. Tom managed to involve students in his work. His selection was all but a foregone conclusion when he was finally able to apply for a tenure-track position.

The last person I hired involves a longer story that goes back to my getting to know Kathy Heid, the woman who evaluated our calculus project for NSF. As we got acquainted, she occasionally expressed her hope that I might meet David Bressoud. She described him as a senior member of the faculty at Penn State, unusual in that he had a genuine interest in the way undergraduates were taught.

In the serendipitous way that some things happen, I one day discovered at a meeting of NSF project directors in Washington that I was sitting next to David. I told him of the great things that I'd heard about his unusual interest in undergraduate teaching, and he acknowledged that it was so.

From that point forward, we looked for each other at meetings. I learned from him what Kathy Heid had intimated, that he'd had such success in directing graduate students that his department resisted assigning him to teach an undergraduate course. The day came when he said something like, "Sometimes I think I'd like to teach at a school like Macalester." I know exactly what I said: "Have I ever got a deal for you!"

There were some routines to be taken care of, but I've often said that the best thing I ever did for Macalester was to hire David. His reputation as a research mathematician was towering. He became a prolific writer of advanced texts. He became a national authority on the way calculus was being taught around the country. In time he was elected to the presidency of the MAA.

It was understood when he came to Macalester that when my term was up, he would be the next department chair. None of us expected that to happen as quickly as it did, but that's a story for the next chapter.

The success of this group in building the department can hardly be overstated. The surest way to authenticate that bold assertion is to point to the place the department holds in our liberal arts college as this is written. Outsiders who are only vaguely aware of Macalester usually think of the political leaders it's produced: not just Humphrey, Mondale, and Annan, but many mayors and legislators known in Minnesota. Some may think of it as the place from which Dale Warland built his famous choir. Several other departments in the college have risen to deserved prominence.

Inside the college, however, the department now called Mathematics, Statistics, and Computer Science is dominant. It is by an order of magnitude the largest in the college, whether measured by the number of grades given each term, the number of majors in the graduating class, or the number of tenured faculty members in the department. Department members occupy key leadership positions in the MAA. As a mathematics department that has developed strengths in computer science and statistics, it could not be better situated at a time when "big data" occupies a key position in the mathematical sciences.

When Bob Gavin became president at Macalester in 1986, he introduced a rigor into the hiring process specifying that positions be nationally advertised, with special attention to underrepresented groups, that the pool of applicants be culled by a committee that included representatives from outside the searching department, and that at least three candidates be brought to campus for interviews. Only then was a recommendation to be brought to the provost.

Those directing searches frequently found the process irritating in one way or another and complained about the iron-handedness with which Gavin enforced each step. It has to be said in retrospect, however, that Gavin left the college academically stronger than it was when he arrived. To that I would add that if it was clear that those conducting the search respected the reasons for the steps and were trying to meet the objectives, they found that exceptions would be made if there were compelling reasons that could be made transparent to the larger community.

That point is illustrated, I think, by the fact that none of our searches conformed exactly to the rules. None of the people hired came to our attention from an application sent in from an unknown candidate responding to an ad. Wagon/Hutchinson called us prior to an ad having been published anywhere. Saxe and Halverson both came as temporary hires recommended by people we knew and whose judgment we trusted. Ballman was contacted directly in hopes that she would apply, and Bressoud first came to our attention through contacts made in the calculus project.

In all cases, except possibly the Wagon/Hutchinson hire, there was a national search. The person ultimately hired, however, had the initial advantage of not having to rely on a paper application being picked out of a large pile. The applicant pile primarily served to set a standard against which known candidates could be compared.

I believe we had success in hiring the candidates we wanted because we respected the objectives of the process. In every search we conducted, we made a point of contacting any Black person in the country getting a Ph.D. in mathematics that year (there were never more than 10 in any year), whether they applied to Macalester or not. This select group was always siphoned off by the big research universities. Among candidates actually available to us, the most under-represented group was women, and of the six new people we hired, three were women.

Many departments have a legitimate interest in who gets hired in mathematics. In our case, two of the six had been teaching on campus and were well-accepted. Ballman was remembered by some as an agreeable student, and she filled the wish of some departments for a statistician. The other three were senior people with high recommendations from related departments in their prior institutions.

Most important, the channels through which our hires came to our attention were reliable. The people they recommended had credentials that compared favorably with anyone in our candidate pools.

My point is that rules and guidelines have their place. The expectation should be that they will be followed, that exceptions made will be made to the rules, not to the objective of the rules. It must be understood that exceptions will be made only for compelling reasons that can and should be openly explained. In this spirit, we had no trouble hiring an exceptional group, able to step in and improve an already very good department.

There are a many things a department chair must attend to personally: attend meetings occasionally called by the provost, fill out reports and questionnaires from the administration and once in a while from a faculty committee, submit annual salary recommendations for each person in the department, find part-time instructors as needs arise, supervise the secretary and student assistants, attend to personal issues brought up by students as well as faculty members.

There are also a myriad of items for which a chair can seek help from departmental colleagues: sit at registration tables when students are signing up for classes; make arrangements for the weekly afternoon "tea" (i.e., get the cookies and pop, and refill the coffee maker); meet with student groups planning the spring picnic, the departmental holiday party, the design of the annual department T-shirt; be on hand on the Saturday morning of Parents Weekend; plan the departmental colloquia series; serve on textbook selection committees. . . . The list goes on.

It is these latter duties that prove most irritating, sneaking up on you, requiring that you run around leaning on colleagues at the last minute—or all too often just doing it yourself. When I became chair, each fall I made a list of all items of this sort that I could think of, and then held an off-campus meeting (several times at our home, once at our lake property) where everyone could see the list and volunteer to cover a few things. It relieved me of attending to these things in an ad hoc fashion, and made everyone feel the obligation to take on a few extra duties.

Attended to in a context of fun and food, this worked quite well. It was my sole innovation to the task of being chair. Because of the opportunity to rebuild the department, I have reason to look back with some real satisfaction about the experience. Nevertheless, I was not unhappy when the time came to turn the job over to David Bressoud.

Undivided Distaste for Algebra

By Colman McCarthy

America's 12.5 million high school students ought to keep a wary eye on Franklin L. Smith, the superintendent of Dayton, Ohio's public schools. He's an algebra lover who's been pushing for years to make the subject mandatory for all Dayton high school students. If Smith's bizarre idea succeeds, it could spread. Currently only one state—Louisiana—has compulsory algebra.

In 1986, Smith tried to force his algebra agenda as a graduation requirement. Rational minds in the community prevailed and told him to take his polynomials and exponentials and bug off. He did. Now he's trying again. One of the Dayton schools under his command—Dunbar High—has given nearly all of its 400 ninth graders no choice but to take Algebra I. A hyper assistant, the supervisor of secondary math, wants compulsory algebra and geometry.

Educators, hearing the periodic frets of politicians that U.S. kids are dopes compared with Japanese student geniuses who can do advanced calculus in first grade and grow up to buy Rockefeller Center, routinely respond with get-tough campaigns for more math. Donald M. Stewart, president of the College Board, has called for "serious consideration of a national policy that all students take algebra and geometry."

It doesn't add up. Would the country be in any less of a mess—failing banks, unprecedented national debt, crime, drugs, pollution and the rest—if algebra had been pounded into the cranium of every high school student unlucky enough to have Franklin L. Smith of Dayton running things? The opposite case can be made: Too many of us were forced to take algebra when the time and energy could have been devoted to subjects that truly were beneficial individually and nationally.

Algebra isn't essential to much of anything. Once adding, subtracting, multiplying and dividing are mastered—by eighth grade usually—why insist on more? Algebra has little to do with mathematics. It's a language, a way of symbolic communication that few people find fascinating and practical, while most of us don't.

The few keep torturing the most. Would millions of high school students trudge into their algebra classes if it wasn't a gate through which they were forced to pass to enter college? Not likely. Algebra is more loathed than learned, more memorized to pass tests than understood to comprehend problems.

Alarmists at the National Council of Teachers of Mathematics, a Reston, Va., group with 75,000 members, is one of the main tormentors of high school students. It wants them to know answers to such questions:

- What are the values of k for which the equation $2x2-kx+x+8 = 0$ will have real and equal roots?
- Find the value(s) of $x+y$ if $x2+y2=36$ and $xy=-10$.
- If $(z)=ax2+bx+c$ passes through the points $(-1,12)$, $(0,5)$ and $(2,-3)$, find the value of $a+b+c$.

These feisty little puzzlers are from a recent council yearbook that carries 34 essays by algebra teachers on their "exciting, living and growing" discipline. The essays are thoughtful and enthusiastic, except no answer is offered to the question: Why teach algebra to those who either don't or can't appreciate it?

I happen to think that algebra is a useless torture. I have never seen a help wanted ad for an algebraist, and in 25 years or so interviewing I have not met anyone who even mentioned algebra, let alone say it was beneficial. But perhaps I'm mathophobic and hopelessly biased. That still leaves unresolved the issue of compulsory algebra. Let students who like it take it. Let them skip gym and study hall to take more of it. Let them wallow. But for those who have no taste, leave them alone.

Minds, like flowers, bloom when ready. Algebra, first offered to the world in 825 by Arab mathematician ibn-Musa al-Khowarizmi, is a language of beauty and subtlety. Like Sanskrit, it's for the few, not the many. This spring, too many millions of high school students of both normal and high intelligence are gutting it out until the last $x+y$ of the final exam. Then they will flush it out of their minds forever.

Is such a large majority to be dismissed as dimwits or incurable rebels? Or should the truly radical be tried— drop algebra for a decade or so and see if it makes any difference. It probably will—for the better.

Algebra:

It's Not Just Math. It's the Language of Science

By Wayne Roberts

Whether by coincidence or design, Colman McCarthy kicked off Mathematics Awareness Week with an April 20 column suggesting that it is algebra that should be kicked off—off the list of courses required in our nation's schools.

He reasoned that teaching algebra to everyone will not address such problems as crime and drugs or pollution, that algebra has little to do with mathematics, and that he has never seen a help-wanted ad for an algebraist.

The temptation to the mathematician, after getting over the initial sputtering and grinding of chalk dust in one's teeth, is to respond with the kind of overstatement in defense of algebra that McCarthy has employed in his attack. The damage he has done is too serious, however, and calls for a more reasoned response.

Do the majority of adults use algebra? Of course not.

I think we can go further, and say that there are a lot of working engineers and other people with technical jobs who do not use algebra on a day-to-day basis.

McCarthy's physician may well have forgotten algebra, but that physician without a doubt needs the background provided by his or her chemistry course, and one can't learn chemistry without first taking algebra. That is the point to remember. Mathematics is not just another science; it is the language through which all of science and much of management science is taught.

The student who closes the door on high school algebra (and so on all of mathematics) closes the door on much more: all of engineering and science; the world of computer programming; anything that requires an understanding of statistics, electronics, medicine and medical technology; most management and MBA programs; and more. Make no mistake. The young person who drops out of algebra has dropped out of a lot more than he or she realizes.

Must algebra be difficult? Not really. Is it sometimes poorly taught? Certainly. Do students get by with memorization rather than understanding? Of course. These are not arguments for abandoning algebra, however, but for teaching it better, a goal toward which renewed efforts of the National Council of Teachers of Mathematics are directed.

McCarthy is certainly right to worry about drugs and crime. We are not experts on the subject, but social scientists have led us to believe that a root cause is the inability of people to get jobs and the resultant poverty and sense of being left out. He is also right to identify pollution as part of the national mess; we do need cleaner sources of energy, and better handling of the waste we generate.

To whom will we turn for help? We don't know. We can't go into our grade schools and identify the problem solvers of tomorrow. We can say with reasonable assurance, however, that they won't come from the ranks of those who decided not to study algebra.

In all of this, we have focused on jobs and said nothing about the need for informed citizens to understand statistics as they face a medical choice, to have a feel for rate of growth when listening to economic forecasts, or to understand the concept of future value when they choose among retirement options.

Neither have we spoken of our need for teachers at all levels to know at least enough about the use of algebra so as to help their students do what McCarthy says he cannot: distinguish between the importance in our society of algebra and Sanskrit. In the best of all worlds, we could even hope for columnists who would not write such nonsense as "Algebra has little to do with mathematics."

Think of your own child, or a neighbor child, or the disadvantaged child in whom you have taken an interest. Do what you can to help that child experience a little more of what it means to have equal opportunity. Tell that young person to keep options open: to take algebra and to follow it with geometry, and all the mathematics he or she can master, and to ignore Colman McCarthy.

IX. The Trials of Administration

A provost must be prepared to lose some battles.

A Turbulent Week

Summer arrives on a college campus on the Monday after graduation weekend. It was particularly welcome on the Macalester campus in May of 1995.

It had been a tough spring. Our provost announced near the end of the term that he was resigning. That in itself was not startling. He was at least the fourth provost to have resigned during Gavin's tenure as president. In Maclaester's organization, the provost is the chief academic officer, but Gavin had a way of inserting himself in anything that interested him, evidently straining relations with his provosts.

The thing that made this spring different was the number of other vacancies in top administrative posts. I can't remember if the dean of the faculty resigned along with the provost, or if he had resigned earlier. At any rate, that position was also open. There was a search going on to fill the position of dean of students, and we had just welcomed a new vice president for development.

Even without taking into account the general discontent of the faculty, it was clear that President Gavin was finding it increasingly difficult to achieve anything like stability in the college. Rumor had it that when the trustees came to campus for graduation and their annual spring meeting, they would be telling Gavin that the 1995-96 academic year would be his last as president.

None of this affected me quite so directly as the fact that the science building on the south end of the campus was to be vacated that spring to allow for a complete renovation. As a result, the Department of Mathematics and Computer Science was being moved into some vacant space on the north end of campus. I was faced with more than packing my own books and files and emptying my desk in preparation for the movers. As chair, I had to supervise moving the department files, the secretarys' desks, and all the equipment in the computer labs out of our building—and then decide how to allocate space in our temporary quarters.

It was during that first week of summer, perhaps even

Monday, when I was walking between the two buildings and a colleague stopped me to ask if I'd heard the newest campus joke. I hadn't. He told me they were installing a menu on the main campus phone instructing callers to press 1 if they want to be president, 2 if they wish to be provost, 3 for treasurer, 4 for dean of the faculty, 5 for dean of students.

I agreed, of course, that we had an extraordinary number of openings in top administrative posts, but I told him he was overstating the situation by including the treasurer. That, I think, was the response for which he was hoping; everyone likes to be the first to spring surprising news. "Haven't you heard? Aslanian is out as treasurer. It's not clear if Gavin fired him or if he resigned, but he's out!"

That news hit the campus like a bombshell. It was during the time of Macalester's most precarious financial situation that Paul Aslanian, then a member of our Economics Department, had been asked to become treasurer. He had performed admirably, even to the point of once convincing a trustee to sign for a bank loan when it appeared the college would be unable to meet its payroll. Everyone who'd been around in those days, from trustees on down, felt that the college owed a great deal to Paul. He had been Macalester's treasurer for more than 25 years. It was hard for me to grasp that just that suddenly Paul was no longer treasurer of the college.

I don't remember if it was later that day or later in the week, but in time I was summoned to Gavin's office. It was true, he told me, that the next year was to be his last. The trustees had asked him to appoint a provost to a two-year term, one year to see him out, another year to see his successor settle in. He asked if I would be willing to take the job.

I was reluctant. He had, after all, just fired a personal friend of mine. Moreover, every time a provost left the office in recent years, my name came up as a possible replacement. I told him I was more than tired of being the foil in a process that always resulted in choosing someone else.

In time, he convinced me that this time around he would be very happy if I would agree to serve. He told me he thought Kathy Parson, a woman in our Chemistry Department, might be willing to serve as dean of the faculty, but I could name someone else if I preferred. I was impressed with being given that choice.

I was enjoying my stint as chair of the Math Department, but I was at the same time distraught over the rancor that permeated the campus. More than once I thought that, given a chance, I would be able to make the college a much more pleasant place to work. This seemed to be my chance.

I'd had a couple of differences with Gavin over the years, but we had worked them out. In one case, I even had a letter of apology from him after he better understood the circumstances over which he had sent me a reprimanding letter. Paul Aslanian told me he thought I was the only person ever to have received an apology from the president. I knew the history of previous provosts who'd tried to work with him, but I reasoned that in this case, if things went badly I would at least have a contract that ran one year longer than his. I asked for a day to talk to Dolores.

Word somehow got out that the provost position had been offered to me. Advice came from every direction. Except for the support of my wife, who thought I should take the job, the advice I recall most clearly came from Emil Slowinski, a senior member of the faculty, author of the country's best-selling chemistry textbook (and therefore a wealthy man), a close supporter of Paul Aslanian, a man well acquainted with a number of our trustees, and a friend of mine.

In a profanity-laden exhortation, he was adamant that I should not take the position until Paul had been reinstated, or the president had been forced to resign, or preferably both. He told me that he'd talked to Richard Ammons, our newly hired vice president for development, and that he was considering resigning now that he was aware of how disagreeable Gavin was. Nothing less than bringing Gavin to his knees would satisfy Slo (as he was known).

I did talk to Ammons and learned that he had listened to Slo and had not disagreed with him (as befits a newcomer listening to a powerful old-timer). He allowed that Slo might have left his office thinking that he, Ammons, might resign, but that he had no such intention.

I also talked with a few close friends on the faculty, and to Kathy Parson, who also had been visited by Slo. After a long conversation, we decided to accept the challenge. And so it was that Kathy and I took on new roles in the college.

I called David Bressoud, reminded him of our understanding that he would take over as chair of the department when my term was up, and wished him well as he assumed supervising the department's move. It was for him a baptism by total immersion.

The next morning I walked into my new office as the provost designate. I was introduced to the administrative assistant, a person I did not know very well. She told me that the stress of her job had led her to look for another one, and that she had an offer on her desk. Then she added (an addition I love to repeat) that she'd heard I was easy to work for and was reconsidering her decision to leave.

This conversation was interrupted by the appearance of a technician from computing services who had been called because the computer that was to be mine was not working. Perhaps to impress me with the aggressive manner in which she cared for the provost's needs, or perhaps to demonstrate how truly stressed she was, my potential assistant assailed the technician for not having responded yesterday when called, so that the computer would be functioning when the new provost arrived. The technician thought of a response to demonstrate that she too was a little stressed. From there the exchanges escalated. By and by, the technician stalked out, her parting shot being that she didn't care if the damned computer ever got fixed.

When things had calmed down later in the day, I advised my assistant to accept the offer on her desk.

When I got a chance to sit down at my desk, I found a letter from Paul Aslanian. He began by writing that Swarthmore College had recently contacted him to ask if he might be interested in coming there as treasurer. His first impression, he said, was that he didn't want to move farther east (his family roots were in Seattle), but given recent developments at Macalester, he thought he should consider the offer.

He then reminded me that he was a tenured member of our Economics Department. It was from that position that he would like to request a two-year leave of absence, allowing him to try the Swarthmore position without severing his tie to Macalester.

The situation illustrated the problem of appointing an insider to an administrative position where he might have to make decisions affecting a long-time friend. I decided not to call Paul to my office, a situation that would underscore the sudden change in our positions. I went to see him on his turf.

In short, the situation was this. His relationship with Gavin had been rocky at times, but they'd managed up until the past week. I learned from Paul that Gavin believed that since Paul had been in administration for so long, he no longer had tenure in Econ. Paul had no doubt that he still had tenure. He also felt that if he were to return to the classroom, he would first need to return to graduate school, call it an extended sabbatical, for two years of study to catch up on his field. I asked him if he would expect a two-year sabbatical if, after two years at Swarthmore, he decided to return to Mac. Yes, that is the arrangement he was seeking.

I was perplexed. The Economics Department could identify a long list of people who'd served as part-timers in what they identified as Paul's position. Well-established policy at the college, conforming to rules of the American Association of University Professors, required that anyone who served at a college for seven years should be regarded as tenured. Just several years before Paul's termination, the Economics Department had a person in Paul's position that they really wanted to retain. I was on the Personnel Committee at the time, and because I was a friend of Paul, the committee had asked me to talk to Paul to see if he would relinquish his tenure so that the current occupant of his position could be tenured. Citing his occasional run-ins with the president, he flatly refused.

The point of my long explanation is that I believed, my colleagues believed, and departmental decisions had been made on the grounds that Paul still retained his tenured position. To deny that would surely result in a lawsuit, one I was quite sure the college would lose; and while the case was being argued, I would be on the opposite side from the president, not a great way to start our new relationship.

I consulted the bylaws. As a tenured faculty member who hadn't had a sabbatical in many years, Paul was certainly entitled to a one-year sabbatical; two years would be a stretch. As to a leave of absence, any member of the faculty could request one. Whether it was granted was up to the provost, who was to make a decision based on the best interests of the college.

It seemed clear that the decision was mine to make, and I decided to do so without inviting a lot of disputation. I put my decision in a letter to Paul, with a copy to the president.

I told Paul that his long absence from the department, while an unquestioned benefit to the college, had certainly worked a hardship on the department, forcing it to get along for many years with a series of part-timers. Now, if I were to grant a leave of absence, I would commit the department to continuing with part-timers for two, possibly four, more years. That, I concluded, was not in the best interests of the college, so I was denying him a leave of absence.

I then turned to the sabbatical. I told him that as a tenured member of the faculty, he was entitled to one and that I was therefore approving one to begin the next fall if he should choose to take it. I no longer recall what I decided about a consecutive second year of sabbatical. I probably left that to the Personnel Committee.

I wondered, of course, how the president would feel about my handling of the case. I didn't have to wonder how Paul's friends felt. That was evident from the quickly growing pile of letters that accumulated on my desk. A letter from a mutual friend of Paul and myself was particularly vitriolic, accusing me of having betrayed a friend, no doubt caving in to the president (whom I had not even consulted). In his mind, I had already dashed any hope that I would be the champion the faculty needed. Others saw the long hand of the board influencing me, a view somewhat balanced by letters from a few trustees who professed disappointment that Paul was denied a leave.

Another storm was brewing. Besides Paul's letter, there was on my desk a proposal to the National Institute for the Humanities (NIH) for a grant to our Social Science Department. It needed the provost's signature as part of the boilerplate that must attach to any proposal. I of course knew nothing about it, so I called Ellen Guyer, a woman in the academic affairs office. I knew from my own experience that she was knowledgeable, thorough, and possessed of good judgment.

Ellen was emphatic in recommending that I not sign the proposal. She had numerous reasons, but most damning was a promise in the proposal that if funded, the college would then develop a new program that would call for some major investment. Such a program had not been approved, she thought, not even considered by the college curriculum committee, much less by the faculty.

Another complaint was that the writers had waited till the very last minute to get their proposal into my office, even after being warned that many administrative people who needed to sign the document might not be in their offices the first few days after graduation, and it was even uncertain if there would be a provost in that time frame. They nevertheless got it in just a few days before it was due in Washington, expecting someone to get all the necessary signatures, including mine, of course.

Having had a lot of experience with grantsmanship over the course of my career, I knew the terrific investment of time that went into writing a proposal. I was very reluctant not to sign it.

I called the two authors to talk to them about their proposed new program. Neither was in town, nor would they be back before the proposal had to be submitted. I knew (though not as well as I thought I knew) how dependent I would be on Ellen in my new job, and I really wanted her to know from the beginning that I highly valued her judgment. I decided not to sign it, figuring that they could submit it in the next round.

The fury of that storm did not hit for a few days, but it packed a wallop. The proposers felt that they had almost a promise from the program officer with whom they were working at NIH that if submitted, their request would be funded. I have never been sure if I made the right decision in not signing it. The proposers never forgave me, and relations with them were never comfortable during my tenure as provost. On the other hand, the longer I served as provost, the more I came to value Ellen Guyer.

By the end of my first week, I was wondering if I had rankled the president, I had a pile of uncomplimentary letters from Paul Aslanian's supporters (though Paul himself took my decision with grace), I had earned the real enmity of two of our most active social scientists, and I had fired my administrative assistant, leaving me with no help in the office for the ensuing summer.

I like to think that my term as provost should be evaluated from the beginning of week two. The first week, after all, was driven by the necessity to respond to problems created before I set foot in the door.

Moving In

The first item to be dealt with was to get a new administrative assistant. Two people worked in the office through which visitors to my office had to pass. One was my administrative assistant, the other a typist/clerk named Jan Peterson.

Administrative assistants had recently come and gone even faster than the provosts they served. Jan, keeping her head down as much as possible, had served in the second spot for a number of years. She didn't work during the summer, so was not present for the first week's excitement.

I thought the obvious first step was to talk to Jan, so I called her home to ask if she would come in. I had chatted with her informally many times over the years on my way to see whomever was provost, but all I knew beyond her being a polite conversationalist was that she maintained a tailored look very becoming to the office.

When she arrived, she had correctly guessed that I might ask if she was interested in moving to the assistant's desk, so she lost no time in expressing her lack of interest in the job. She very much liked being at home with her teenage daughters during the summers, a perk that did not come with the assistant's job.

Later in the conversation, as we got better acquainted and a bit more free in expressing ourselves, it became clear that she wanted no part of the guff that came with the assistant's job. She asked if I'd noticed the hasp and padlock on one of my desk drawers. As a matter of fact, I had. The ugliness of this appendage to the desk couldn't be missed. That, she explained, was the result of a brouhaha that resulted when a previous provost accused her assistant of having taken papers out of her drawer and then misplacing them.

Several more war stories followed. She then explained that in her position, if she just kept quiet and did the work put in her basket, she avoided all the controversy that attended the coming and going of provosts and their assistants.

In time she did allow that as her daughters approached college age, she and her husband would appreciate the extra money she'd get as my administrative assistant, but she just didn't want to put up with the grief that seemed to come with it. I tried to assure her that things were going to be different while I was in charge, and I gave her the home phone numbers of the secretary in the Math Department and that of Kathy Grundhoefer so she could check me out. She agreed to talk to them and to her husband, and to come back in a week.

Before she returned, I talked to several people who worked with her and accumulated a variety of reports. Those who'd had lunch with her described her as pleasant company, fond of talking about her teenage daughters, quick to laugh. Those who worked closely with her in the office described her as quiet, very much to herself. I was told that she had trouble keeping track of the office budget, which was part of her job, and evidently complained a lot to friends, though never in the office.

Paul Aslanian, after reading my letter, had called Swarthmore and accepted their offer. Our friendship had survived the recent experience, making it possible for me to ask him about Jan, particularly about her trouble keeping books. I learned that the main part of the academic budget for which I was responsible—faculty salaries, departmental budgets, etc.—was managed by Lynn Hertz, an associate of Ellen Guyer in the academic affairs office. He had high praise for her keeping track of a budget that ran into millions.

Jan managed the relatively small fund that supported activities directly associated with my office: bringing candidates to campus for interviews, my travel, a discretionary fund, etc. As things were set up, this budget that Jan managed was just a line item in Lynn's overall budget. The troubles came when Lynn tried to get periodic reports from Jan. Paul had occasionally had direct interaction with Jan, and he assured me that finance was not Jan's forte.

When Jan returned, she was willing to talk about my expectations. We hit it off very well. When I told her about reports of her complaining, she agreed that she was probably guilty but that in this office there had been a lot to complain about. I told her that henceforth she was to do all her complaining to me. I then told her what I'd learned about the budget troubles, that I'd talked to Lynn, and that she was willing (in fact had been very happy) to take over managing the budget for my office.

With the provision that she could have the rest of the summer off, Jan took the job of being my administrative assistant. It was one of the best decisions I made while provost. She was made for the job. The three provosts who succeeded me all kept her in the position.

Moving Jan to administrative assistant solved a major problem, but it created another. We now had to fill Jan's old position. I thought the best way to convince Jan of my confidence in her was to put her in charge of the search for a new typist. She was reluctant at first, but I assured her that the personnel office would take care of placing ads and doing some initial screening, so that her main involvement would be to interview a few finalists and make a recommendation to me. I reminded her that she was the one who would work most closely with the new person, and that compatibility was the new keyword in the office.

She proceeded with several interviews, then selected a woman she thought would be good. This was how I met Winnie Farley, whom we hired. I think the experience did a lot for Jan's confidence in her new role. Jan and Winnie became great friends, and Winnie was still working in the office when Jan retired.

Details transferring financial responsibilities of my office to Lynn Hertz were worked out with Craig Aase, the new treasurer. Clarifications that put Lynn in charge of tracking all funds that passed through my office was another arrangement that has persisted ever since; so also has the friendship I developed with Craig as he coached me on things he thought I should understand about managing a multimillion-dollar budget.

There was another part of my responsibility for which I felt in need of extensive coaching. I'd always been pleased with Macalester's reputation in the area of internationalism, but at the same time I always felt that we had a hodge-podge of programs that lacked coherence. As I came into the office of provost, I was vaguely aware that Bob Gavin had brought in a new person to develop an international studies program, and I was eager to meet him and hear his ideas. I made a point of visiting as soon as possible the office of Ahmed Samatar.

I caught him by surprise. He hadn't anticipated that someone coming out of the Mathematics Department would make it a priority to learn something about his plans, but he recovered quickly. He didn't hesitate to belittle much that the college did in the name of internationalism. Programs that took students abroad amounted to little if students did not first learn something of the place they were to visit, and then have some specific things they hoped to learn while there. A few courses offered here and there by various departments did not constitute a respectable academic program. Faculty members, he said, should see their own discipline in an international context. We should capitalize on our splendid reputation by starting a Macalester journal of international affairs. There was more.

Ahmed Samatar

I left thinking that Ahmed was intense, ambitious, confident of his own ideas of how to build one of the finest international programs in the country, and somewhat oblivious to the possibility that even Macalester might not have the limitless resources he would need. I admired his vision; I anticipated that he now felt he had a friend in the administration, and that he would expect great support. I think that first visit helped us trust that we had each other's friendship, a trust that would be sorely needed during the many times to come when we would lock horns over budgetary matters.

Some things I learned just by walking around. One day I wandered into the academic programs office and was amused, surprised, and ultimately puzzled by what went on. The furniture in the outer office had been shoved to one side, creating space on the floor for about 30 neatly arranged piles of paper. When I asked what was going on, I was reminded about the freshman seminar program that we'd been using for a number of years.

The seminars had been instituted during the years when we needed new ways to attract students, and new ways to be sure that every new student experienced the ideals of a small liberal arts college. Faculty members were encouraged to offer seminars. They didn't have to be directly related to a faculty member's discipline; in fact, for a while seminars could not count towards a major in any department, a rule that was later relaxed. Every seminar had to have certain characteristics. Enrollment was limited to 16 students (guaranteeing that everyone immediately experienced claims made that in a small college, students get to know faculty members). The instructor automatically became the academic advisor of everyone in the class. There was to be a lot of writing and discussion of the goals of a liberal arts education.

To accommodate the usual entering class of 400 students, about 30 seminars had to be offered. A list of seminars, each augmented by a brief description written by the teacher, was sent to each entering student. Students were asked to list their first, second, and third choice.

Although I'd known all this for years, I'd never wondered who decided which students got into which seminars. Inevitably, some seminars would be the first choice of more than 16 students. Which 16 should be chosen? Was it clear that every one of 400 students could be given a first, second, or third choice? What rules of sorting were used?

I was seeing how all this was done. Ellen Guyer and her secretary were walking, sometimes crawling, around with pages submitted by students, on which they'd indicated their top three choices. Each page was dropped onto a pile. Occasionally some pages would be moved from one pile to another. Here was the staff at work, carrying out, somehow, the faculty decision that every student should get one of his or her top three choices.

I watched the process, thinking to myself that it's a finite optimization problem. Assign a number—1, 2, or 3—to each student according to the choice that student got. Then add all the numbers. If there were exactly 400 students, the ideal total would be 400. That's unlikely, probably impossible. The goal would be to assign everyone so that the total is as small as possible.

Years later, one of the young men hired in the Math Department wrote a computer program to do the sorting. Its effectiveness was gauged by whether it could perform as well as Ellen and her secretary did crawling around the room on their hands and knees.

There are a lot of things that go on in a residential college to which the faculty is more or less oblivious: news and publications, alumni affairs, the health service, counseling, the operation of the physical plant. During that first month of popping into offices and chatting with people I met as I wandered about, I learned a lot. I tried, especially in the evening hours, to think of things I might do as provost, not only to improve programs but to make working at the college a satisfying, even a rewarding experience, for the many people making contributions that I had rarely thought about as a faculty member.

It was easy to identify problems that should be addressed, not only to prepare the way for a new president but also to make Gavin's last year as good as possible for him. I certainly wanted to effect some changes, but I didn't want to establish myself as a thorn in the side of a man who, in spite of an abrasive style, had done a lot for the college. I felt good about prospects for changing the atmosphere in my office, but I thought it best not to try changing the way things operated in other administrative offices. What could I change?

Words of encouragement are always appreciated, I thought, and when passed to individuals on a wide variety of subjects, they could hardly be offensive to the president. I ordered some 4 x 5 note cards made of sturdy stock, engraved with an Office of the Provost letterhead, and promised myself that I would try never to go to bed before writing a note to someone. When you start looking for nice things to say to people, it's surprising what you begin to notice. The cards went to people in all areas of the college: faculty, of course, but also to people who served the numerous dinners Dolores and I attended, departmental secretaries, custodians . . . . The notes proved to be a much-appreciated gesture, one that I kept up for all four years in office.

The student newspaper, produced with no faculty or staff supervision, had been very tough on the president. I called the editor to my office and asked if he had any idea what a provost does. Few students do, and he was no exception. I listed for him some things in which I was quite sure he would be interested: how decisions are made on faculty salaries, which departments get to hire an additional member, whether to cancel a class because of insufficient enrollment, whether to support a new course or a new major in the curriculum. In time, I asked if he thought the paper would be willing to carry a weekly column by the provost. A week or two later he called to say that the various section editors felt that once a week was too much, but they would be willing to try an every other week submission—for a while, at least.

There was at the time a cartoon carried in various daily newspapers around the country called Wayne's World, so that was the title they put over my column. It gave me a wonderful soapbox from which to pontificate about whatever was on my mind: the loutish behavior of someone I encountered when taking a late-night bus home from campus, jokes I heard from our rabbi chaplain, the thoughts of a custodian I interviewed about cleaning up dormitory bathrooms on Sunday mornings that followed Saturday night parties, changes I'd like to see in graduation requirements, peculiarities of professors I had as a student, etc. Feedback assured me that the faculty and the trustees made up part of my readership, and the column went on as long as I was provost.

No group on campus was more stressed than young, untenured faculty members. Their first hurdle was a third-year review. It was not perfunctory. Gavin always sat on the review committee, and everyone knew a story about someone for whom the third year was his or her last at Macalester. Those who were continued always got a few suggestions about how they might improve. Unfortunately, these were accepted not as well-meaning but as something that could be pointed to as a warning if they were let go at the time of tenure review in their sixth year.

I decided to invite this group of about ten or so to meet with me for several dinners in one of the college dining rooms, and give them some idea of what I'd be looking for if and when a new president would probably choose to be much less involved in personnel decisions. The first dinner focused on those thinking about their three-year review. I told them that within the first three years, they needed to establish themselves as first-rate classroom teachers, and as good citizens of the college (attend faculty meetings, serve on a committee, perhaps volunteer to teach a first-year seminar) as well as in their department.

I thought that this would be a good place to indulge a hobby horse of mine, stating that being an easy grader was not a good way to get favorable student evaluations. Students want to feel that you know them, care about their progress, and take steps to help them improve. They appreciate prompt return of their papers, and regular feedback should make them well aware of how they're doing in the class. I told them I'd always received good student evaluations in spite of having a reputation as a hard grader.

This would be a good place to tell a favorite story. During

one of my weekly dinners in the student dining commons, a student who'd noticed that I sometimes signed official things as A. Wayne Roberts asked why I went by my second name. I told him that my parents started me out this way, and by the time I was old enough to realize that it causes more confusion than one might think, I was too accustomed to Wayne to change. The student gave an embarrassing laugh and asked if I knew what students called me. "They call you B. Wayne Roberts."

Grade inflation on college campuses almost makes grading meaningless, and I intended, if possible, to make grades at Macalester meaningful. It was an ambition not to be realized.

At another of these dinners, I addressed the publish-or-perish syndrome. I said that although getting original research published in a refereed journal was everybody's gold standard, I took a much broader view. I told them of my experience with Miss Tucker's largely worthless recommendation, from which I concluded that everyone should be engaged in something that makes them visible beyond the borders of the campus: writing textbooks, providing leadership in a professional society, using one's professional skills to provide needed public service in the larger community.

By the time the 4th of July rolled around, I was beginning to relax in my new surroundings. We'd settled all the personnel issues in my office, I'd gotten to know the key people with whom I'd be working, and I felt I was establishing a good working relationship with President Gavin. I made the office my own by getting a less modern desk from college storage. Even without a padlock on the drawers, I didn't like sitting behind a desk when people came in, so I ordered a small round table at which I could sit and talk with whomever happened along.

And people did happen along. Most came to wish me well in my new job. A few came with suggestions they hoped I could implement. The principal thing I learned in August was that so long as I was provost, I was going to have to find someone else to write the questions for the high school Math League.

Establishing New Routines

As the fall semester was about to begin, I felt good about the plans I'd made for sending appreciative notes, writing a column in the student paper, and trying to relieve the anxiety of our newest faculty members. These ideas all served me well in the years to come, but I soon realized that I should also have prepared for the routines of my new office.

Handling daily communications with faculty was one issue that caught me by surprise. I knew how memos to the provost worked. You wrote your question or suggestion on a pad of some sort, put it in the out basket on the department secretary's desk, waited two or three days, and an answering memo would appear in your inbox. That at least is how things had worked during most of my career.

The expectations of my colleagues were altogether different. A faculty member used email to send you a message, went to teach a class, and looked for your response when he or she returned to the office. If you answered the next day, the feeling seemed to be that you must have decided their message was not very important. When I got computing services to route my email through Jan's computer so she could call something of urgency to my attention, much as she would open and sort my mail, people often seemed to feel that their confidence had been breached, that a message intended for me was being read by someone else.

I decided I should try to create a sense on campus that if anyone communicated in any way with Jan—by phone, memo, or email—they effectively had my ear. There were, after all, cases in everyone's memory when provosts and their administrative assistant didn't get along too well. I therefore began taking Jan on little walks around campus, stopping in departmental offices, and trying to convey the idea that if they contacted Jan, their concern would get to me. I also found, however, that things worked much better if, after everyone went home, I stayed in my office and answered as much email as I could. Dolores adapted to the idea that suppers, if they were to be eaten at home, should be planned for 7:00 or 7:30.

I also learned that it was a real problem to get control of my own schedule. I found out quickly that the president had a meeting of the administrative staff on Monday mornings, and attendance was not optional. If meetings of some sort absolutely required that you be off campus on Monday morning, it was required that you arrange to be at the meeting via speaker phone from wherever you were. It was often inconvenient, it was heartily disliked, but you just learned that it was required.

Part of my scheduling trouble was self-inflicted. Having been chosen so abruptly by a widely disliked president, I wanted as quickly as possible to emanate good will from my office. I determined to accept as many invitations from academic departments as possible. They usually involved attending a lecture by a distinguished visitor, often preceded by a formal dinner. Dolores often accompanied me to these events, and Jan learned that the easiest way to handle these invitations was to call Dolores and get the event on our home calendar. Sometimes we'd be on campus three or four nights in a week.

So long as Jan understood that my noon hours on Monday, Wednesday, and Friday were reserved for handball, I regarded it as a happy arrangement. I got out of the habit of looking at the appointment book that I had, up until entering the provost's office, kept in my pocket. The one Jan kept was much more accurate. I didn't quite realize that I had so completely abandoned my own book until I missed reading a note reminding me that real estate tax was due. The penalty I had to pay for being late suggested that I needed to make further changes.

I had read with disapproval of corporate executives who expected their secretaries to take care of their personal lives as well as their business responsibilities. It surely is out of bounds to expect one's secretary (now one's administrative assistant) to remind you to buy your wife some flowers on your anniversary, but I did develop a better understanding of the value of relying on just one appointment book, and I became all the more appreciative of the good working relationship that Jan established with Dolores. I had two women telling me where to go and when to be there, and that arrangement worked well.

A Year with Bob Gavin

It wasn't long after the semester started that I learned the ongoing renovation of Olin Hall was not behind me. It's characteristic, I was to learn, that major building renovations uncover numerous problems not anticipated when contracts with construction companies are signed. For example, the spot to be excavated to house some nuclear equipment was filled with concrete footings supporting concealed beams that supported equipment on the roof.

The problem of surprises hidden in the old structure was aggravated by the fact that the architects designing the changes, though with a large and respected firm, had never done a science building before. One of their failures was that though they included in chemistry labs the emergency showers that code required, they forgot to put drains under them. Since city inspectors make an annual visit to test the sprinklers, drains had to be installed. Tearing up the newly finished floor was complicated by the fact that the floor already concealed gas, water, and electrical connections to each student station in the lab. It made for expensive drain pipes.

Mark Dickinson, our director of buildings and grounds, served as liaison with the head of construction. Going to President Gavin with news of yet another unexpected expense was the bane of his life. Either there had been no contingency fund built in at the planning stage, or it had been used up. At any rate, his visits with the president were unpleasant. He was an early visitor to my office, hoping I might be able to relieve him of this ordeal.

I found that everyone associated with college finances in any way knew about the problem and was sympathetic to Mark's position. I convened a meeting of people who managed various budgets, and the sympathetic spirit that prevailed enabled us to cobble together a contingency fund that Mark and I managed. It enabled us to handle at least minor problems as they arose without bothering the president.

I don't doubt that Bob Gavin knew a contingency fund of some sort had been set up. Very little happened that he didn't know about. I suspect he was as relieved as anyone to be rid of aggravating run-ins regarding cost over-runs. I was happy to think that I had a part in working out something that kept things running rather smoothly.

There were times I got caught in the middle of arguments the president was having with someone else. In the most notable case, the chair of the Geology Department wanted to see a member of his department promoted. The president, ultimately responsible for promotions, was sure that a misstatement of fact in the dossier prepared by the chairman was a deliberate attempt to strengthen the case. He not only denied the promotion but relieved the chair of his position. Members of the department, siding with their chair in an explanation of what they saw as a mistake, were united in their protest, and all refused to take over as chair. That's how I wound up as acting chair of geology until the president's departure from the college.

I've already mentioned that Dolores attended many dinners (that she usually enjoyed) and sat through a lot of lectures (at all of which she gave the appearance of enjoying). Doing as much as we could together was, of course, good for us, and it made her much more helpful when I ruminated at home about some decision I was facing. Most of all, the two of us together could, I think, bring a little warmth to situations in need of some relaxation. This comes to mind when I recall the evening when Dolores and I hosted a rather tense dinner for the demoted chair, the members, and the spouses of the Geology Department of which I was the nominal chair.

It's also true that while the provost is the chief academic

officer of the college, he or she had better be prepared to be on the losing side of an argument with the faculty. Macalester's January interim term, introduced the year before I arrived on campus, was a month during which each student took just one course. It periodically came under fire. It served some disciplines very well. Language students could spend the month in a country where the language they were studying was spoken. Theatre students could spend the month in the New York theatre district working behind the scenes, talking with producers and actors, and attending their performances. Geology and biology students could do field work. But there were admittedly many creative ways for students to simply waste the month, and publicity of extreme examples regularly embarrassed the college and brought critical letters from parents.

Since one purpose of interim was to encourage students to try something out of their comfort zone, interim courses were graded pass/fail, and each department was encouraged to offer some courses that would attract students normally reluctant to venture into the area. One could see how this would work in creative fields: explore your ability to draw and paint, revisit the piano that you abandoned in grade school, etc. Admittedly, it didn't work so well in mathematics. Students not in the sciences could seldom be lured into a month dedicated to mathematics.

Those opposed to interim finally mustered enough votes to eliminate it in my first year as provost. I argued, as usual, for retaining it. And as usual, colleagues responded that for most of us in mathematics, January was a month we could dedicate to our own writing and research.

Faculty time was the issue that finally sunk interim. As President Gavin continually raised expectations for scholarly production (i.e., publication), faculty, especially younger faculty, resented the time devoted to devising courses that would attract dilettantes not majoring in their departments. As I said, a provost must be prepared to lose some battles.

Because circumstances under which I became provost

precluded what I suppose might have been explained in an orientation under more normal circumstances, I was still learning about some of my basic responsibilities well into the second semester. One snowy day, I headed to the gym for my regular noon handball game. The lunch rush was over when I stopped in the cafeteria for a bowl of soup on my way back to the office. The woman who ladled up the soup was unhappy. "Hamline, Augsburg, St. Thomas, even the university have shut down because of all the accumulating snow. I think we're the only school in the city that's still going."

When I got back to the office, I told Jan what I'd heard and wondered out loud why we were still open. "That," she said, "is because it's your responsibility to call off classes."

My colleagues were in fact quite understanding about such lapses. So also was the president, making me occasionally wonder why my predecessors had so much trouble working with Bob Gavin. I attended the Monday morning meetings of the administrative staff, I met with him once a week in his office, and I felt that we got along quite well. I was aware that one requirement of years past had been relaxed. He had made it known that as a consequence of an increased travel schedule in his last year (perhaps interviewing for a new position, I figured), he was not requiring that candidates for faculty positions only be brought to campus when he was available to meet them.

It was in the spring of the year that I got my lesson on how difficult Bob could be. The Linguistics Department was conducting a search and had been authorized to bring three candidates to campus. Scheduling worked out such that Bob was out of town and so did not meet the first two candidates to visit. The chair of the department, reasoning that the playing field should be kept level, did not schedule the third candidate to meet Bob, even though he was in town and could have met her.

As it happened, the third candidate, Sarah Dart, was not a newcomer to the profession and had established an attractive record while teaching at a college in California. While at Macalester, she made a very positive impression in the department, with the faculty personnel committee, on several people who taught foreign languages, and, I must say, on me.

When the three interviews were completed, the search committee met with me and, following protocol, with President Gavin. Everyone except Gavin had met all three candidates, and among them there was quick and unanimous agreement that an offer should be made to Sarah. Bob listened quietly until I, getting wary of his silence, asked if everyone in the room was in agreement that I should call Sarah to make an offer.

It was then that Gavin spoke for the first time, saying that he didn't feel he could make the recommendation unanimous since he hadn't met her. Everyone at the table took this to mean he was just recusing himself, but I took it as a possible red flag. I rephrased my summary statement, saying that with the understandable exception of Bob, who had not met her, I was getting the message that I should call her that evening to make an offer. Everyone nodded in agreement, but again Gavin said that he hadn't met her, so he couldn't make it unanimous.

By that time, I was more determined than ever to get Bob on record approving an offer. I sensed that the group was getting impatient when I reiterated my intentions for a third time. I still didn't get the endorsement I hoped for from Bob, but neither did he demur. I hung back a bit as the group left the room, wondering if Bob would have some further comment. He did not.

My call to Sarah was unusually pleasant. The usual pattern in these calls, I had learned, is for the candidate to be pleased but a bit undecided, either because he or she has another offer, or because there's an interview at another college yet to be completed. In any case, I expect to be asked about such details as salary, moving costs, etc., and then for time to talk to a spouse or someone special to the candidate. Sarah was not coy. I learned that she was married but that her husband was not leaving California, leaving me with the impression that separation may have been part of the motivation for moving.

She told me who else had made her an offer but said Mac was

her clear choice. She thanked me for the quick response because she'd been stalling the other school. She told me she was going to call the other school as soon as we hung up to decline their offer.

The next morning I went to the president's office to tell him how enthused our candidate was to get our offer. He looked up from his desk and said, "I haven't met her, and I won't sign her contract." I considered reminding him that I was the one who signed contracts, but I supposed he could override me, and anyhow, that didn't seem consistent with the good mood with which I had started the morning.

I can't recall the ensuing conversation, but I remained civil while repeating that Sarah had, on the basis of our conversation, turned down an offer for another job. I do recall very clearly how the conversation ended. I said, "Bob, what am I supposed to do now?"

He said, "Wayne, that's your problem."

Feeling that civility had run its course, I got up and left. A few minutes after I had settled back in my office, Bob's secretary (known on the floor as his apologist) appeared at my door. "What in the world happened?" Thinking that Bob might have given her a clue as to what he expected, I asked what made her think something had happened. She said, "If you think you came out of Bob's office looking like your normal self, you're wrong. I looked twice to see if smoke was coming out of your ears."

Eventually, I called Sarah and gave her all the details. Then I asked if she could fly to St. Paul the next morning to meet the president. Poor woman; what choice did she have? She said she would do it.

I checked Bob's schedule, ascertained that the problem would be resolved if he found her as good as everyone said, and made arrangements (costing more than $1000 in 1996) for her to make a round trip from California to St. Paul the next day.

She impressed Bob as she had everyone else, I took her to a nice restaurant for an early dinner, dropped her at the airport, and with the change in time zones, I assume she got to bed at a reasonable time. Whether she went right to sleep might be a different story.

So ended my only major run-in with Bob Gavin. Of the incident, I said to Dolores, "It's as if Bob noticed that the year was running out and said to himself, 'If I don't do something soon, Wayne is going to think I'm a pretty easy guy to work with.'"

There was some real opposition to the idea, but I planned several appropriate farewell events for the Gavins and received several thank-you notes from him. I still have them. I have always felt sorry for the man. He was good for Macalester; he left it a stronger college than it was when he came. It was only because of how he related to people that he was denied the approbation that should have been his.

X. The Joys of Administration

I treasure the relationships I built with students,
colleagues, and in the larger community
over more than 50 years associated
with one school.

Changing the Atmosphere

Mike McPherson, the new president, closed the door behind him and settled into a chair in my office. "What the hell is wrong out there?"

I laughed. "It's all your fault," I said. "You asked Joan [Craig's administrative assistant] after the staff meeting where Craig was."

The fall term was just getting underway, and Mike had decided that until he had a reason to change things, he would continue with the routines to which we were accustomed, which included Monday morning administrative staff meetings. He didn't know, of course, the turmoil that had in previous years accompanied someone's absence, and his question about Craig's absence was, for all he was concerned, something polite to say as he passed Joan's desk.

Mike McPherson

That's not the way the question was heard. Joan, still accustomed to the old regime, had reported to Kathleen (the president's assistant) before the meeting that Craig was out of town, and she assumed this would have been reported to the president. It hadn't, evidently, and here she was being "blamed."

She quickly made her way to Kathleen's desk. Kathleen's defense was that she didn't think the new president was requiring reports on everyone's schedule, but Joan assured her that he had just asked her where Craig was. Things escalated, soon involving the opinions of most of the women (all the administrative assistants, once called secretaries, were women) on the floor.

As Mike began to sense the defensiveness and pains everyone

took to make sure that the occasional mistakes that occur in any office could not be traced to their desk, he asked me what he could do to change the general atmosphere. I told him that as I'd observed the climate the previous year, an idea had occurred to me that I'd like to try.

There was nothing novel about my idea. Whether I'm trying to work with officers of the student Christian fellowship, keep a group of editors working together, build esprit de corps in an academic department, or develop rapport with untenured faculty, gathering around good food always comes to mind. In this case, I asked Jan to reserve the trustee conference room for a fancy lunch: tablecloths, fine china, real flowers on the tables, a lunch that would appeal to anyone concerned about their waistline—but nevertheless topped with an irresistible dessert. All the office help on our floor was to be invited.

It so happened that a friend of mine, Alrick by name, had recently told me about his effort to meet someone for lunch at a restaurant that was part of a chain in St. Paul. They'd gotten mixed up over which link of the chain was to be their meeting place, and when, after a protracted wait, Alrick guessed at what might have happened, he decided to call a nearby restaurant to see if his friend was there. It was before everyone carried a cell phone, so he asked the manager if he might use the store phone.

The answer was no; the phone at the reception desk was for incoming calls only, but there was a pay phone just outside. So, after looking up the phone number, he made his call. But he made a mistake. He had copied down the number of the restaurant where he was. He got the manager to whom he had just spoken, but neither of them recognized the other's voice. The ensuing confusion was the stuff of a slapstick comedy.

I told that story before dessert was served, drawing the moral that we all make mistakes, and in retrospect, they were the object of laughter. I expressed the hope that we could, on our floor, learn to laugh at mistakes, and then pitch in to help right whatever may have gone wrong.

Mike McPherson had a wonderful sense of humor, and he was inspired to add a story or two and his own appeal for a lot more fun and laughter on our floor. He concluded by asking me to write up the story I'd told, and distribute it to everyone in attendance.

It would stretch the truth, to say nothing of the reader's credulity, to say that everyone worked in happy harmony forever after, but there was certainly a very different spirit going forward. That was much to my benefit because I was the next one to make a mistake of embarrassing proportions.

A member of our faculty, unknown to him, had been chosen to receive a prestigious national fellowship. The chair of his department had been notified and asked to see that the award be presented, as a surprise, in an appropriate setting. The chair invited me to present the award at a department meeting.

I thought it was something our new president would like to do. The chair agreed, so I made the necessary arrangements. But I made a mistake—a big mistake. It would be both difficult and painful to describe what went wrong, but the result is easy to describe. The president wound up in the wrong department and presented the award to the wrong person. We did achieve complete surprise, but that's all that can be said in my favor.

The mistake came to light just hours after it had been made. To call it awkward would be to understate the situation, but I did hurry to the office of the happy recipient to explain my error, apologize profusely, and disabuse him of his good fortune. The next step in my mea culpa was to go to the president and tell him that I had sent him to the wrong person.

After digesting my story, he offered one of his own. As the new president, he had been hosting a series of dinners at his home for trustees, major donors, and educational leaders in the Twin Cities. The night before, when all the guests had left, he got to thinking about his teenage son who had so frequently been eating solitary dinners in his room because his parents were hosting guests downstairs.

"I decided that I should devote some attention to him," Mike said, "so I went upstairs to ask if he would like to go out with me for a pizza." His son happily accepted, not only because he liked pizza but because it would be his first opportunity to ride in the fancy new car made available to the president by one of the trustees who ran a large automobile dealership. "So," continued Mike, "we went out to the garage, got into the shiny new car, and I backed into the caterer's truck still parked in our driveway.

"I've been fretting all day about why I did such a stupid thing. Now I know. It's so I could have a story to tell to you when I said, 'Wayne, we all make mistakes.'"

Near the end of the term, the trustees had their first meeting since Mike had become president. Aware that previous provosts had difficulty in getting along with President Gavin, they asked me after I had given my report how Mike and I were getting along. I said a number of positive things, and concluded with the story just told. There was general laughter, after which Mike stood up and said, "There is a bit more to that story. Every morning now, I try to make a mistake so I'll have something to say to Wayne when he screws up."

I made other efforts to introduce Mike to the campus that turned out better. One good idea was to ask department chairs to invite Mike and me to attend one of their department meetings. Small departments often get by without formal meetings, it being more natural to attend to common concerns in the coffee room, so it took most of Mike's first year, but eventually we did meet with every department.

These meetings went well, giving both of us a chance to hear about activities of both faculty and students that would not ordinarily come to our attention. Departments went out of their way to make the meetings pleasant, regularly making sure there were cookies and coffee on the table, and almost as regularly telling us of some idea they would love to try if only they had a little more money in their budget.

I recall only one meeting that was contentious, and that was owing to a young astronomer who started in the Physics Department the same year I started as provost. She told me when we first met that she had an understanding with my predecessor that she would teach much larger classes than usual, in exchange for which she would teach just one course each semester, making her load just two courses per year instead of the usual five. This concession was made because she had as a graduate student established herself, in her mind at least, as a top-notch researcher, and she would need relief from a five course load to pursue her research program.

I tried my best to be pleasant in that first meeting, but I was also firm in telling her that no one at the college had such a teaching arrangement, and that I would not approve one for her. I cited David Bressoud, whom I'd hired in the Mathematics Department. His research record, established over the course of many years, made him an international leader in his field, but he taught five courses each year, like everyone else at Macalester.

She did not take that well, but it was only the beginning of our troubled relationship. She needed more money for equipment, more student assistants, more of most everything. It was merely the continuation of her lament that she took the opportunity when meeting the president to vent her unhappiness with the restrictive way I treated her. At one point, this young woman said (I wrote it down at the time), "I'm not sure that either one of you guys understand what the teaching loads of active researchers look like."

On our way back from that meeting, I learned that Mike thought it quite humorous to be described as a guy who didn't understand the cost of research. (I should mention here that he was an economist by training who, before his administrative days, was regarded as a national authority on the costs of higher education.) He advised me to pay no attention to her. "She's unhappy here, is likely to become more unhappy, and she will eventually leave us for a research university where the world will find out if she is as good at research as she thinks she is."

I think she left us in the next year or two.

I had during my first year carried out my intention of hosting two dinners for our untenured faculty. With the singular exception of the young woman just described, these were well received. They also set me to thinking about the colleagues with whom I arrived during the 1964-1966 hiring spree. They had led the college's early climb to national recognition, been active supporters and critics during the Flemming era, and worked faithfully and unitedly during the 10-year comeback led by John Davis. They then joined Bob Gavin, even if highly critical of him at times, to achieve the goal set in the early 60s. Macalester was, according to the annual *U.S. News* poll, and according to polls by other academic organizations, one of the nation's leading liberal arts colleges.

Some of that group had moved on to other schools, and some had begun to retire, but the majority were still around. I decided it was time to recognize them and to have the new president recognize them. I chartered a tour boat for a dinner cruise on the St. Croix River for this group and their spouses.

Mike moved around the boat in an effort to visit with as many as possible and gave a short talk congratulating the group on what they had accomplished over a 30-year span. One of my colleagues, noting that I was a part of the group being honored that night, chided me a bit about giving a party for myself, and I guess it was so. I certainly enjoyed the event and got appreciative comments about it for months afterward.

These events stand out as highlights during Mike McPherson's first year as president. They surely suffice to make it clear that I greatly enjoyed working with him. The feeling was evidently mutual because as the year was drawing to a close, Mike asked if I would be willing to stay on the job for another two years. I was more than happy to do so.

Since I had not come to the office of provost in the traditional way of working up an administrative chain, assistant dean, then dean of some academic program, etc., my three years as provost under Mike were a continual learning experience. I would like to conclude this chapter commenting on things I learned. They don't lend themselves to a chronologic ordering, however. Indeed, I would have trouble locating many of these events in time, so I've organized them by categories with which a provost deals.

Searches

The most contentious part of hiring new faculty members occurs in the spring, when decisions are made about which departments or programs will be authorized to conduct a search during the following academic year. These decisions must be made within the financial framework of the college, which pretty much dictates the total size of the tenured faculty.

Departments experiencing growth in the number of students served naturally feel entitled to an increase in staffing. There are always interdepartmental programs, usually growing out of student demand (women's studies, ethnic studies, environmental studies, Ahmed Samatar's international studies) that need faculty whose primary allegiance is to the program, not to a department from which he or she has been borrowed. Of course, no one ever assumes that a sudden swing upward in student interest is temporary and can be met with temporary measures.

Departments or programs from which someone retires always feel the position vacated is theirs, and permission to fill it should be automatic. Departments experiencing declines in student enrollments will always argue that the decline is temporary, that to decrease their size would be short-sighted. And even if it's clear that steady declines in enrollment call for decreasing the size of faculty in that area, tenure rules may prevent such adjustments if no one is of retirement age.

A real believer in the traditional liberal arts (who just happened to be from the Classics Department) came in once to say that the ideal structure for a liberal arts college would have seven departments made up of the Trivium (grammar, rhetoric, logic) and the Quadrivium (arithmetic, geometry, astronomy, music), that students would select their courses from these departments, and that these seven departments would all have the same number of faculty.

When I explained this idea to Mike in one of our weekly meetings, he maintained such a thoughtful composure that I thought for a moment that he was taking it seriously. Then, after a pause and no change in his manner, he said, "And wouldn't it follow that all faculty members in each department should be the same size?"

It was the job of the faculty Personnel Committee to review all the requests for positions and then to make recommendations to me. I found their work to be helpful, and seldom found any reason to disagree with them. I got very little flak in a process that inevitably disappointed a lot of applicants.

My next involvement was to approve the make-up of a search committee submitted by the chair. In small departments, it often included the entire department; in larger departments, some subset of the department was proposed. Department representation was often supplemented by a member from an associated department, and sometimes by a woman or a minority person if there was no such representation among the departmental representatives.

It might seem that approval of the committee would be perfunctory. I never treated it that way. My idea was that this was the time to anticipate arguments. If there were factions in the department, if the department was under fire for ignoring a point of view in their discipline, or being male-dominated, or vulnerable in any way imaginable, this was the time to be sure that contrary opinions were heard. I wanted disagreements to be fought out in the committee, not in my office after the committee made its report to me. I might still get minority opinions expressed to me, but it was certainly helpful if everyone knew I had a recommendation that came from a balanced committee.

The searches that were authorized were conducted within well-defined guidelines, and statistical analyses of applicant pools were monitored in my office. Search committees were then to pick from the pool, sometimes numbering several hundred candidates, three they wanted me to bring to campus for interviews. Usually, when I met with the committee, they either had agreement on three candidates, or they had narrowed it down to four or five, deadlocked at that point, and agreed to accept my decision on which three to bring to campus.

When the committee, meeting with me, agreed on a candidate they wanted to hire, it was my job to notify the candidate and work out a contract. This was usually a pleasure. The reputation of the school usually made it a candidate's first choice, and we were in a position to be financially competitive with other offers the candidate might receive.

Macalester did have one unusual policy that on a few occasions gave me trouble. We never granted tenure, never, to someone coming in the door. When trying to attract an experienced, even a mid-career teacher who had tenure at another school, this sometimes become a stumbling block. I disliked the policy when I was chair of the Math Department. It seemed insulting to the likes of David Bressoud, Joan Hutchinson, and Stan Wagon to tell them they would be considered for tenure after finishing their first year at Macalester. It never became a problem with any of them; they were confident it would be forthcoming.

It was a big problem only once. Our highly regarded Political Science Department had passed the chair position back and forth among three people who'd been the heart of the department for as long as anyone could remember. As had been the case in mathematics, they were all approaching retirement together, and when they got a chance to search for someone new, it made sense to look for a mid-career person to come in as chair.

After a long search, they settled on a candidate from Canada. He strongly resisted the idea of a move from Canada into an untenured position. In this case, on the day he was being interviewed on campus, Dolores had lunch and showed his wife around the Twin Cities. When I told Dolores that I was going to have trouble over the tenure question, she told me there would be no problem because it was clear to her that his wife was determined not to leave her family roots in Canada.

Several days after their visit, the department chair got a letter in which the candidate waxed eloquent about how wonderful the department was and how much he would like to come, but he just could not think of moving at this stage of his life to a nontenured position. The department descended on me in mass, wanting an exception to the tenure rule, and they made it plain that they thought I was being unnecessarily rigid. My own suspicion was that the candidate was happy to lay the blame on me for a decision his wife was pushing at home.

They resumed their search the following year, and we got a wonderful chairman who was a very popular teacher—and a real builder who was relentless in pushing me to increase the size of the department.

As time went on, I had reason to appreciate the policy of not granting tenure in the first year. We hired a senior professor who was raised and trained in China before coming to a school in California, where he was tenured. It turned out that he was a real authoritarian in the classroom, highly unpopular with students. Everyone agreed in that case that it was good we had denied him tenure when he arrived, making it easy to bid him good-bye.

In describing the transition of Macalester from a small Presbyterian college primarily serving a four-state region to a school with aspirations to be numbered among the nation's elite, I made much of the foresight of Ezra Camp, then chair of the Math Department. He was ready for the change, having positioned the department to hire the kind of people that would build the program he had in mind.

The English Department, the largest department on campus in those days, was at the other extreme. The percentage of its staff holding a Ph.D., invariably regarded as a measure of academic prestige, was very low in a staff chosen to teach with enthusiasm the freshmen rhetoric course required of all entering students in those days.

By all accounts, the department was popular, very effective at what they were hired to do; but that counted for little to those hired to pursue what disenchanted English teachers called "the holy grail of academic prestige." In short order, a Ph.D. was brought in to bring about the desired change, and one can imagine the spirit in the department as young people with a focus on literary criticism were brought in to replace venerated professors who taught the fundamentals of clear writing.

Somehow, the department never did come together as a cohesive unit. As time went by and it appeared that old wounds might be dissipating, one of the new hires, a gifted classroom lecturer with a magnetic personality, arrived not yet having quite finished his thesis. Always promising, but somehow never finishing his thesis, he arrived at the all-important sixth year without a Ph.D when a tenure decision had to be made.

His situation revived again the question: Must a very popular teacher be dismissed because he does not have a Ph.D.? It was ultimately decided that this extraordinary teacher would be tenured, a decision that did not sit well with the few remaining old timers who had managed to get their Ph.D. but were still bitter about friends who'd been let go over this issue.

An altogether different issue arose when two members of the department divorced their respective spouses in order to marry each other. The subsequent marriage of the abandoned spouses to each other did not restore harmony in the beleaguered department.

When faced with the impending retirement of a good many of the once-young intruders, there was wide agreement that the department should be authorized to hire an outsider with an established reputation to come in as chair to lead a fresh start. The usual search procedures were undertaken, but (surprise) the search committee could not agree on anyone to recommend to me. It is Einstein who is credited with the observation that it is a sign of idiocy to try the same steps again, hoping for a different outcome, but try we did.

As the second year of searching was winding down, the chair of the committee, who was retiring at the end of the year, dropped in to tell me that once again, the search had failed. He suggested that I try to form an altogether new committee, preferably a more compatible group.

I took the unprecedented step of deciding that I would undertake the search myself. My plan was clear. I would call the chairs of the English departments of Big Ten universities. I would be candid in explaining my need to rebuild our English Department. I would tell them that I wanted to offer a two- or three-year contract to person near retirement so that tenure would not be an issue, a person of sufficient stature so that present members of our department and candidates we wanted to hire would respect his or her qualifications. I asked if they might have a person who, nearing the end of a successful career, might be attracted to the opportunity of building a good department in a respected college as a final legacy.

I naturally took people by surprise. Happily, chairs seemed not to take offense at my desire to hire away one of their senior faculty members. Most thought that if they had a person in the circumstances I described, they would be doing that person a favor by alerting him or her to an unusual opportunity. One chair joked that he had one rather well-known person near retirement that he would be happy to see go.

My venture came to a happy ending when I called the University of Michigan. Stuart McDougall had built a center at the university for specialized studies, then gone on sabbatical, and returned to the regular faculty. His chair thought his successful work at the center had been stimulating, so that his return to the regular faculty was proving to be something of a letdown.

Whether that was the case or not, Stuart responded positively to my proposal, came to Macalester, and when I left the office of provost, he was happily engaged in rebuilding the English Department.

Negotiating contracts with senior people of stature was always interesting. David Lanegran, chair of our Geography Department, was an urban geographer who played the key role in saving St. Paul's old federal court building from the demolition ball. Restoring that magnificent old building anchored what in time became a downtown square bordered by the courthouse turned office space, a new concert hall home for the St. Paul Chamber Orchestra, the restored city library, and a restored high-end hotel. That project was just part of what David did in restoring sections of the city, and in this work he became a close friend with the mayor, George Latimer.

Lanegran was a happy man when he stopped in my office to tell me that after a stint in Bill Clinton's cabinet, Latimer was returning to St. Paul and would be open to joining the Geography Department on a part-time basis. It turned out that Latimer was taking a half-time consulting job in Chicago but wanted to live in his St. Paul home. Of course we jumped at the chance to hire him for the other half of his time, and he proved as popular with the students as he had been for many terms with the voters.

When his Chicago responsibilities came to an end, we had to renegotiate his Macalester salary. He had become so active on campus that I asked him what more we would be getting for the additional salary. For some reason he seemed never to have thought about that, and it struck him as funny that I should ask.

In time, Latimer and I became good friends. Having lunch with him is an experience. People recognize him in any restaurant, and he never tired of telling people how much I expected him to do to earn his money. That would come up after he introduced me as his boss, the provost at Macalester, "a man who has become a legend in his own mind." We still have occasional lunches together in our old age.

Tenure

Tenure has its critics, and I understand why. I have already alluded to the difficulties it can cause in hiring, and I'll have more to say about the problems it can cause when a professor becomes a classroom liability. But it also serves very useful purposes that go beyond the historic purpose of guaranteeing a teacher's right to express convictions that may be out of step with current norms and beliefs.

Granting tenure is a statement that the faculty believes you are and will continue to be an asset in achieving the institution's purposes. It comes as an official welcome, a promise of support, an affirmation of the faith your colleagues have in your ability to contribute to a community of scholars. And as time marches on, tenured people do develop a sense of community, a sense of loyalty to the institution, as we saw at Macalester during our darkest years.

Young people value this declaration of acceptance, and usually develop a feeling that they are part of a group trying to achieve something worthy of their best effort. I tried to reinforce this feeling by instituting a ceremony each spring. We celebrated the achievements of the newly tenured, talked a bit about our hopes for our future together, and presented the newly tenured with cap, gown, and a gift certificate to be used at the college bookstore to put some commemorative books in their personal library.

Granting tenure is a large financial commitment. Institutions surely should enter into the agreement with due caution. Agreements worked out years ago with the American Association of University Professors give institutions six years to make up their mind on an individual. Macalester, in the case of a young person just coming out of graduate school, typically uses the full six years. A thorough review of progress in the third year, thought by some to be too severe in the Gavin era, nevertheless proves helpful both to the institution and the candidate.

A principal function of the dean of the faculty at Macalester was to monitor the progress of untenured faculty and help them prepare their dossier as the sixth year approached. Each fall, I would get a list of faculty members coming up for tenure.

I was particularly pleased the fall that I saw Karla Ballman's name on the list. I recalled having taught first-year calculus to her and learning from her the great value of a student assistant during her four years of help in the formative years of the Math League. I'd kept in touch with her after graduation, steering her to MIT, and had taken steps to attract her back to Macalester.

I was chair when she answered the call to develop a more robust statistics program in the department, and as I expected, she plunged in with her typical energy and enthusiasm. The one introductory statistics course we had as a kind of service to the social sciences was revamped, and she took leadership in developing two more advanced courses.

I recalled trying to dissuade her when I found she was writing books for both advanced courses as she went along. I told her from my own experience that writing a book was a major undertaking, and that she should focus on just one.

Her argument was that she had a point of view she wished to develop that differed from available texts, that students were responding well, and she was keeping up with producing materials as needed. I backed off as I recalled when I tried to change her method of keeping track of exams as they poured into my office from the high school math test (AHSME). She had persisted with her own methods, and I was surprised at how well they worked.

Course work was only a part of what she took on. People who begin a study that will rely on statistics typically make their biggest mistakes in how they collect data. They unconsciously get biased data, forget to get information from subjects that they need later to classify their results, and more. Karla made herself available to colleagues in the social sciences, helped them avoid these early mistakes, and ultimately decided that such counseling would be a terrific training ground for students. She set up a program in which she helped students who were in turn assisting a professor in another department.

I also recalled that she approached me one day to say that she found at MIT that her own ideas about statistics developed best by working on real problems. She wondered if through my contacts with industry in the area, I could put her in touch with someone needing statistical help. That was fairly easy to do, and I soon had her aware of a problem described to me by an actuary at the St. Paul Companies, a casualty insurance company in St. Paul.

In short, I felt that I'd played a large part in Karla's mathematical development, and I was delighted to think that it would be my privilege to preside over granting tenure to her.

My first indication that there might be a problem came when the dean of the faculty, Kathy Parson, came to see me after having reviewed Karla's dossier. She told me there was record of many good projects, but that in five years, distressingly little had been finished. Moreover, a relatively new hire in the department, a mid-career man who also had impressive credentials in the area of statistics, did not agree with Karla's approach to the subject.

It was when Karla's case came up for an initial, somewhat bleak review in the Personnel Committee that I heard that Joan Hutchinson had decided to undertake a very thorough review of Karla's record. That relieved me. Joan by that time had become very active at the national level, as well as among our own students, in encouraging more women to enter mathematics.

It was after I read Joan's review that real worry set in. She detailed numerous projects, including the two books, that had been started but not completed. The department was right, she felt, in not supporting Karla for tenure. The Personnel Committee followed suit.

On the morning that I was to visit candidates to announce decisions, the president was waiting for me when I arrived at my office. He knew what Karla meant to me, and he offered to go to her office in my stead. I could not imagine that.

The walk to her office was a long one. I berated myself for not having been more forceful in getting her to focus on just one book. I should have leaned on those she had helped in their research to acknowledge her help in their published papers. I never should have introduced her to the St. Paul Companies. I should have kept closer contact with her and her work after I became provost.

Though she fully anticipated a negative decision, she was nevertheless furious at having been turned down after the effort she'd put in. Several projects, including the books, were, she said, near completion. A lot of time had been spent on curricular development, for which she was getting no credit.

The walk back to my office was longer. With watery eyes, I avoided meeting anyone and entered the administration building through a side door for which I was grateful to have a key. I asked Jan to cancel my appointments for the rest of the day, and took a long bus ride home. It was then, and it remained to the end, the single worst day of my career at Macalester.

That being the case, I must bring the story up to date. Thoroughly disenchanted with academia, Karla obtained a job at the Mayo Clinic, where in time she became their chief statistician. She then moved to the Weill Cornell Medical Center in Manhattan, where she is as of this writing the division chief of Health Policy and Research. Several years ago she was invited back to Macalester as a distinguished alumnus to give a talk on her life as a medical statistician. I was retired by then, but when invited, she specified that she would like to visit with me. I greatly enjoyed that, and I'm sure she's made a lot more money than she would have as a tenured member of the Macalester faculty.

Karla Ballman

Now, what about the stories of tired old professors, reading from dog-eared notes, hanging on for years after they would have been retired if not for their tenured status? In my experience, such stories are greatly exaggerated. After evaluating about 130 tenured faculty members at Macalester from the office of the provost, only four might have been thought of as problematic, and of these, only one was past normal retirement age.

Another myth is that tenure makes it impossible to replace someone. Of the four referred to, three left while I was provost, and the fourth had agreed to retire the year after I left office. In many cases, and certainly in public high schools (where they don't have tenure, per se, but union rules that play a similar role), administrators prefer to ignore rather than address the problem of an under-performing teacher. A chorus I learned in Sunday School about Jonah provides a useful suggestion: "God did not force him to go against his will; he just made him willing to go."

The first of the four who decided to go under my watch was a bit past mid-career. He taught a foreign language. While in the Math Department, I knew him only casually and regarded him as a quiet, very nice person. It was while I was having one of my Wednesday night "dinner with a student" conversations that I met a first-year student who told me she intended to transfer after her first year because she was not being sufficiently challenged. She included this teacher in her list of disappointments, saying that he told the class on Day 1 not to worry about grades because he was going to give everyone an A.

I called him in the next morning to ask if it was true, and if so, why. He told me he was getting very hard of hearing, that pronunciation was a big part of teaching language, and that he hesitated to downgrade anyone on the basis of not having heard them correctly. Within a week, he came back to negotiate an early retirement. I had addressed a problem, but I certainly did not feel good about it as I bid him farewell.

The second person was a chemistry teacher of Japanese descent who had begun teaching an ethnic studies course in which she told the story of her family's mistreatment during WW II. As she researched her own family's story and met with other faculty who talked about abuse in one form or another of minorities in this country, she committed less and less of her time to chemistry. It got to the point where we were hiring part-timers to cover her absence in chemistry. By the time I became provost, she was wanting to commit full time to ethnic studies.

I pointed out that she was tenured in chemistry, that she had no training and certainly would not be hired from the outside to teach ethnic studies, and that her salary dictated that she ought to be making the contribution of a full senior professor in her home department. She had a sabbatical coming, and I said I would only agree to it if she used it for full-time study in a graduate department of chemistry. After some back and forth on these themes, she decided to quit teaching.

The third faculty member to leave was a woman in our Music Department whom I think was a very popular teacher when she started at the college. In a great misfortune, her husband died at a very young age, and sometime after that, she declared herself a lesbian.

I was vaguely aware of this. I became more aware of it when advisees of mine began to complain about her militant criticism of male privilege, and in some cases change their minds about getting a double major in math and music. She became a part (in fairness only a part) of the continual problems of that discordant department, and took particular umbrage when I brought in an outsider to chair the department as they were concluding 20 years of internal wrangling.

She came to my office to tell me it was not very collegial of me to bring in an outsider when a majority of the department had not agreed to it. I told her that I thought collegiality had disappeared from the department years ago. It was only a year or so after that, perhaps after my term in office had expired, when she left the college. I genuinely hope that she found a place to be happier.

The last person in this quartet was a senior member of the Education Department who for a number of years had very few students sign up for her courses. She acknowledged the obvious and agreed to revise her courses to attract more students in the near future. We worked out an agreement that included specific target numbers, and when not reached a year or two after I left office, she did retire.

I heard many complaints about faculty that stayed too long when I attended meetings of provosts from other colleges in our ACM consortium. It seemed clear to me that Macalester had much less of a problem, a fact I attributed to our rigorous screening of candidates for tenure, and for our rich programs of sabbaticals and other opportunities that kept our faculty abreast of new developments in their fields.

Tenure does not protect a faculty member who is guilty of various forms of unethical conduct. Here is another situation that administrators often prefer to sweep under the rug rather than deal with, however.

In my four years as provost, I only had to deal with such charges once. A faculty member was accused of sexual impropriety with a female student while he led a group of students on a several-day field trip. The charges were pressed by a former boyfriend of the young lady involved.

This was one time I felt that some prior training in how to deal with such things could have been helpful. As it was, common sense seems to have been adequate. Since the young lady herself denied any wrongdoing, and the charges were brought by a jilted young man, I questioned the story from the beginning, but I felt I had to pursue the matter as thoroughly as possible. I eventually concluded that the faculty member should have been more careful about appearances, but that the charges owed more to imagination than evidence. I wrote such a report, showed it to the accused, and after he agreed that it stated the facts, I put it in his file in my office.

Years later, I happened by his office one day, apologized for all the questions I had asked, and thanked him for the gracious way in which he cooperated. He told me he understood that when such charges are made, a responsible administrator must take them seriously.

Setting Salaries

As the time approached during my first year for chairs to submit activity evaluations for each member of their department, an aggressive chair came in to request a significant boost in pay for a member of his department. The person he had in mind did not have his Ph.D., had been part-time in the department for many years (as a part-timer, the seven-year rule of "tenure or out" never applied), as a Black man brought a view of the history of civil rights that was based on his own experience, and was enormously popular with the students. Yet, as a part-timer, he had remained low on the salary schedule and had no fringe benefits.

I told him I thought the case deserved a careful look and that I would consider it. I then asked Ellen Guyer (met previously as the one who assigned students to their first-year seminar and who advised me on a host of issues) to produce a list of all comparable people in part-time positions across the college.

The results surprised me. The Music Department alone listed about a dozen such people, usually drawn from the ranks of the Minnesota Symphony or the St. Paul Chamber Orchestra, who worked with students on a particular instrument. The situation was similar in the Art Department. We didn't have a business major, but the Economics Department wanted to include accounting in their offerings, so they had a long-term part-time accountant. By and by it dawned on me that before we decided to offer some advanced statistics courses, Jean Probst had functioned in exactly this way in the Mathematics Department, a part-time faculty member who taught elementary statistics courses.

I explained all this to the chair who asked me about it, told him there was a large group that ought to be paid more and that

I would bring this need up when we discussed next year's budget, but it would take some time to bring so large a group up to a more satisfactory level. I thanked him for calling it to my attention.

He was not satisfied. He assured me that if his man got the raise he deserved, they would certainly keep the raise confidential so as to not provoke a stampede to my office. To his dismay, I stood firm. When he got up to leave, I said, "Take a little comfort in the fact that I don't strike deals with the most persistent. Others are not getting a better deal on salaries or department budgets or equipment because they exerted more pressure than you did." And I did begin a systematic effort to get a special allotment in the salary budgets in future years so that we could pay this group something closer to what they deserved.

The experience also prompted me to seek more input than only recommendations of department chairs when setting salaries. After all, they had a view only of their own departments, and it was their role to advocate for their departmental colleagues. My office staff knew a great deal about which faculty members would be quick to help out on problems that transcended an individual department: accepting a few more students in their class after enrollment limits had been reached, taking on a particularly demanding role in a college committee, being available for a program on parent's day, and much more.

Staff members were pleased to be included in faculty salary discussions. I invited Kathy Parson, dean of the faculty, and Ellen Guyer to meet with me for two full days in a conference room at an off-campus nonprofit organization where we could discuss the situation of each faculty member. I firmly believe that over the four years we did this, faculty members were treated as fairly as possible, and we discovered a few people who had grown accustomed to being overlooked.

I added one more wrinkle to issuing yearly contracts. On each contract I signed, I appended a personal note that included a specific compliment. It was easy to find something to say since I had in front of me a chair's report on each individual. This effort drew many appreciative notes. Coupled with my note per night to someone (those went to staff as well as faculty), we made relations with the provost's office much more personal.

Graduations

I was surprised at the effort it took to correctly pronounce the names of the graduates, including international students, as I read them at the graduation ceremony. The International Center invited all international students to make a recording of the correct pronunciation of their names. A week before graduation, I got a list of all the names, together with the recordings. I still invited these students to my office to rehearse me, and some did come. The test came when, on the big day, an international student stood at the bottom of the stairs waiting for me to read the name. If a student slapped his or her forehead when stepping forward, I knew I'd blown it.

Students always want the graduation ceremony to be on the lawn in the middle of campus. It's picturesque, of course, and the college is eager to please everyone on this celebratory day. At the same time, one must plan for the possibility of rain. Should we accept the expense of a double set-up, placing a couple thousand chairs in carefully arranged rows so that the right student is in line as names are being called, and then duplicate this arrangement in the gymnasium in case of rain? Should we do a set-up on the lawn only, hoping we get enough warning of rain to allow moving all the chairs before the ceremony?

Several weeks before my first year on the podium, a committee of students came to my office to say that the graduating class wanted to change the practice of having graduates sit in rows in alphabetical order at the graduation ceremony. They wanted to be able to sit with their friends, in some cases with their fiancés.

It was an understandable wish, made politely to the right office. My first inclination in such a situation is to be accommodating, but this request raised a number of problems. It seemed impossible with such a seating arrangement to have the piles of diplomas on stage arranged so that each graduate gets presented with the right one as they come across the stage. Parents like to get into position to take pictures of their graduate, and they rely on the alphabetical order to know when to leave their seat and get down to the front for that all-important picture.

The students saw the possibility of chaos, but they thought the details could be worked out. I told them I would think about it, and when they left I employed one of my most reliable methods for solving problems. I called Ellen Guyer.

As usual, she worked out a plan. It involved having a practice graduation in the gym where chairs were set up exactly as they would be on the lawn. Ellen paid me the compliment of saying that I had the student's trust, so if I spoke to them at the practice about the necessity of everyone doing exactly as they were told, she thought they would do it.

The programs distributed to the audience listed the graduates in alphabetical order, but an insert listed them in the order they would cross the stage, enabling parents to anticipate the appearance of their student. As she always did at every graduation, Ellen stood at the bottom of the stairs to the platform, checking the name of each student before they ascended the stairs.

Ellen's presence at the bottom of the stairs almost did me in when I presided for the last time. It was the conclusion of a story that began in my first year as provost. In one of the few times I ever saw Ellen at wits end, she told me of a blind student in that year's freshmen class who came from a family with the means to provide a private tutor for the girl through high school. The intentions had been good, but the girl hadn't learned the things she would have learned fending for herself in public schools, or even in a special school for the blind.

The girl had no idea how to cross the busy street that ran through the campus, how to survive life in the dorms, how to take notes in a classroom, and more. Since providing help for disadvantaged students was one of the jobs that fell under Ellen's responsibility, most of the girl's problems fell in her lap.

After several weeks of doing her best, Ellen called the parents to suggest that the girl needed one year in a special school for the blind, not for academic reasons, but to learn to manage personal care and safety. The parents would not hear of it. They'd provided a tutor for the girl throughout her pre-college years so she would be prepared for study at a first-rate college, our college catalog said we welcomed special-needs students, and now it was time for us to make good on that claim.

Ellen took it on as a challenge. The first year was tough going, but they got through it together. Of course, it got easier as the girl adapted, but she did depend on Ellen in unusual ways through all four years. When I congratulated Ellen on how well it all turned out, she deflected the compliment, telling me it was a team effort involving the dean of students, who helped with the details of living on campus, and many faculty members who were accommodating in many ways. I told her I was sure it was a team effort, but it was my opinion that the team had a captain extraordinaire.

On graduation day, I of course recognized this girl's name when I saw it was the next one on the list. I glanced to the stairway. There stood Ellen, her hand extended to help the girl find the handrail. Somehow, it struck me forcefully as a metaphor of what Ellen had done for this girl for four years. I had to pause to get control of own voice before I could continue.

The most memorable graduation by far occurred the year it was decided to give an honorary degree to Kofi Annan. He was Macalester's most famous graduate, a winner of the Nobel Peace Prize, then serving as secretary general of the United Nations. Honorary degrees are intended to honor the recipient for work that represents the college's ideals. In this case, while we certainly wanted to honor Kofi, it was clear that Kofi also honored the college by clearing his schedule to be at our graduation ceremony.

That is not to suggest that Kofi did not enjoy coming back to campus. He enjoyed recalling his first arrival on campus, having come as a somewhat bewildered young man straight from the heart of Africa. Students always enjoyed hearing him tell stories when he came, and he was pleased to be a member of Macalester's board of trustees.

Ted Turner

Not long before the degree was to be presented, Ted Turner had drawn national headlines with an announcement that he was making an enormous contribution to the UN in honor of Kofi's outstanding work as general secretary. This prompted our president to invite Turner to participate in the ceremony honoring Kofi. Turner was quick to accept.

That's when the troubles began. Clyde Bellecourt, a long-time activist in pushing Native American causes, immediately announced that he would be leading demonstrations at our graduation because of the involvement of Ted Turner, owner of the Atlanta Braves. Turner was a target of Bellecourt because he would not change the name of his offensively named team.

On the Monday of graduation week, we learned the nature of the planned demonstration. Clyde appeared on campus that morning with the biggest drum imaginable. The office of the president faced the mall of the campus, where chairs get set up for graduation, but my office faced Macalester Street, along which there ran a public sidewalk on which Clyde had his helpers place his drum.

Wearing ear protection, he began beating the drum, which was easily heard for blocks around. His endurance was remarkable as he beat that thing nonstop all day under my window. That went on every day of the week. I believe the furniture in my office was vibrating. Pne night after we had been in bed for a few minutes, I asked Dolores if the bed was shaking or if it was just me vibrating.

The promise was that the drumming would accompany the graduation ceremony. The city police assured us that they would not attempt to move Clyde because he was on public property, exercising what would pass in the courts as freedom of speech. This was something they knew from previous encounters with Clyde. Clyde and his lawyers knew it as well.

Clyde Bellecourt

Predictably, there were students who joined in support of Clyde, and they helped him monitor the doors to our building, alerting him whenever I or the president entered or left. On those occasions, the students packed the doorways until Clyde arrived and with great sarcasm admonished them, "Stand aside; be sure you don't touch him because he is a very important man who could have you arrested." This was followed by other mockery, at which Clyde excelled.

The administrative staff, wondering how to avoid major disruption at the graduation, had numerous meetings and consultations with lawyers and city officials, all to no avail. Always optimistic about being able to work out some compromise, I asked Clyde if he would go to lunch with me. He instantly agreed. It was a new experience for me. For two hours I listened to a litany of ways in which White people have abused Indians.

I had little doubt that most of what he said was true, and even my most carefully phrased rejoinders got me in trouble. I recall, for instance, trying to defuse his personal attacks by saying that I understood that in his position of national leadership, he spoke not just for himself but for Native Americans everywhere.

He jumped on my use of "Native Americans," asserting that the term was used by academicians and others who hoped to disassociate themselves from past oppression of Indians by using new terms for the oppressed (or something like that). He asked, "When you call me a leader, do you know what I lead?"

I said, "You lead the AIM." He asked if I knew what AIM stood for, and I responded, "The American Indian Movement." Then he asked if I'd heard what I just said.

"You answered correctly. We call ourselves Indians. We're not ashamed of that. It's you high-minded White people who are afraid of the word Indian because you know what you've thought and continue to think of Indians. But I'm proud of the word. I am an Indian!"

I won no concessions. I did learn that Clyde had one other plan for graduation day. The thing he found most offensive about the Atlanta Braves was the chant that fans used as a simulation of a war cry when they were calling for their team to rally. He told me he had a recording of this chant, familiar to any baseball fan who listens to broadcasts of games from Atlanta, and that he might arrange for loudspeakers to be set up next to his drum.

About mid-week, really worried that our attempt to honor Kofi was going to turn into a major confrontation, the president, by then in possession of a petition signed by a good many students, stopped in my office one morning to tell me he was flying to Atlanta to ask Turner for advice. "He must run into this everywhere he goes," Mike thought, "so perhaps he has a way to deal with it."

It was the evening of that same day when Mike again

appeared in my office, having just returned from his one-day round trip to Atlanta. "That's not going to help," he told me. "I showed him the petition and asked how he handled these things."

Turner took a look at the petition calling on him to change the name of his team and said, "I know exactly how to handle this. You take the thing, crumple it into a ball (accompanying his words with the prescribed action), and throw it into their damned faces."

One of our trustees ran a public relations office in Washington, D.C. At Mike's request, he came to St. Paul a day early to advise Mike what to do. The trustee was upbeat. "You'll see. Papers all over the country will carry a picture of Kofi Annan and Ted Turner and his wife (Jane Fonda) in front of the campus flag pole. A caption under the picture will tell of Macalester's decades of flying the United Nations flag under the American flag. It will be great."

As to any disruption, his idea was that Clyde Bellecourt had no idea of how to sway public opinion in his favor. The public has learned to disregard him as a rabble rouser.

Mike was not consoled. "With the way things have been going ever since announcing that Turner was coming, the picture you envision will probably include Jane Fonda putting a match to the American flag." Mike went on to say that even if the story played well in the newspapers, that wasn't going to stop the planned disruption of the ceremony.

I think it was the day before graduation

Kofi Annan

that Mike got a note from Ted Turner saying he had high regard for Kofi Annan and did not want to detract from a proper recognition of his achievements by his alma mater. Therefore, he was cancelling his plans to accept our kind invitation to be present.

All's well that ends well. Kofi treated his honorary degree as if it was the greatest thing that ever happened to him, and he told again a story he had told often enough on campus so that it had even been given a name.

The Earmuff Story

Having come to St. Paul directly from Ghana, where he had been raised in a climate common to countries near the equator, he was apprehensive about the Minnesota winters that he'd read about. As an international student, he was assigned to a host family, and as fall was threatening to turn into winter, the family took him out to shop for appropriate winter clothing. They introduced him to coats with linings he had never imagined, gloves, scarves, sweaters, and boots. But he put his foot down when advised to buy some earmuffs. He thought them the most ridiculous looking things he'd ever been asked to wear.

The time came when, while waiting for a bus, he needed ear covering that he didn't have. He had to be treated for frostbite on his ears. And that, he concluded, taught him a lesson that has been valuable to him throughout his career travelling the world for the UN. Never assume that you know more about how to live in a country than do the people who live there.

Some Notable Trustees

There are certainly some perks to being provost. One was the opportunity to interact with some notable people I might otherwise only have read about in the newspaper; and because they were notable people, it seems worth recording the impressions they left.

Having just written about graduations, I'll start with a graduation week event. Most departments have awards they give to recognize outstanding work done by graduating seniors. These range from adding the student's name to a departmental plaque all the way to awarding a sizable stipend for graduate study. Someone had the idea that if these awards were presented at a convocation on the Friday night preceding the Saturday commencement, parents could arrive in time to see a son or daughter honored.

It turned out to be a bad idea—a very bad idea. Scheduled for an evening, it had to be held indoors, meaning the gymnasium. It was a hot, sultry evening, and the gym was packed. There was no air conditioning. I'd been asked to begin the proceedings with a short talk congratulating those to be honored, and then with several others wearing our caps and gowns to preside over the program.

By the time I finished a 10-minute talk, I was sweltering, and that was only the beginning. The aggregate of awards to be given by all departments was more than had been realized, and of course each department chair had prepared a few remarks explaining the nature of the award and why Sally Witquick had won it.

We were more than an hour into the program when I spotted Joan Mondale in the audience. She and other trustees were on campus for their spring meeting, held in conjunction with the graduation, but she was the only trustee in the gym that night.

I sought her out when the program finally came to a merciful end and asked why she was there. She said the young people being recognized were the ones most likely to emerge as future leaders of our country. She wanted to see them, hear about their accomplishments, and encourage them. She was, she said, disappointed that all the trustees were not there to join her in this effort.

Previously introduced as the daughter of a long-time chaplain and an alum of the college, Joan Mondale took her role as a trustee very seriously. Since her husband was at that time the U.S.

ambassador to Japan, she had to make transpacific flights twice a year to attend trustee meetings, and when on campus, she made it her business to walk around and take note of things.

On her first visit after Mike McPherson assumed the presidency, she came to my office for some reason. On her way through the outer office, she noticed the absence of a large urn. I'd always heard that it was the work of an artist of note, that it had been purchased on a trip abroad by a trustee of yesteryear and donated to the college. At least since I had come to the college, elections of faculty committees had always been by "urn election." One went to the office of the provost, signed next to your name on the list of eligible voters, and dropped your ballot in the urn.

I was not surprised that Joan noticed the urn was gone. She had become known when her husband was vice president as an advocate of public art, and her lively interest in all forms of art was well-known about campus.

I told her the new president's wife, on her first visit to my office, noticed the urn, ascertained that it was a gift to the college, and decided it would be a splendid adornment next to the fireplace in the living room of the president's house.

I did not tell her that the two women in my office charged with getting ballots out of narrow-necked, heavy, four-foot urn were not unhappy to see it go. They had gladly cut a slot in the cover of a cardboard box meant to store file folders, decorated the box to identify it as a ballot box, and found counting votes a much more palatable assignment.

Joan's reaction was mixed. She was happy to learn that Mrs. McPherson had an interest and good taste in art. At the same time she hated to lose the college tradition of urn elections. She gave me the name and address of a friend who ran a gallery and told me to choose a new urn suitable for the office. On her next visit to campus, she checked to see if I'd followed through. I had!

Several years later, while campaigning for a second term as U.S. senator from Minnesota, Paul Wellstone was killed in an airplane crash. With just weeks left until the election, the

Walter and Joan Mondale

Democratic Party called upon Walter Mondale to run for the office. To my great surprise, he lost the election.

I wrote a note to the Mondales expressing my disappointment. Joan answered it, saying that it had been an honor to be asked to run, that she and Walter had once again enjoyed meeting people of the state as they campaigned, and that they now wished the winner of that election wisdom as he began six years in the senate.

I learned that Joan Mondale's interest in public service was genuine. In what had to be one of the more menial jobs of her life, she took very seriously her responsibilities as a trustee of the college. She viewed the students as potential leaders of our country. She was quick to be at Walter's side when he was involved in a campaign, and she was respectful of the elective process, even in losing.

While my admiration for Joan as a public-spirited citizen was growing, Dolores was enjoying opportunities to employ the skills she acquired years ago in the Carley living room, entering into good natured repartee with Walter.

One night we were sharing a table with the Mondales at a dinner on campus. Somehow the discussion turned to Walter's success in having the St. Croix River that separates Wisconsin and Minnesota declared a national river. It led to a lively discussion when Dolores informed Walter that because of his bill, eminent domain had forced us to sell land along the river we'd purchased to use for camping.

She pointed out that when we owned the land, we'd take large bags to collect the rubbish that canoe enthusiasts left behind when they camped on our land. She wondered if he planned to introduce another bill to run garbage barges down the river to clean up the now-public lands. Walter wondered if she would continue to clean up our spot if he provided her with a supply of big bags.

One of my favorite exchanges between Walter and Dolores was related to the favorable impression she formed of Madeleine Albright when she gave a talk at Macalester. After a talk about her years as secretary of state, there had been a time for questions. The first one came from a student who'd come primed to be abrasive. Referring to a well-publicized remark she'd made after a U.S. bombing had killed civilians, including some children, he asked how she could be so callous as to describe the deaths of innocent children as collateral damage.

She was aggressive, meeting the question head on. As best as I can recall she said, "Well I'm glad that question came first so we can get it out of the way. I made that comment in the give and take at a press conference with reporters hostile to the action we had taken. I never should have said it, and I have apologized repeatedly, but I still get the same question you just asked from people who would rather cause me embarrassment than kindly accept a sincere apology.

"But let me add that we stopped that thug Milosevic, and I'll not apologize for that."

It was the kind of answer Dolores often wished for but seldom heard when she thought students were being "smart alecks." She loved the way Albright handled that and other questions thrown at her.

It happened that the next night there was a reception where we ran into the Mondales. Dolores was still enthused over the previous night and told Walter that Hubert Humphrey used to be her hero, but he was gone now, and she thought Madeleine Albright would now be her hero. Walter replied, "Haven't you skipped over one?"

The fact is that Walter Mondale had become something of a hero to both Dolores and me. We admired the time he gave to interacting with students on campus, we admired the positions he took, and we admired the way he spoke of those who opposed him politically.

It's an admiration that seems to be shared widely by those who got to observe him up close. Years ago, a friend from our teenage years, Don Holt, had become chief of the *Newsweek* bureau in Washington, D.C. One year he scratched out a little note on the Christmas card he sent to us, saying. "I think your man Walter Mondale is the most decent man in the Senate."

The Daytons are another prominent family with strong Macalester ties. The founder of the first Dayton department store served on the original Macalester board, and there has been a member of the family on the board almost continuously ever since. The family was represented on the board while I was provost by Ruth Stricker Dayton. Ruth read my columns in the Mac Weekly, often sending me notes when a particular column struck her fancy.

Ruth had married Bruce Dayton, founder of the Target stores after his first wife died. Bruce was a major benefactor of the Minneapolis Institute of Art. I once got to tag along when he led a tour of the galleries displaying major works he'd brought from China. I thought at the time that I understood some of what he said made these paintings so valuable, but I'm afraid I couldn't repeat much of it now.

My favorite Dayton story relates to a grant the college had

received from the Kresge Foundation. Over a given time period, Kresge would match gifts to the college up to a total of $10 million. One morning the president stopped in my office to say that he was not looking forward to the day ahead. He had his reason. The Finance Committee was to meet that afternoon, and he would have to report that the Kresge grant was going to expire and we had only raised $9 million—that is, we were leaving a million dollars on the table.

That was of course his problem, and I forgot about it until about 6:30 that evening, when he again stopped in, this time grinning like the Cheshire cat. He told me he included the Kresge story in his report, and after the meeting, Ruth came up to him and said, "Bruce is picking me up. Why don't you follow me down to the car and tell him your story."

He said he felt like a puppy following her down to street level. Sure enough, there sat Bruce in his car. Ruth motioned for Mike to get in the back seat, and said, "Tell Bruce your story." Apparently he got just far enough into the story so that Bruce could see where he was headed. He interrupted and explained that they were to meet friends for dinner, but that he would be happy to send a million tomorrow for such a worthy cause.

Those who made plans in the early 60s to raise Macalester's standing in the academic world saw that they would need to attract both faculty and students from around the nation. Nothing was said at the time about the board of trustees, which in those days was largely made up of businessmen and church leaders from the Twin Cities. Inevitably, as students from around the nation made their mark in the world and began to return as trustees, the board also took on a national look, tilted of course toward the financial centers of the East Coast.

Perhaps that's why it was decided that the board should hold one of its meetings in New York. Or perhaps it was because in New York, Kofi Annan could be a guest of honor at a meeting that was to launch a major fund drive.

At first Dolores did not plan to come with me to the meeting.

She began to reconsider her plans when she heard that the group was having dinner in an old brownstone home, now used exclusively for groups wishing to schedule a private dinner. Her mind was made up when she learned that the chef in charge was the woman who'd been chef for Jacqueline Kennedy.

It was, in every respect, a new experience for us, not likely ever to be repeated. We were met at the steps going in by the Secret Service, which prepared the way wherever Kofi was to go. That was nothing compared to the excitement in the street when his car and personal attendants pulled up. Inside, the chandeliers, the cabinetry, the carpeting, the furnishings of the house guaranteed that Dolores and I would feel out of place for the duration of the evening.

I shall not try to describe the meal. The chef did that for us, describing in the interlude we needed before dessert the preparation of the various courses that had been served. Then as the formally dressed waiters circulated among us with trays displaying a variety of desserts, she described our options. I remember her last words. "Finally, for those of you who love chocolate, you must try my own chocolate creation." (It probably had a French name.) Her description ended with, "You will worship at my feet."

After dinner, Kofi addressed the group, starting, as was his style, with a story. He told of his early years helping his father harvest crops. It was essential, he'd learned, that one carefully preserve seeds at the time of harvest to be used the next spring.

He then cited the bountiful dinner and the obvious affluence of those present as the harvest that comes to those who have worked, and then came the reminder that some of the bounty must be used to see that there will be more harvests in the future. He cited what it had meant to him to come to a college where someone else had prepared the way for someone like him.

No fundraiser could have asked for a better after-dinner talk.

More Notable People

Sometimes a provost, by virtue of the position he or she holds, gets invited to participate in an event not an integral part of the college program. One such opportunity came to me by way of a phone call from a member of House of Hope Presbyterian Church.

Armed with a generous gift, the church was planning a symposium emphasizing the need for more civility in public life. They had secured the participation of Václav Havel of the Czech Republic for their keynote speaker, and they were now wondering if they could expand the impact of their symposium by involving institutions from the larger community. In particular, they noted that House of Hope, the governor's mansion, Macalester, and St. Thomas occupied a relatively short stretch of Summit Avenue. It would be wonderful, they thought, if the church, the state government, and two educational institutions got involved in their effort.

So far as I knew, this was the first attempt anyone had made at cooperation between the church and the college since tensions had arisen during the days of student protests of the Vietnam War. I thought we were well past the time when colleagues would worry that I was trying to restore our identification as a Presbyterian college, and that cooperation among the invited parties would be a good thing. The president was a bit indifferent to the suggestion, being specific only on the matter of his own involvement. He made it clear that if we joined the effort, I would be the one to make time in my schedule for whatever was required. I decided to proceed.

It was Governor Arne Carlson who first convened representatives of the sponsoring institutions, inviting us to breakfast at the governor's mansion. Arnie's reputation was that of a Republican on the liberal side of his party. If that was so, it was not evident that morning.

I don't know if he was Catholic; I don't know if someone at

Macalester offended him in some way; I do know that he lost no opportunity to make digs at Macalester, sometimes by way of comparison with St. Thomas.

After perhaps half a dozen such remarks, none of them subtle, I finally spoke up and said that I had been happy to respond positively to the invitation from House of Hope, but if those present were as offended by Macalester's participation as the governor seemed to be, we would withdraw and I would leave the meeting. That awakened enough support from the others to get the governor more in the spirit of the Václav Havel Symposium on Civil Society that we were planning.

Arne Carlson

With the House of Hope committee carrying on all communications necessary to entertaining the president of a foreign country, I thought one meeting to plan a schedule would do. Since planning started a full year before the visit, however, there was time for the various representatives to meet several more times, so of course we did. I read somewhere that a committee is a group of people who keep minutes and waste hours. Mike McPherson never tired of reminding me that I had brought this on myself.

The schedule agreed upon had a welcoming luncheon for the Havels at St. Thomas, then a late-afternoon public speech in the Macalester fieldhouse, followed by a dinner for invited guests in the Macalester boardroom. I think the governor also hosted a small event for political leaders to have an opportunity to converse with President Havel.

St. Thomas, with every intention of honoring President Havel, planned a luncheon that would have been appropriate for visiting royalty. The things that went wrong are what stick in my mind.

To begin with, beautiful long-stem fresh flowers were set in the middle of every table. Harry Webb, a neighbor and good friend of mine, taught photography in the St. Thomas Art Department, did all their photography for special events, and was himself a fastidious artist with a camera. As a good photographer should, he went to the dining room ahead of time to plan locations from which he would work, and he was dismayed at the height of the flower arrangements, which would interfere with his sight lines.

He quickly hit upon a solution. He removed every arrangement from its vase, cut a couple of inches off the bottoms of the stems, and put them back as they were, more or less.

I must interrupt the flow of my story here to record that when Harry died years later, there was a luncheon after the service for guests of the family. At this event, there was a time for telling stories about Harry. The St. Thomas director of special events was there, and told the story of finding all the centerpieces cut down and restored "as best as a photographer could arrange flowers." She told those assembled that Harry was lucky to have lived as long as he did.

With flowers arranged as Harry wanted them, the guests of honor entered the room on a red carpet leading to the head table. I admit to being quite interested in seeing Mrs. Havel, Dagmar by name, a woman who had been famous in Czechoslovakia as a pornography star before Vaclav married her. I'd read that political opponents of Vaclav delighted in playing reruns on late-night television of movies of the first lady in her former life, and not much else.

President and Mrs. Havel were in formal attire and made a highly photogenic couple as their entry was announced by a brass quartet playing the Czech national anthem. Behind them came

Minnesota Governor Jesse Ventura, who had displaced Arnie Carlson in an election since the event had been planned. Always characterizing himself as a man of the people, our former wrestler turned governor was dressed in a flannel shirt, blue jeans, and gym shoes. Photographers present tried hard, of course, to capture the Havels and Jesse in the same picture.

Tickets for the public lecture, even in the expanse of our fieldhouse, were at a premium. The provost at St. Olaf, knowing that I had to scramble every year to get tickets to the St. Olaf Christmas concert, called to suggest that for a couple of tickets to hear Havel, he would see to it that I got concert tickets next Christmas. It was the most tangible reward for my work on the symposium.

Madeline Albright was the speaker at the next year's symposium, an event to which I have already alluded in describing my wife's esteem for her. That symposium went much more smoothly, but I think Macalester's participation in these events ended with my term as provost.

Not all the special opportunities that came to me as provost involved public figures or magnificent social events. Macalester, like many colleges, has funds earmarked for bringing to campus several times a year a distinguished academician who can draw on his or her own expertise to give a lecture that will be of interest to members from the surrounding community as well as students and faculty.

Since such speakers are usually not the guest of a particular department, it sometimes fell to me to meet the speaker at the airport and act as host during the visitor's stay in the Twin Cities. This was an assignment I relished. The people I met and the subjects about which they were well-informed provided enough snappy conversation starters to keep me supplied for the rest of my life.

I was on such an assignment when I met Ron Takaki, a professor of ethnic studies from the University of California-Berkeley. In pleasant conversation during the half day we spent together, he made me aware of how seldom-taught aspects of

American history can help one understand relations among ethnic groups in our country.

We had barely finished introducing ourselves at the airport when Ron asked me if I knew where Fort Snelling was. When I told him that we would shortly see it from the freeway on our way to campus, he asked if we could stop there to visit the museum. I learned on our way to the fort why he was interested.

Ronald Takaki

He told me that sometime after citizens of Japanese descent had been incarcerated at the beginning of World War II, it occurred to our government that they needed people who understood Japanese culture, who knew the location of strategic resources in Japan, and who could read Japanese messages when they were intercepted by intelligence sources. They decided to screen Japanese people in the camps where they were being held, and then bring those deemed likely to be useful to a place where they could work with the U.S. military.

Those in charge of establishing such a group perceived early on that it would be hard to secure their cooperation if they were being held in detention, apart from their families, while being asked to perform a vital service. Given the hostility that Americans felt toward the Japanese, finding a location for establishing a Japanese community became an issue. After due consideration, it was decided that Minnesotans might be as welcoming to some Japanese families as could be hoped for, so this group was established at Fort Snelling.

Takaki wanted to see if this episode was commemorated in the museum exhibits. I was surprised and he was pleased when we found several panels of pictures and commentary from the period of interest.

It did not surprise Ron that I knew nothing about the group assembled in Minnesota. Americans, he assured me, know the stories of immigrants who arrived along our Atlantic coast much better than they know about those arriving at points along the Pacific shore.

To prove his point, he asked if I knew the name of the island where most immigrants arrived in New York. I was happy to be able to respond with Ellis Island, but that was not the point of his question. That question was a setup for his next one. Did I know the name of an island on the West Coast that played a similar role for immigrants from the Far East? I didn't field that one so well.

We talked a bit about the troubles of the Irish, the Russians, the Jews, and others when they first arrived, but here too I was being readied for questions about those who arrived from the East. Did I know that Chinese and later Japanese men were brought over for the specific purpose of building our railroads? That they worked and lived under conditions not much different from slaves? That they were not allowed to bring their families because the intent was to send them back home when the railroad tracks had been laid? Could I name a few Asian immigrants who have made specific contributions to America?

When I mentioned that I had trouble handing out awards at the annual Math League Tournament because most of the winners had Asian names that I didn't know how to pronounce, Ron observed that even the success of Asian young people in school created problems.

At Berkeley, where the competition to get admitted is intense, the academic prowess of Asian students results in them securing spots in the freshman class all out of proportion to their numbers in the general population. This creates resentment among Whites who don't get in; it also fuels resentment among Black students who, when they claim discrimination because of race, are rebuffed, using Asian groups as evidence that students aren't refused admission because of their race.

At some point in the evening, conversation turned back to

the internment of Japanese citizens during WW II. Ron said he enjoyed the irony involved in setting up schools for the Japanese children in the camps. There, the kids, American citizens who had been taken out of their homes to live in makeshift compounds, started class each morning with a patriotic song, including the familiar lines:

> My country, tis of thee,
> Sweet land of liberty,
> Of thee I sing.

Our conversation extended well beyond the time it took to eat dinner, during which time I began to realize in a new way the inadequacy of thinking of minorities as groups with the same attitudes and problems. Those that were here before White people arrived have very different viewpoints and problems than do those who arrived from Western Europe or the Far East. Those who come from Mexico or places geographically close have still different problems. Those with physical distinctions are more likely to live in segregated communities (Chinatown, the Black ghetto, the Mexican village) than are those whose appearance enables them to blend in with the White population. Tensions arise not only between minorities and the White population, but among the various minority groups.

I was prompted to buy and read *A Different Mirror*, one of Takaki's books. I was reminded again of the advantages of being in a position where I met and interacted with knowledgeable people who, just by being themselves, made me aware of beliefs and attitudes I didn't even realize I had.

As to some of the less pretentious but nevertheless memorable social occasions, one event planned entirely by Dolores and myself stands out as particularly gratifying. As my last year as provost was coming to an end, we got to thinking of the close relationship we'd developed with the Macalester wait staff. They often served us several meals a week. They catered to our preferences and covered for my multiple faux pas (such as my battle with napkins, usually still on my plate when they came with the food, often on the floor, sometimes still tucked in my belt as I was leaving the room).

We decided there should be an event where these people were served in style. We reserved a room at a nice restaurant, invited the waiters and their spouses to a dinner where they were waited upon, and had them back to our home, where we served them dessert. It was well received, of course, and had the effect of guaranteeing that we are still treated warmly on those occasions when we attend a dinner at the college.

More about Internationalism at Macalester

As introduction to the final two events I want to describe, I must return to Ahmed Samatar, whom I left in this account after meeting with him in my first week as provost. Ahmed did indeed give structure to our international program. He designed a curriculum, selected those who were to teach prescribed courses from the ranks of cooperating departments, and opted to teach the introductory course and the senior seminar himself. He started a Macalester journal of international affairs and integrated the various study abroad programs so that they complemented the in-class experiences.

He had great concern for maintaining rigor in the international studies major. Faculty members he invited to teach in the program were selected with this in mind, and he himself set the bar high. Comments I picked up during my weekly dinners in the student union made it clear that students found his classes to be well worthwhile, but demanding in the extreme.

Just how demanding, or perhaps I should say just how extreme, was brought home to me when a young woman in Ahmed's senior seminar came in to let me know how she was being treated. Her complaint was that Ahmed's comments in the margins of her papers were insulting. He would write, "How did you ever get to be a senior at Macalester with writing like this?" He made it clear that he thought the paper might serve as a first draft, but that if presented to a future employer, "it would be an insult to Macalester College." Her account was punctuated with tears.

I asked if she had one of these papers with her. She did not, so I asked her to drop one off so I could read it. I was glad when I read it that she was not present; I don't know what I would have said to her. She was certainly correct in describing Ahmed's comments as insulting. He was every bit as blunt as she alleged. He was also correct!

The paper in no way represented the kind of work I hoped to see from a senior at the college. I called Ahmed in to discuss ways he might address her obvious problems in ways that were more constructive. He did agree that there might be a better way to handle the situation, but he also thought I should call in some of her former teachers and ask why they had passed this young woman without letting her know that her work was a disgrace.

Ahmed believed that if Macalester was to live up to its reputation of instilling an international outlook in its students, then every faculty member ought to be presenting material as his or her subject is seen in the context of international thought. It was before I became provost that he developed and got approved a very expensive program that he believed would over time internationalize the college curriculum.

Every other year he led a summer trip for faculty members to a foreign country. He announced the country a year ahead of time and asked faculty members to write an essay describing how they thought a visit to that country would enhance their teaching and/or research. On the basis of the essays, he selected 10 colleagues to accompany him on a trip paid for by the college.

The group spent the first two weeks in residence at a major university in the selected country, where the local faculty lectured on the history, geography, major religion(s), economy, governing structure of that country, etc. The group then separated, allowing each faculty member time to pursue interests described in his or her essay. They came together for the final two days to report to each other on how they had spent their time.

Ahmed lost little time after I became provost in telling me that he wanted me to accompany him on these trips. It was a sure way, he said, to address my lack of international experience. I expect he also reasoned that getting the provost involved in the program was one way to keep this expensive program in the college budget.

The first trip planned after I became provost was to Malaysia, picked, Ahmed told me, because it had sizable populations of Muslims, Hindus, and Christians that got along uncommonly well. It also represented the rapid development taking place in Third World countries.

I knew that in recent years we'd been attracting large numbers of students from Malaysia, whose way was paid by their government, and that they were expected to study mathematics and science. Ahmed said he would arrange for me to address the Malaysian Math Society and to speak at several universities while in the country.

I would have been more attracted to the trip if Dolores could have accompanied me, but in defending the use of college funds for these trips, Ahmed made it clear that participants were to be fully engaged in the seminars and other planned activities during the first two weeks, and they were also to put full time in the last two weeks on the individual projects they'd described. He therefore made it a condition of participation that spouses not accompany the group. I certainly did not want to seek an exception. I decided that even without Dolores, it was too good an opportunity to pass up.

Plans were well under way when terrorists brought down the twin towers in New York and hit the Pentagon in Washington. By the time we were to leave the next spring, American travel to countries with sizable Muslim populations had dwindled badly, and there was considerable debate about whether we should go.

Fortunately, we went. We were treated well on the airlines and at places where we stopped, all of them feeling the economic pinch caused by the drop in international travel, all of them eager to treat well the few who still came. On our first evening in Penang, Malaysia, we were encouraged by our hosts at Universiti Sains Maaysia to attend an international festival. Here we first encountered some anti-America feeling. Vendors were selling t-shirts depicting Osama bin Laden as a heroic figure. That was not the worst thing to happen to us, however. Ahmed assured us that because the festival was planned with international guests in mind, the food served would be safe for us to eat. That was wrong.

I was plagued with severe diarrhea for the entire four weeks. Ellen Guyer was on the trip also, and suffered not only my problem but also an inability to hold down anything she ate. We were housed in what had once been barracks for English soldiers and were now dormitories for university students. People with gastronomical problems wished for bathrooms of the kind to which they were accustomed. Ellen and I commiserated each morning at breakfast, trying to decide who'd had the worst night.

The lectures were wonderfully enlightening in every way. The English had been the first Westerners drawn to the South China Sea. In large part, they'd been drawn to the Malay peninsula to deal with the pirates who interfered with their shipping. As they established colonies, they ended a great deal of fighting and brought stability among the peoples living in settlements along the coast. The infrastructure they created (huge curbs along the streets to deal with the monsoon flooding, for one obvious example) was a great improvement. To my surprise, the lecturers were at points quite generous in citing some of the good things that came out of colonial rule. They also had a good deal to say, of course, about the reasons for ultimately shaking off colonial rule.

The arrangements for my lectures had been made by Rohaizan, a woman who'd been my advisee while getting her degree in mathematics at Macalester. Ahmed had warned me not to hug her or even attempt to shake hands, both forbidden in a country with a sizable Muslim influence. So warned, I was more than surprised when she first spotted me at our welcoming reception. She rushed right over and embraced me. Later in the evening, the dean of the university asked me how I had managed that. "I've been trying for years to get my arms around her," he said.

I was even more surprised when she told me she'd made arrangements to take me out to dinner, and that she would be picking me up the next night at the entry to the building where I was staying. When we got to the restaurant, we were met by two of her friends, and it proved to be an entertaining and enlightening evening.

Her two friends were both divorced, one from a Chinese man, the other from a Malay. Rohaizan herself was married to a Muslim man who was an official of Malaysian Airlines. The women, for my benefit, were speculating as to which of these groups, all well-represented in their country, produced the better husband.

Chinese men, they agreed, were too driven by their desire to succeed in business. Once married, said the woman who'd divorced her Chinese husband, family took a poor second to work. The complaint about the Malay man was quite the opposite. He was too easy going, too nonchalant about getting ahead, more than willing to let his more ambitious wife try to improve their economic situation.

Rohaizan was the one content with her husband. Her friends weren't willing to attribute that to the qualities of Muslim men in general, arguing that Muslim men expected their wives to be their servants. Rohaizan's marriage succeeded, they avowed, because her husband realized that she had become very Americanized while at Macalester, so he had made the necessary accommodations in order to have a very attractive wife. The two friends then began laughing among themselves until one of them said to me, "You know that Rohaizan is very religious, having made the pilgrimage to Mecca, and you probably attribute her successful marriage to her religion." Then, with great hilarity, they described in detail the absurd things she did to please her husband.

I already said that it was an entertaining and enlightening evening.

The university maintained a research station in the heart of the jungle, accessible by a lengthy hike from a town on the edge of the jungle, or a much shorter walk from a point on the coast. Those of us who opted to visit the station were asked if we would rather take the hike or go by boat to the access point on the beach. Assured that we'd be safe from wildlife, we were unanimous in wanting to hike through a real jungle.

It was an experience not to be forgotten. Monkeys swung from the trees; logs served as bridges across numerous streams. A sloth was pointed out. Our guide explained how he knew that a carcass along the path was the remains of a jungle cat's dinner. I almost wrote that the heat was unbearable, but obviously we did make it. We were about two hours into the hike when we asked our guide if it was too late to ask for a boat to take us back. His cell phone wouldn't work from our location, but he did eventually get through to ask for a boat to meet us; we were relieved.

During the 10 days for individual projects, I had a chance to visit Singapore, to accompany two colleagues on a visit to an offshore island, and, as previously arranged, to lecture at several schools.

The group reassembled in Kuala Lumpur, the capital. The prosperity of this emerging country was everywhere evident. To my embarrassment, I learned that the local officials had reasoned that though the group was to be housed at the nearby Universiti Kebangsoon Malaysis, their provost should be housed at the opulent Equatorial Hotel. It was at this hotel where we were hosting a dinner to which we'd invited all the Malaysian graduates of Macalester. It was luxurious to the point of making me uncomfortable, especially as my companions headed off to more life in dormitories. But honesty compels me to add that I was also grateful for a bathroom suitable for someone then surviving almost a month of gastronomical anguish.

There were about 70 Macalester alumni at the dinner that

night. I was surprised at how many of them asked me about my children, often calling them by name. When given a chance to greet the crowd, I told them how much their warm greetings meant, and I asked how many of them had at some time during their stay at Macalester had a meal in our home. More than half of those present rose to their feet.

It was a time when many Americans were wondering what could be done to improve Muslim understanding of our country. I wished Dolores could have enjoyed with me the fact that we had done at least something.

While in Kuala Lumpur, I had opportunity to walk the streets with David Lanegran, our urban geographer. It was odd to see a new building going up using the cranes and equipment we're accustomed to seeing at our own urban building sites, and then to see in the next block a building going up using floor-by-floor bamboo scaffolding, workers mixing concrete by hand, etc.

As we approached what was then the tallest building in the world, Lanegran pointed out several places where a panel of siding was missing; he took me to the 50th floor, from which we had to walk to the 51st floor because the escalator didn't work. He explained that in developing countries, they were anxious to build modern facilities but didn't have the trained support system of skilled tradesman to build or to maintain them. A French company had won the bid to put up the world's tallest building, and when finished, they went home. When things needed repair, there was no one to do the work.

On the flight home, I reflected on the fact that one of the great blessings I seldom considered was that I lived in a country where there were tradesmen who knew how to build things and to maintain them. I take for granted everything from buildings where toilets flush and escalators work to reliable phone systems, and much, much more.

Two years later the faculty seminar was held in Brazil. Once again the lectures showed me very quickly how little I knew about our host country. I was impressed with the idea that if one substitutes Portuguese settlers for English settlers, there are a lot of parallels between the early history of Brazil and that of the United States.

Start on the East Coast, push the native population ever farther west, introduce the slave trade, set up a governing structure that puts the settlers in charge. It was even the case that when railroads were introduced, laborers from Japan were brought in with the idea that when the work was completed, they would be sent home.

I don't know why I thought it would be any different; I don't think I'd ever thought about the matter at all. Once you notice the similarities, however, the differences raise questions. For all the difficulties in this country, ours has been a model of stable government that serves its people far better than anything realized in Brazil. Brazil, it seems, did not have founders intent on setting up a model country of free, self-governing people. I believe the two weeks of lectures that were part of this experience made me much more appreciative of the men who had a vision of what our country could become.

My time during the period devoted to individual projects was prescribed on this trip. There were quite a few Macalester alumni in Brazil who were regular contributors to the college, and there were several current students from Brazil whose parents were generous contributors. When Richard Ammons, our vice president for development, heard that the faculty seminar was to be in Brazil, he decided that this was the time for him to take a trip he'd been planning to call on our supporters in that country.

He told me that contributors were always polite to him when he called, but they knew he was a fundraiser, and that an occasional call was part of his job. What impresses them, he said, was a call from a senior officer of the college. This was his build-up to asking if I would use my unscheduled time to accompany him on some of these calls. I was happy to agree.

It turned out that Rio de Janeiro was a good location from which to make our various calls. Rio further provoked my thinking about the state of two countries with such similar beginnings. Rio is a beautiful city, but the attractive homes lining its streets are each surrounded by imposing fences and locked gates. Obviously, those who own homes have to take security into their own hands to feel safe from the multitudes of people without homes who are attracted by the city's favorable climate.

The practice of providing one's own security was dramatically illustrated by a call we made one evening to the parents of a current student. We were picked up by a limousine and taken across town to the entry of a gated community. A guard met us and checked our names against a list our hosts must have provided ahead of time. Then began an upward climb on a winding road passing through a neighborhood of beautiful large homes. Eventually we came to the driveway of our destination, where we were stopped at another gate. Once again a guard verified our identity before we were allowed in for the drive up to the house.

I came to understand that our student's father was one of Brazil's largest contractors, whose company was then building (or perhaps it was rebuilding) Rio's main airport. The view from the swimming pool in front of the house was stunning, taking in twinkling lights of the city below, its beaches, and the ocean. It was not clear to me right away where the huge living room of the house ended and the outdoor patio furniture began. A huge buffet table was laden with tempting food that we took to poolside tables. We could not have been treated more graciously.

I was nursing a cold when we arrived in Rio, so I begged off from calls for the first two days. I felt quite miserable the first day, and stayed in my room, not exactly a privation since I had a view out my window of an expansive beach across the street. I did think that I should at least have a picture, so I stepped out onto the balcony, set the telescopic lens, and snapped a couple of pictures.

I was feeling better the next morning, and the part of the Macalester group then in Rio had decided that they would meet for dinner that evening. It was agreed that they would stop on their way to a restaurant to see how I was feeling by dinner time.

It was to be an evening I have never quite lived down. When they called, they had arranged to pick up another member of our group at a location across town, so I was to be picked up about 4:30. I went down a little early to be in the lobby when they arrived.

The elevator terminated in a hallway just adjacent to the bar. As I got off the elevator, there was just one woman in the bar that I noticed (any man would have). Her rather formal looking low-cut blouse seemed a bit out of place at that time of afternoon.

I proceeded to the lobby and sat down. Moments later, the woman followed me in, enabling me to make a guess at her profession from the rest of her attire now visible. She came right up to me, introduced herself as Michelle, and asked my name. A little—actuallym a lot—befuddled, I made the mistake of answering. She followed that up with other questions. Was I visiting in the city? Was my wife travelling with me? What was I doing tonight? Did I know the song, "The Girl from Ipanema?" Did I realize the restaurant made famous by that song was just a few blocks from where we were?

When I told her I was waiting for friends to pick me up for dinner, she told me it was much too early for dinner, that I should instead wait until a little later, and then join her at the aforementioned restaurant. She assured me that we could have some fun. By then I realized it had been a big mistake to get involved in a conversation, and I risked a little rudeness, telling her quite firmly that I was going to join my friends. I was relieved when she left me and headed over to the reception area.

The stage was thus set for the ensuing situation comedy. Sherry Grey, a member of the Macalester group, entered the front door of the hotel, spotted me, and headed toward me. Michelle was headed back from the reception desk. She spoke first. "Wayne, I drew a map for you. You should meet me at this restaurant about 8 o'clock. We'll have a lot of fun."

Sherry stopped in her tracks. "Wayne! Who is this?"

I decided there was no use explaining the naivety of my

having answered all of Michelle's questions, so I stood up and said, "Sherry, I'd like you to meet my new friend, Michelle."

Michelle glared at me and said, "I thought you said that your wife wasn't with you."

As the 10 members of the faculty group began to arrive from around the country, Sherry got better and better at telling that story. When we were assembled to hear everyone's account of their individual projects, I decided to contribute a limerick:

> Michelle had been taught to lead with her best,
> And so she displayed her so-ample breast.
> She invited me to dine,
> But it's for Dolores I pine;
> So I'm quite able to leave the rest.

I of course requested that my composition not appear in the issue of the *Macalester International Journal* that would carry reports produced by others, and in this they complied. They did not feel inhibited, however, in telling Dolores all about my adventure.

My protestations of complete innocence were not aided when I had my photos developed. Those were the days when you didn't see your pictures until you got home and had them developed. I didn't know that from the balcony of my sick room in the hotel, I had with my telescopic lens photographed a group of topless young women playing volleyball on the beach.

A Happy Ending

An idyllic picture of higher education portrays an accomplished scholar sharing what he or she has learned through years of study with an able student anxious to absorb all he or she can master. Peripheral to this activity are administrators hired to tend to the necessary but mundane business of providing the facilities and accommodations necessary to bring scholars and students together in a supportive setting. Many teachers regard administration as work to be avoided; at the extreme, there are teachers who regard administration with contempt. I am not one of them.

Early in my career, I developed the self-perception that I was adept at explaining to young people the ideas, even the abstract ideas of mathematicians who have given us great insight into the world around us. At the same time, I came to believe, after exerting real effort, that I did not have the insights and imagination necessary to add to accumulating mathematical ideas. I learned to enjoy my role in the world of mathematics as one who could convey to young people the accomplishments of those gifted with creative mathematical minds.

I also learned, as I saw how colleges work, that I not only had a knack for administration but that I actually enjoyed it. I've been asked, and have wondered myself, if I should have gotten into administration sooner than I did. I don't know. It's unlikely, had I done so, that I'd have had years of conversations with students who had questions about the Christian faith. I like to think those conversations were useful to at least some students. I know they have given me a more mature understanding of my own faith.

It's also the case that those who rise in administrative ranks almost always do so by moving from one school to another, taking on more and more responsible roles as they move. I treasure the relationships I built with students, colleagues, and in the larger community over more than 50 years associated with one school.

I did get to serve as provost for four years, and I'm happy to say that I enjoyed the opportunity. I came into a situation that called for the restoration of good will, the feeling of community that is so vital if people are to devote their energy to learning and to contemplation. I was blessed with a staff that seemed to enjoy the work we did together. The party that was given when I left the office of provost, those that spoke that evening, and the many letters I received allow me to think that in many ways, I succeeded in the task I was given. I have nothing but gratitude for the opportunity.

XI. The Joy of Teaching

A good teacher will know what he or she is good at,
and will choose materials appropriately.
It's a mistake to try forcing everyone
into the same mold.

Back to the Classroom

Retirement was a possibility when my term as provost was over, but it wasn't a possibility I considered very seriously. I hadn't had an opportunity to teach calculus after the reform effort, having moved almost immediately into administration. Also, even though I'd enjoyed my years as provost, there was real appeal to retiring from the friendly confines of the department where I'd spent my first 30 years at Macalester.

The calculus course I taught after returning to the classroom was quite different, and I think much better, than the one I taught for most of my career. The biggest change was the introduction of group work, an idea that hadn't even been under discussion when the reform effort began. It was an idea introduced, or at least popularized, by Uri Treisman, a professor at the University of California-Berkeley.

It had been noticed at Berkeley that of the minority groups on campus, the Asian students stood out for their superb work in mathematics. Treisman undertook an extensive study to find out why. He went so far as to have graduate students live in the dorms around campus to observe the various groups. The thing most noticeable was that Asian students regularly gathered in study groups during the evening, and their intention was clear. Everyone in the group was to understand the concepts under discussion. Everyone did his or her own homework, but help and encouragement were instantly available to anyone having trouble.

Uri Treisman

I heard Treisman describe this extensive study several times. Sometimes he was asked how he, a full professor in a very active research department, could devote so much time to the study he had undertaken. The answer was always the same. "It's not work for the untenured."

I adopted the idea of group work. The more I used it, the more convinced I became of its efficacy. Still using the Friday quiz routine, I used the results of the first two quizzes, together with grades students earned in previous math courses, to guide me in forming groups of three or four. The idea was to be sure that each group had one very able student, and that students who were struggling got into a group where help was readily available.

I tried to get them working as a group by telling them early in the term that on that week's Friday quiz, I would average the scores of everyone in a group, and they would all get that average recorded as their grade on that quiz. During the semester, groups would be required to complete two projects selected from the *Resources* books. Each group turned in a finished paper, and everyone in the group got the grade assigned to that paper.

Sometimes the better students, accustomed to getting high marks, came to my office to complain about their grades being dragged down on group assignments. My first response was to tell them about the industry-related institutes I used to run during summers. I told them that invariably, the first thing to happen was that the company assigned the student to a group within which to work.

I told them the true story of the only student a company ever asked me to reassign during one of my summer programs. His academic record indicated he was a strong student, and the company assigned him to a group working on a recurring problem for which they needed a solution. He came up with some excellent ideas, but he had no interest, indeed he thought it a bit below him, to write up a solution other employees could understand and use. Company irritation reached the point where they wanted him gone. Clearly, he needed some experience in working with a group.

Then I talked about learning to use the differing skills of group members. If there are one or two members who quickly see how the problem can be solved, let them sketch out a solution. One or more members should carefully proofread this work to make sure they think it's correct and that they can't think of a better solution. Identify and turn the work over to the best writer in the group, because the presentation of a report counts in the evaluation. Assign the computer guru in the group to produce required drawings. Don't forget that the final product needs to be proofread by one or two careful readers.

Finally, I also pointed out that with at least a dozen Friday quizzes, a midterm, and a final exam, I'd have plenty of opportunity to evaluate their individual work and to make appropriate adjustments if I saw that various group grades were pulling them down.

During the four years of my absence from the classroom, the controversy about using technology had disappeared. The students saw to that. Calculators in the classroom were ubiquitous, the young people used them with aplomb, and it was soon apparent to even reluctant faculty that they needed to be conversant with the new technology if they were to keep up.

Calculators were used whenever they could illuminate a key idea. I held one of our early classes in the computer lab, where students learned to use programs that had been developed for the course. Classrooms were outfitted so that anything on the instructor's computer or taken from the Internet could be projected on a screen. Four years after my early support of using technology, I was suddenly aware that my own computing skills were badly outdated.

Of course I used ideas and materials from *Resources*. A favorite research project for a group was to develop a model for U.S. population growth. A group could choose census data from, say 1750 to 1850, use it to develop a model, then check to see what their model would predict for 1900 to 1950, and finally, compare their predictions with the data available for those years.

Besides seeing what's meant by exponential growth, this gave students an understanding of how much models depend on initial assumptions. It also gave them some healthy skepticism about projections they saw in newspapers. I encouraged them to use their model to predict the U. S. population in 2050, keep their work, and check it out in their old age.

Depending on the interests of the class, I also used some readings from *Resources*. I always included one describing the controversy that developed over whether Newton or Leibnitz invented calculus. Historians mostly agree that Newton had it first, but everyone agrees that Leibnitz came up with far better notation, pretty much what is used today.

English mathematicians, loyal to their man, tried to use Newton's notation, but it was far too cumbersome, suitable only for the master himself. Consequently, mathematical progress for the next generation was largely made on the continent, where mathematicians were using the notation provided by their man, Leibnitz.

This article always led to classroom discussion of consequences that national and ethnic pride can play, even in the supposedly dispassionate fields of science. Students were generally surprised to learn that the United States did not assume its role as a world leader in science until Hitler drove all the Jewish scientists out of Europe.

Group work, use of technology, research projects that don't have answers in the back of the book, readings that provoke discussion of assumptions about ethnicity or gender—as I said, I think it was a better class than what I taught for most of my career.

I also had some things to learn about teaching in a new environment. I'd only been back in the classroom a week or so when I complained to the department secretary that maybe I wasn't up to lecturing for an hour anymore, that I felt myself getting dizzy while standing before the class. She laughed and said she knew my problem. "I've seen you lecture. You get to talking with your hands held out in front of you. That was okay when you were holding chalk, but now you're holding markers (Chalk had been banned because of the dust that settled on all the computers in the room), and the fumes from the solvent are getting to you." She was right. For a while I talked with my hands in my pockets until I learned to keep them away from my face.

Far more serious was an experience I had when collecting a homework assignment. I sometimes did this once a semester just to see how many students I had who were up to a real challenge. I'd print a difficult problem on a paper on which they were turn in their solution. At the top of this page, just above where they were to sign their name, I wrote, "The work submitted on this page is my own. I have not consulted anyone about this problem."

I did this in my first semester back in the classroom. The first few papers I graded didn't get very far with the problem. Soon, however, I came across a curious paper that started out correctly, then had some extraneous work that, with the help of an error, suddenly got back on track and went on to a nice solution. I figured the student had been working on scratch paper, that one such page included the digression with the mistake, and that he had inadvertently copied from this page while transferring the solution to the page he was to submit.

Very shortly, however, I came across another paper with the same digression, the same error, and ultimately a solution; and then another, and another. More than half of the submitted papers had this same "solution."

When I returned the papers, I did so at the very end of the hour. As I handed them out, I explained that I had put a question mark on some of the papers, and since there was no time left to discuss them in class, I'd like those who received a question mark to see me in my office.

It was, on the face of it, the most egregious case of cheating I'd ever encountered. The manner of approach by the students who appeared in my office would have made a nice study for some psychology student. Some walked in, dispensed with any attempt at excusing themselves, and simply said, "I copied someone else's work." Some explained that they were unable to solve the problem but heard that someone had discovered a solution on the Internet, that the solution was circulating among members of the class, and that they didn't want to be the only one to turn in a blank paper, so they copied the circulating solution.

One young woman, very quiet in class, was the daughter of a prominent woman often mentioned in the newspapers. She came in, sat down, visibly tried to compose herself, and then burst into tears. She was worried that her transgression would somehow get known and embarrass her mother. I spent quite a bit of time with her. It was not to scold her.

The incident reminded me of an economics class I had at Morton Junior College. The incompetent who taught it was the quintessential professor who, year after year, read from the same dog-eared notes, rarely looking up, certainly not knowing anyone in the class. Students who showed up for class came with a set of notes passed on to them from someone who took the course a year or two earlier. The game was to see if you could improve the notes where a word or phrase had been missed.

To this sloth, the guy added the unpardonable sin of giving a final exam available from the publisher of the text we used. It was no trick for some enterprising young entrepreneur (it was a class in economics, after all) to get a copy of official departmental stationery on which to order a copy of the final.

On the basis of a few quizzes, I was in line for an A in that course, but with self-righteous indignation, I refused to buy a copy of the final when it was offered. I'm afraid I was insufferably proud of the B I got from that man. I didn't think of the students who bought the final exam as cheaters; I thought some much worse things about a teacher who would through his own laziness subject students to the pressure to do what they felt they had to do to keep up with everyone else.

When I realized that solutions to many of the classic challenging problems of calculus were worked out on websites that had sprung up since my previous teaching days, I felt that I was at least partially responsible for what had happened. The extraneous-looking digression, I learned, occurred where the online solution had left a gap for the student to fill in.

The student who first copied the solution did his best to fill in the gap, couldn't provide the needed step, so made a convenient "mistake" that would let him pick up with the online solution.

I discussed the incident with several of my colleagues, asking how they would handle the situation. Most suggested entering a zero for the score on the offending papers. A few said they would lower the grade in the course by one step. An English teacher told me about a student who had submitted as his own a poem he copied from a book so old and obscure that he figured he could get away with it. When my suspicious colleague located the original with the help of Google, he flunked the student on the spot.

I knew that the dean of students wanted all such incidents reported to her. Her reasoning was that if each professor handles such an incident individually, no one sees what for a given student is becoming a way of life. It was her practice, when she learned of a student's cheating in several courses, to get help for that student by way of counselling.

In spite of the logic of wanting incidents reported, I chose to handle the situation myself, in part because I felt that I should not have assigned a problem at least partially solved on the Internet. I devoted a part of one class to discussing the self-esteem that comes with personal integrity. We also discussed the lasting damage to one's reputation if caught cheating. Finally, we discussed some ideas of what a student might have done when he or she learned of the circulating solution.

I also told them a story from my experience as a paperboy. We had to collect the subscription fee in those days, and more than once, when I knocked, a kid about my age would answer the door. When my purpose was known, the kid would announce my presence, often by yelling to a parent in another room. It was not unusual for the parent to yell back, "Tell him I'm not home." The embarrassed kid, sometimes one I knew from school, would shrug and say, "He said to tell you he's not home."

The moral of that story, and it extended to me and to my economics teacher, was that we should not only be honest ourselves but we should try to make it easy for people around us to be honest if they are so inclined.

Appraising Calculus Reform

Shortly after the annual math meetings in January of 1995, I received a phone call from one of the program officers at the National Science Foundation. He reminded me that the meetings in 1996 would mark the tenth anniversary of calculus reform. He said that officials at NSF, thinking of the huge investment they had made in the movement, would like to have for distribution at the 1996 meetings a published assessment of what had been accomplished. He wondered if the CRAFTY committee that I chaired would, with NSF support, produce a report. The committee agreed, and with less than a year to work, we moved quickly to plan a four-part report, each part to be edited by a member of the committee.

We were only five months into producing this report when I was appointed provost, so my contributions were largely limited to initial decisions as to what we would do, who would be responsible for each part, and trying to keep everything on schedule. Near the end, drawing on what each of the section editors had learned, I did write "A Modern Course in Calculus," the lead article of the report. Our report, *Calculus, The Dynamics of Change* appeared in the Notes series of the MAA. It was available for sale at the 1996 meetings, much to the pleasure of the NSF.

As I write now, I have the perspective of another 25 years. That advantage is offset by the fact that I haven't been active in academia for six years, but that doesn't prevent me from having some opinions about the reform effort.

It's obvious that the use of calculators and computers in teaching is and has been for some time as common as chalk once was. No one worries anymore about students not learning basic facts and techniques the way they once did. That's true partly because it's no more convenient to look up basic mathematical facts on a screen every time you need them than it would be to look up the spelling of basic words when writing a sentence. And it's true partly because there never was a time when students were as uniformly proficient in the basics of mathematics as aging professors seemed to recall.

Many senior faculty, not being directly involved in teaching calculus, primarily heard early calls to make the course "lean and lively," and references to "the disgraceful number of students who, having enrolled, failed to complete the calculus sequence." They envisioned a reformed course "dumbed down" and made lean and easier to pass by dropping the most challenging topics.

As it turned out, attempts to make the course lean largely failed; reform had much more to do with pedagogy than with content. Had this been anticipated, it's possible that much of the opposition would have melted away. As it was, the controversy had the salutary effect of attracting the attention of faculty members who had not thought about the course for years.

I visited the University of Michigan to see for myself the ambitious approach they were taking to reform. I visited a classroom where a senior faculty member was teaching a first-hour calculus class on a cold morning. It was clear from a preclass conversation that he had some reservations about the reform effort, but he added, "I'll tell you one thing. I will never abandon this idea of having students work in groups. In the old days, kids who showed up at all would wander into class late, hunch down into their coats, and dare me to keep them awake.

"Now they meet in a group the night before class to prepare the one paper they will be turning in. They leave that meeting with agreements on who will prepare what, intending to staple their efforts together the next morning, just before class. But one or two of them have trouble getting their problem to work out, so everybody gathers round to try fixing the difficulty before I collect the papers. By the time class starts, they're all engaged, eager to ask about the problem on which they've been working."

Reform had less effect on textbooks than I would have thought. At first, there were a lot of new, some radically different, texts. The most radical were effective in the hands of those who developed them, but rarely attracted much of a following. There were two "reform" texts that ultimately dominated the national market, one by Zorn and Ostebee from St. Olaf, the other by Gleason and Hallett from Harvard. They were both adaptable to a variety of uses, with or without computer-aided instruction.

A good many of the texts popular before the reform effort remained popular by adopting whatever their authors regarded as useful ideas then in favor. Problems easily destroyed by a calculator disappeared. Traditional pretenses at applications disappeared, usually replaced by at least alluding to real applications.

A visit I made to Purdue impressed upon me the primacy of a good teacher. Ed Dubinsky had become a well-known advocate of using a computer lab in connection with classroom lectures. In a visit to his lab, I witnessed a perplexed young man come up to Ed with a question about instructions for numeric integration. The instructions said to partition an interval into "a convenient number" of subintervals, then pick an arbitrary point in each interval, and have the computer add up the products obtained by multiplying the

Ed Dubinsky

length of each interval by the value of the function at the arbitrarily chosen point. The young man had compared his answer with that of a young woman at the next table. Her "convenient intervals" were different, as were her arbitrarily chosen points, so of course her answer was different.

The instructions said to do this over and over, each time choosing smaller intervals. How, the young man wanted to know, was it possible that he and his classmate would ever get the same answer?

Ed asked him how many times he had tried making the intervals smaller. Whatever the answer was, Ed told him to do it a dozen more times, easy to do with the computer. When he walked away, Ed grinned at me and said, "By tomorrow, he and the young woman will understand what it means to say that Riemann sums will converge."

The next day I sat in the back of his classroom. It was bedlam. Kids were gathered at blackboards around the room, arguing vociferously, then trying to get Ed's attention, hoping he would settle the argument. Rarely did he do more than make a suggestion, or tell them to go look at what that some other group was doing. With about half of the class time so used, he finally called for order. Inspecting the various attempts to solve problems that were left on the boards, he pointed out the errors and the good ideas. He had the kind of personality that enabled him to get a laugh when he made a caustic comment, Grouch Marx style, about the effort he was reviewing. When he launched into his lecture in the last 10 minutes or so, he had the undivided attention of everyone in the room.

I left Purdue thinking that Ed was one of the best classroom teachers I'd ever seen.

Ed was certain that his methods were the only way to teach. He was certain that the programs he'd written for students to use in the lab were the best available. His mannerisms went over better with students than they did with his colleagues, and very few chose to emulate him.

There was one senior member in the department, however, who thought he would give Ed's materials a try. I visited his class. He had none of Ed's verve, wit, or rapport with students. He would ask a question. No one would respond. A student would ask a question, and get a question in return, very much as Ed would have done. In this class, however, I heard the student who got nothing but a return question mutter to the kid next to him, "How the hell are you supposed to learn anything from this guy?"

One needs good materials, but not as much as one needs a teacher who knows how to choose materials that match his or her style. A good teacher will know what he or she is good at, and will choose materials appropriately.

Ed's materials could be carried across the hall. His personality and his style could not. It's a mistake to try forcing everyone into the same mold.

It follows that just as there are a variety of personalities, there is a need for a variety of materials. I am, in my old age, more pleased with the approach we took in producing *Resources* than I was when we finished the project. We made good materials available. Good teachers may now choose what best suits their style.

Scholars of Distinction

The caller said, "We think that we could set a tone of academic excellence in Minnesota's secondary schools if at graduation time in June the governor would host an event in the Capitol Rotunda at which he would recognize a few students as Scholars of Distinction in each of several basic academic disciplines."

The woman talking to me was from the Minnesota Department of Education. She asked if I would consider developing a program through which Scholars of Distinction in Mathematics might be selected. I had just retired from full-time teaching at Macalester, I liked the idea of having such a program, and I thought the compensation they offered me for directing it was quite generous.

As I got a better understanding of what they had in mind, I did express a reservation about the way the program was to be funded. A minority businessman had come to the department wondering what he might do to promote scholarship among high school students. They'd responded with this Scholars of Distinction idea that had been floating about in the department for several years. Beyond his commitment to fund the program, they had no plan to work it into the department's regular budget.

My first concern was that putting their idea into place would be quite an undertaking for a program that had no plan for long-term stability. I wanted to get a promise that they'd begin to work the program into their regular budget. They assured me that their funds were far too tight to consider that, but they felt certain that their benefactor was in for the long haul. I then pointed out that the prospects of having minority students appear among the state's top scholars in mathematics were poor, and I wondered if their benefactor might not be disappointed about that.

Eager to start a program they'd been talking about, they felt the first concern was to get a model program in place. My concerns would have to be dealt with as we proceeded. I liked the vision they had, their enthusiasm was contagious, and I agreed to take on the job.

Fall term had already begun. The principal concern seemed to be that we should have about six students to present to the governor the next spring. With this as my only guidance, I felt free to initiate procedures that would, in time, make people realize that it really meant something to say that you had been a Minnesota Scholar of Distinction.

I lost no time in forming an advisory committee. Tom Kilkelly had coached the Math League all-star team that we took to the national tournament for several years, a position from which he knew a good many of the best mathematics students in the state. I surely wanted him involved, and he was quick to accept. Jack Sorteberg had retired from teaching, but I knew him to be a man who always had in mind projects on which a student might work, something I wanted for the program I had in mind. He was very glad to be involved.

The third person I wanted was a stretch, but there were several reasons I wanted Joe Gallian involved. First, Joe had become widely known for a summer program he ran at the University of Minnesota-Duluth. It involved undergraduate students from around the country in substantive research. I couldn't think of anyone who would have more ideas for papers that students could write. Second, Joe was at the time president of the MAA. His involvement would give our program instant recognition, not just in Minnesota but around the country.

The trick would be to get him to fit one more thing into his schedule. The MAA president makes many trips to the office in Washington, he is in demand in this country and abroad as a speaker, and of course he still teaches courses. Joe was a friend, however. We had worked together on various projects, and I knew he'd want to see this idea succeed. I asked him; he accepted.

As soon as I had this committee formed, I scheduled a meeting. In deference to Joe's desire to meet his afternoon class, I scheduled it at a restaurant on the freeway to Duluth, somewhat closer to Duluth since the three of us from the Twin Cities could all get away in time to do more of the driving. As I shall note later, this decision became an issue.

The meeting was quite productive. We agreed that each participant would write a paper, on a topic either the student or we would provide. Each of us would, with the involvement of the student's teacher, supervise one or two students. Drawing on his experience, Joe thought we should set up three meetings over the course of the year where the students could confer in person with the supervisor and give progress reports on their work to each other.

The committee liked the idea of choosing participants on the basis of letters from one of their teachers. Guidelines for these letters of support were listed, the first of which was to advise teachers only to recommend truly outstanding students, the kind that only come along once every few years. Then we wanted to know what math courses the student had taken and what grades had been received. Finally, in what extra math activities had the student participated? (Mathcounts while in junior high? Summer enrichment courses? The University of Minnesota program for talented youth? Math League? School Math Club?)

We then designed a brochure that described the program in glowing terms. It specified that to be considered, we needed a letter of recommendation from a teacher (our outline for such a letter was included with the brochure). We also made it clear that the student participant would be required to write a paper, attend three meetings—one in Marshall, one in Duluth, and one in St. Paul—and of course come to a closing recognition event at the State Capitol.

This was all accomplished in one evening, which I took as evidence that there was great value in having a small committee that was long on experience in working with gifted students. I came later to understand that we should have had more input from someone who could have alerted us to the expectations and restrictions that went with working for the Department of Education.

My liaison in the department was their specialist in education programs for gifted and talented students. I sensed that she was unhappy that my committee had met without her. She didn't say that; I just got that feeling, and I immediately regretted that I hadn't thought to invite her.

She did let me know about other concerns. She told me several times, in several ways, that I was to understand that this was not to be run as an extension of the Math League, that it must be widely advertised in all schools in the state, and that participants couldn't all be from the Math League. She had in mind some teachers she would like to see added to my committee. The bill I'd brought along for the dinner meeting failed to meet department guidelines that frowned on meetings in restaurants, and required that if such a meeting was unavoidable, it should be held in a restaurant on an approved list—i.e. restaurants with modest prices, all in the Twin Cities.

I responded that the plans we'd made started with sending our brochure to the chair of every math department in the state. No one, I assured her, had suggested anything that gave preference to schools in the Math League. I did go on to say that the schools in the Math League were the ones with a teacher interested in providing extra opportunities for gifted students, precisely the kind of teachers one would expect to respond to our brochure. She made it clear that when applications came in, she wanted to be involved in the selection process.

I told her I would be happy to add to our committee a teacher or two she could select, but the expectation was that committee members would contribute suggestions for projects and be ready to supervise students as they worked on them. I never heard any more about adding members to the committee. As to my having met in a restaurant up toward Duluth, I had my reasons, which I explained to her.

She, in turn, had some things to explain to me. The department worked under rules largely determined by those who kept track of the public's money. If I'd held the meeting during the day, there would have been no questions raised about paying substitute teachers for the teachers involved. It was understood that meetings were necessary, that you couldn't expect teachers to work evenings or Saturday, so substitutes were frequently used. The rules sounded firm and were presented with such clarity that I didn't even argue that if we had needed three substitutes, the cost would surely have exceeded the cost of our dinners. I paid for the dinners out of my stipend.

She in turn could see that we tried to have a statewide program by scheduling the three meetings in three parts of the state. It apparently made a difference that in this case, participants in the program were the ones for whom meals were to be provided, and I promised to try holding the meals on college campuses, where costs would be controlled.

The big lesson for me was that working under a grant from the state was very different from working with one from the NSF. No one at NSF would have expected the program officer to be involved in administering the project, and one's only financial constraint was to get the job done within the agreed-upon budget.

My next meeting with the program officer occurred when selections were to be made from the applications that came in. It turned out that we only received seven or eight. The good news was that we had certainly succeeded in conveying the idea that nominees should be truly exceptional students; and with extraordinary good fortune, when the homes of the applicants were pin-pointed on a map, it looked as if geographic distribution had been the major criteria in gathering applications.

The bad news was that, as I feared, all but one of the applicants were active in the Math League. Even worse, from the point of view of the program officer, was the totally predictable fact that only one of the applicants was female. That really put me on the defensive. I explained that in the Math League, gender distribution of participants was roughly equal, but when individual high scorers came to the state tournament, it was an almost all-male show. This is true in all mathematics contests worldwide. The seven-member team the United States sends each year to the International Mathematical Olympiad is frequently all male, as are teams from every country that participates.

I failed to be persuasive with my explanation of efforts made at every level to have females succeed with anything like parity with males in the upper echelons of mathematics. The usual conclusion of outsiders is that there is a pervasive old boys network that perhaps unintentionally but nevertheless effectively stacks the cards against women. I told her that if she could solve the problem, a lot of us who deal with criticism at every level would be grateful. I think she is trying.

As it turned out, the lone female in the group, Jean Huang, selected a project I proposed, so I had the privilege of supervising her. She was truly exceptional in everything she did. She was an accomplished musician. We had to change the date of one of our three meetings because it conflicted with a statewide physics competition in which she was a top contestant. Once when I called her home for something, her mother said she wasn't there, that she had gone with her father to meet a man who wanted to buy the painting with which she had won first prize at the State Fair the previous summer. Even allowing for the preference I'd feel about a project I supervised, I believe her paper was clearly the best produced by our participants.

That is not to denigrate any of the other papers. I felt that in our first year, we had a group deserving in every way to be called Scholars of Distinction. The ceremony at the Capitol was fitting, and our committee was very pleased. To no one's surprise, all the honored students were accepted into prestigious colleges or universities.

Alas, the entire program was short-lived, enduring only one or two years after that initial run. The generous benefactor continued his sponsorship for only two or three years before he moved on to other interests. I was replaced by a graduate student from the University of Minnesota and my committee was disbanded. I have no doubt that the Department of Education was able to control things more easily.

I did attend the ceremony at the Capitol the year after I was replaced. I thought the idea of having such a program was a good one, and I thought I might look petulant if I failed to show up as soon as I was dropped as director. I probably should have stayed away.

It turned out that the group of scholars honored in mathematics all came from the same private high school in Minneapolis, and I couldn't resist observing to the Department of Education representative that they evidently found a deep pocket of talent I'd completely missed. She responded that they were a wonderful group of young people who deserved to be honored. I don't doubt it.

As recounted earlier, grants from the Department of Education played an important role at a critical time in helping get the Math League started, and it has been helpful to have the department's mathematics specialist on the League board. My experience in working under supervision of the Department of Education convinced me anew, however, that the League has been able to stay closer to its mission by being controlled by a board made up of coaches who work directly with student participants.

Serving the MAA

It was either 2000 or 2001 when, as the summer meetings of the Mathematical Association of America approached, I got a call from Ann Watkins. Previously mentioned as a fellow member of the ad hoc Ombudsman Committee, Ann was by then the incoming president of the MAA.

She came quickly to her point. A huge controversy had arisen in the MAA and would be coming to the floor at the first meeting at which she would be the presiding officer. She claimed to know nothing about parliamentary law and wondered if I would accept appointment as parliamentarian of the MAA.

I immediately protested, telling her that just because my name was Roberts didn't mean I was in command of the Rules of Order. She didn't even laugh. I learned that in our work years ago on the Ombudsman Committee, she had formed an inflated opinion of my sense of fairness, she was sure that others in the MAA had the same opinion, and she wanted me next to her on the platform. Flattery will, as they say, get you somewhere, and pretty soon I heard myself agreeing to serve.

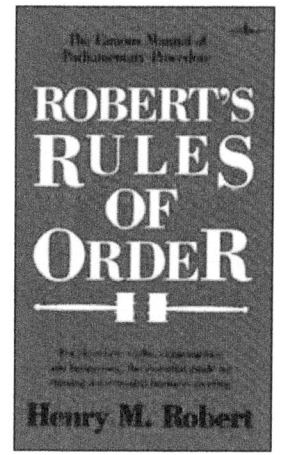

I bought my first copy of *Robert's Rules of Order*. I was dismayed to see how thick that book is, but I began to study it. I soon learned that even among the few things I thought I knew, I had some wrong ideas. I was surprised to learn that ex officio members of a governing board are entitled to vote. In fact an ex officio member has all the rights but none of the duties of a regular member. The presiding officer has much more leeway than I'd thought. If there are no corrections to the minutes as read, there is no need for a motion to approve them. The presiding office simply declares them approved. There is no need for a motion to adjourn; the presiding office simply says, "We stand adjourned."

That's all trivial stuff, of course, but it impresses people if you know it. It's more useful to know that a motion to approve a treasurer's report or a committee report is almost always a bad idea. Seldom is anyone in the assembly in a position to know if the report is correct. A treasurer who has made a mistake or falsified a report should not be able to defend the mistake later by saying that the assembly approved it. Misunderstanding is more likely if having just heard a committee report, someone moves to approve it. Does that mean that a recommendation made in the report has also been adopted?

I learned to interrupt such motions. "In order to avoid possible later confusion as to what has been approved, might I suggest that you move to thank ___ for the report?" The most useful task of a parliamentarians, I learned, is to keep track of amendments, amendments to amendments, substitute motions, etc., helping the presiding officer know what needs to be voted on next. In this capacity, I served the next three presidents, for which service the MAA paid my travel expenses to meetings.

Ultimately, I got an opportunity to earn my keep. The MAA decided that after operating for more than 100 years under the original bylaws and their many amendments, the time had come to rewrite them. And who would be better to chair the committee charged with this task than the parliamentarian? To make sure that this would be a challenge, I was given a committee of four or five people dispersed from Oregon to Maryland, and no travel money that would allow us to meet face to face.

To collapse a very convoluted procedure into a manageable description, the committee was to write drafts (always delayed by committee members who would take a week to answer their email), get the executive director and officers to approve them, submit them to the 40 or so sectional officers across the country so they could be discussed in sectional meetings, incorporate suggestions that came back, submit the proposed new bylaws to the board at one of their two meetings a year, and then, if approved at that level, submit them for approval by two thirds of the entire membership.

Actually, it wasn't that simple because at every stage, our conscientious executive director would notice something she regarded as a problem, resulting in another change to then run through the entire gamut again.

I vividly recall a response I got from one of the officers during this process. I thought I was pretty inured to criticism of my written work after years of writing textbooks, memos to the faculty, proposals to foundations, and more. None of this prepared me for a withering critique taking issue with the formal style I'd used in drafts I'd written. ("Committee chairs shall be elected to two-year terms.") He demanded to know, "What's wrong with plain English?" (Committee chairs serve for two years.) It was a lengthy letter, expressed in very plain, one might even say colorful, English. He must have sent copies to the other officers, for very quickly I had letters from each of them, encouraging me not to quit.

The next time I ran into my critic, he was jovial as could be and insisted that I accompany him to the hotel bar, where he could buy me a drink. I think he was surprised when I ordered a Coke. I was surprised when he had to pay $3 for it.

After two years or so of this endless loop, I noted that most of the work was falling to me and Ken Ross, a former MAA president who was on the committee with me. We got along well, so I finally suggested that he and I go to Washington, work all day on the bylaws section by section, meet late in the afternoon with the executive director to show her what we'd done that day, and send the result of that discussion to the rest of our committee. The committee was asked to read their email every night and respond by the next morning or forever hold their peace. Following this procedure for a week, we managed to get a finished product at the next annual meeting.

I owe a great debt to the MAA. In my early years in Minnesota, it was at MAA section meetings that I established friendships with colleagues throughout the region—and especially at Carleton, St. Olaf, Hamline, and the University of Minnesota-Duluth—friendships that lasted throughout my career. It was through this section appointing me to coordinate the American High School Mathematics Exam that I saw the need to start the Minnesota Math League. It was at the book exhibits at national meetings that I made contacts with editors and was able to get a number of books published. It was during my appointment to the CRAFTY committee that I saw the opportunity to lead the project that developed *Resources for Calculus*. Service on the Ombudsman Committee gave me opportunity to visit departments all over the country, and ultimately led to working with national leaders in writing new bylaws.

I am sorry to see not only the MAA but many professional societies struggling to attract young people to membership. These organizations have much to offer, and they represent the interests of one's profession.

A Broader Role for Private Colleges

Private colleges could not exist without the generous support of foundations, the beneficence of many individuals, the indirect support of the federal government through grants and tax breaks, and the willingness of supportive communities to provide many services to non-tax-paying enterprises in their midst.

In turn, private colleges do a great deal for the society of which they are a part. Because I am a mathematician and read a great deal about the scientific enterprise of this country, I know that private colleges have produced an altogether disproportionate number of the students who enter graduate schools to study the natural sciences and medicine. I assume something similar can be said about the number of graduates of private colleges that can be found in places of political leadership and in other leadership roles in our country.

Nevertheless, I think private colleges could do more to contribute directly to the society of which they are a part. One example quickly comes to mind. It was a real disappointment to me when looking for someone to replace me as director of Minnesota's Math League to realize that the League leadership would not be staying at Macalester.

That is not a criticism of my colleagues in mathematics. At the time, most of them were young people, looking forward to tenure reviews or laying the groundwork for future promotions. I've quoted Uri Treisman as saying that intensive work with undergraduate teaching is not work for the untenured at Berkeley (or any other major research university, I would add). In the same way, I'd say that administering a program serving secondary schools is not work for the untenured at Macalester (or any other of the liberal arts colleges with which we are compared). I didn't approach any of the young people in my department about leading the Math League.

In different circumstances, there might have been a senior colleague with the time and interest to take on directing the League. As it was, the few senior people we had, all of them successful by the well-understood expectations in place as they'd developed their careers, were usefully immersed in the activities for which private colleges reward faculties. I did not approach any of them about taking the job.

When I arrived at Macalester in 1965, I heard a great deal about a summer institute titled something like American Studies. It was team-taught by faculty members from political science, history, English, and perhaps sociology. It was an effort to understand how these disciplines illuminate one another, deepening one's understanding of our country's development. I got the impression that it was very popular among secondary teachers.

As was the case in those days, many of the contributing faculty members did not hold a Ph.D., and the people coming in as their replacements were too focused on meeting expectations in their disciplines to spend their summer on an interdisciplinary project such as I have described. The American Studies program was a casualty.

Very little happened during my 50 years at the college to provide any attractive alternative useful to secondary teachers. As I have made plain, David Lanegran in geography and I were the only ones on the Macalester faculty who had significant long-term contact with secondary teachers.

That's not because my colleagues have no interest in secondary education. It's just that the rewards for college teachers dictate that energy will be put into research and writing that pushes forward the boundaries of one's discipline.

I do not want in any way to minimize the importance of these things. I'd just like to see colleges also recognize and reward faculty members who use their professional expertise in the service of a broader community.

In the dark days when financial distress seemed to threaten the very existence of our college, it was heartening to see the imaginative ways faculty members reached out to serve the larger community. A program for adult scholars brought neighbors to the campus in the evening. Some came to earn credits to finish up the degree work they'd abandoned for one reason or another earlier in life. Some came for the joy of learning.

A Summer Institute for Teachers

The Math League started as a competition among 13 high schools in the Twin Cities. As the league grew, with divisions forming all over the state, the original 13 schools simply became the Twin Cities Division. When a season-ending tournament became a regular part of the program, the top team from each division was invited to the tournament. Most divisions consisted of seven to nine schools. The schools in the Twin City Division, feeling that they had to beat an unfairly large number of schools to earn a birth in the tournament, decided to split into St. Paul and Minneapolis divisions.

By the time I returned in 1999, from service as provost, to the Department of Mathematics, Statistics, and Computer Science, Kathy Grundhoefer had retired, and a new secretary was handling the business side of the Math League. As I resumed a more active role as director, she told me the Minneapolis schools had fallen on hard times. There was a growing dissatisfaction around the league with the fact that the winner of the Minneapolis Division always had a spot in the state tournament despite the fact that many teams around the state had higher season scores than did the winning team from Minneapolis.

It was true that the Minneapolis schools were in disarray. There had been several recent changes in administration, and the district was operating without a mathematics coordinator. I decided to try and revive the district's interest in the Math League by visiting all the math departments of Minneapolis high schools.

I began my tour at Edison High. I hoped to appeal to their pride as the site of the first meet when the League was formed. I was fortunate. They had a young man, David McMeyer, just beginning his career in the district. He was a natural teacher, eager to make his mark. He warmed instantly to the idea of the Math League, something that evidently had not even been mentioned to him as a newcomer to the school.

He quickly gathered a large group of students. I attended a few of their practice sessions and gave Dave numerous materials helpful to working with gifted students. It was not long before he was drumming up a competitive spirit in the division by contacting other schools in the district. It was a fortuitous beginning.

My next stop was at Southwest High. The school served a

prosperous part of the city, and because seniority rules allow teachers in the Minneapolis system to shift schools when openings occur, many teachers manage to retire from Southwest. It was the school that usually topped the Minneapolis Division of the league, and I knew a number of teachers in the department. They were supportive of my visiting other schools in the division, and thought some increased competition would help in developing their team.

The third stop was at Washington High, where I found two young women who were quite new to teaching. As the newest teachers in the department, they had formed a friendship, and they thought they would enjoy serving as co-coaches for a team. I joined them in meeting with a small group of students once a week for a month or so. It took several years, but the young women persisted, and in time they had a competitive team.

Several other visits were made before I got to North High, the place I must admit that I deliberately left for last. I think it's worth telling the story of that visit in some detail, illustrating as it does the problems of a big city school serving a tough part of the city.

I was met at the door by two armed policeman. When I explained my mission and showed them my Macalester ID card, they agreed to let me pass through the metal detector and enter the school. I was on my own to find the cluster of administrative offices.

I introduced myself to the woman at the front desk who appeared to be in charge, and explained my reasons for wanting to visit with the principal. She told me he was busy, and that she doubted very much that anybody would be interested in forming a math team. I persisted, asking if I might then see the chair of the Mathematics Department. With obvious resignation that she took no pains to hide, she consulted a schedule of some sort and then informed me that the chair of the department was in class and would not be available for an hour.

When I told her that I was willing to wait, she motioned me

to a chair, from which I had a clear view through an open door to the principal's office. He seemed quite at ease as he worked his way through a pile of mail, and I wondered if he might be more welcoming than the woman protecting his time, but I thought it best simply to wait. As I watched people come and go, I got to wondering if I might be the only White person in the building.

I was disabused of that idea when after the anticipated hour of waiting, an attractive young blonde woman came into the office, walked over to me, and asked if I was the one who wanted to see the chair of the Math Department. I hope I hid my astonishment. When I said I was the one, she asked the woman in charge for a key, and we went through the door next to which I had been sitting. It led to a small conference room.

I learned that she had graduated from Luther College with a math major and a determination to teach in an inner-city school. North was the first place to which she applied, and she was in her second year on the staff. She told me that she lived in an apartment within walking distance of the school and said that students were good about walking with her back and forth from her apartment.

The idea of a Math League was new to her, and she thought coaching a team might give her one more chance to build rapport with students. I told her about my stint as an assistant coach at Washington, but she didn't think an old White guy showing up once a week would work so well at North. She was much more interested in having me send her materials designed to help a new coach.

When we rose to leave the room, she surprised me by ushering me across the hall and into the principal's office. She walked right in, in spite of the fact that by then he was visiting with another man. She introduced me, did a very creditable job of describing the Math League, and told him she intended to start a team and would need a school van to transport students to meets.

It could not have been more clear that she had the principal's full support, and I suspected would have had it no matter what she suggested. He said all the right things about the importance of getting students interested in mathematics, and was effusive in expressions of appreciation to me for having taken the trouble to come to North High.

He then thought to introduce me to the visitor in his office. It turned out that he was the school's football coach and that he and the principal were old friends dating from when they had both come to North as gym teachers. The coach now occupied the office next door to the principal. North was generally a football power in the Minneapolis Athletic League.

It's an old story. An athletically inclined young man goes to college, where he plays sports, earns a degree in physical education, and finds work as a P.E, teacher in a high school. As he approaches middle age, he tires of trying to keep up with kids running laps and doing calisthenics, decides to take some summer courses in academic administration, and trades the whistle around his neck for a necktie. I knew of several examples of that transformation while I was still a student at Morton High School.

I don't know if that pattern is as entrenched as it was in my youth and when I was on the road trying to sell the Math League to principals. I hope not. I am not anti-sports. I've been a life-long member of the Chicago Cubs Diehard Fan Club, and my years at Wisconsin turned both my wife and me into football fans as well. It remains the case, however, that people whose main interest in college was sports rarely turn into thoughtful, visionary academic leaders. They are most at home sitting back and talking sports.

I left North High full of admiration for the young woman who was exerting such influence in the school, hoping she would indeed find some young people willing to work at mathematics. It might have happened; instead she found some young man, married, and away they went.

Having met so many new teacher/coaches during that school year, I decided to replicate in miniature the summer institute used years ago to kick-start the Math League. I invited the Minneapolis coaches to bring a couple of students to a weeklong summer institute at Macalester. Coaches in St. Paul had heard about my fraternizing with the Minneapolis coaches and asked if they might join the summer fun. The League board thought it was a good idea and decided their treasury could afford to provide lunches for participants.

It was in the dining hall that summer that I ran into my colleague, David Lanegran, the only other Macalester faculty member who conducted summer activities for secondary teachers on a regular basis. When he learned what I was doing, he told me it was well and good that I was willing to undertake such a thing without compensation, but also a little silly. He asked if I knew that the Minnesota Office of Higher Education Commission (MOHE) gave grants to colleges that conducted institutes for secondary teachers.

"If you'd do things right," he told me, "you could be paid, and your participants could receive a stipend and credits that secondary teachers need once in a while to renew their licenses." Well I certainly wanted to do things right, so I looked into his suggestion.

I learned that MOHE did indeed give grants, and that they felt there should be more opportunities for mathematics teachers. The only requirement I was lacking was someone who had a degree in mathematics education, a requirement for their program.

One of the teachers in Minneapolis who'd voluntarily stepped in to perform the functions of a district mathematics coordinator heard about my need and introduced me to Terry Wyberg from the University of Minnesota.

We formed a team that was meant to be. I was known to secondary teachers involved in the League. Terry was known to far more teachers, and they thought highly of him. There was a generous sprinkling of math teachers throughout Minnesota who'd taken their teacher education courses under Terry. Supervising student teachers made him a regular visitor to classrooms around the state, and he'd served as president of the Minnesota Council of Teachers of Mathematics, the professional association of secondary math teachers.

Terry was a good deal younger than I was. He had an endless supply of manipulatives intended to illustrate mathematical ideas, and his command of technology continually astonished me. I knew more mathematics than he did, and he was more than happy to let me choose a mathematical emphasis for our institute. We had no trouble designing a routine to be followed each day.

I got the morning off to a substantive start by posing a challenging problem that the class, sitting in groups around tables, could work on while Terry and I circulated among them. It was an informal time during which we could see various approaches to the problem, make a suggestion if a group needed one, and engage in chit-chat with the teachers. By the time several groups had presented solutions (and I had invited one or more presenters to come to the back of the room and try to read what they had written on the board), it was time for a morning break. After the break, I lectured on the topic introduced by the morning problem and posed some more problems to work on until (and sometimes through) the lunch hour.

Terry Wyberg

After lunch, Terry took over, usually able to use the classroom's ceiling projector to illustrate software related to the topic of the morning, always able to introduce another site on the Internet aimed at secondary students. After pausing for an afternoon break, teachers worked on developing materials they could take back to their classrooms.

These summer institutes proved quite popular and were offered for about 10 years. They were usually oversubscribed, not a problem because MOHE, happy to see a popular institute for mathematics teachers, was almost always able to increase the size of our grant to cover additional participants.

There are many topics touched upon in a high school curriculum that teachers are happy to review: complex numbers, analytic geometry, trigonometry and polar coordinates, probability, and more. We changed topics every year, making it attractive for teachers to return for several years.

Many comments we received on evaluation forms each year had a similar message. Having been attracted to a math major in college because they loved to solve problems, they found that in-service institutes for teachers focused almost exclusively on somebody's new theory of how students learn, that they seldom got chances to do "real mathematics." Our institute was not like that.

Evaluators always commented on the quality of our refreshments. Our grants included funds for the traditional "coffee and," the "and" being an assortment of pastries. The expectation was that this would be delivered by the college food service. I quickly discovered that if we made our own coffee in the department, there would be plenty of money left for me to get fruit, orange juice, even peeled hard-boiled eggs to serve. This required time after supper every evening to get fresh fruit, clean it, and arrange it on platters, but it was appreciated, especially by our middle-aged, weight-conscious participants.

Each morning, in preparation for the afternoon break, I'd fill a large cooler with some pop and lots of bottled water (the most popular drink among the teachers). I'd then pull it down to the chemistry lab and help myself to their large ice maker used to provide chipped ice for experiments. By midafternoon the drinks were cold enough to serve with popcorn, Triscuits, and other cookie substitutes.

Things were going well, grants from MOHE had become automatic, and I was greatly enjoying the interaction with teachers in 2014, but that was the summer I would turn 80. I had begun to think I should quit while things were still going well. Then one day there came an incident that pushed me over the edge.

I had, as usual, started the day posing a problem. Terry and I were making our rounds when he came upon a group attacking the problem in a most unusual way, one he could see was going to be successful. It was the kind of situation where you invite someone in the group to go to the board and show the others. That's not what Terry did.

He took the iPad that he always carried, held it over the table, and snapped a photo. He sent it to the cloud, retrieved it on Macalester's system, and had it projected on the wall, all in the space of 10 seconds or so. The rest of the class could immediately see not only the method that was going to work but the scratch paper strewn about the table that showed the work leading up to the key idea.

I watched this, realized it would never have occurred to me to take a photo, and if it had occurred to me, I wouldn't have known how to get it projected on the screen. Moreover, because it showed the various dead ends that ultimately led to the solution, it was better than just having the solution presented in polished form. The teachers, all of whom routinely use "smart boards," laptop computers, and PowerPoint presentations in their secondary classrooms, took all this technology for granted.

I decided that it was certainly time for me to quit.

For the afternoon break on the final Friday, Terry surprised me by inviting participants from the previous 10 years, members of our Macalester department who happened to be around, and even the head of MOHE, who made some nice remarks. In honor of the event that had helped me finalize my decision to quit, the group chipped in to buy me my own iPad. Counting my taking leave of the provost position, my official retirement from full-time teaching, and the big party thrown when I retired as director of the Math League, this was my fourth retirement party. And my last.

Students

As I come to the end of a long career, I realize that some of the most memorable students I've had are those who struggled in one way or another. A couple of stories will illustrate my point. For obvious reasons, I'll omit their real names even though I know them well.

A young man, let's call him Bob, identified himself as he entered college as pre-med. By the time he had his calculus and his chemistry grades at the end of his first year, it was clear to him that he was probably not headed for medical school. His disappointment was keen. I was at that time chair of a committee that was negotiating with Rush Medical Center in Chicago to establish a cooperative program in which a student could, in five years, earn a B.S. from Macalester and a degree in nursing from Rush. In this way I had come to know Luther Christman, who was head of nursing at Rush.

Christman had impressed upon me that nursing was a career for men as well as women. I began to talk to Bob about a career as a nurse, and eventually he embraced the idea. To make a long story short, Bob became a nurse and served several terms as a medical missionary in Africa. When his wife's health problems forced them to leave Africa, he began teaching and ultimately became the chair of the nursing program at a liberal arts college. When I retired, his letter of appreciation for my encouragement was moving.

A young woman I'll call Jane was my advisee. She wanted a major in math and chemistry. The math was tough going for her, and being a bit withdrawn, she told me she was worried about chemistry as well because as part of a major in that department, she'd have to give an oral presentation based on her senior laboratory project. She absolutely could not bring herself to give a talk in front of the chemistry faculty and fellow majors.

I talked to the chair of the Chemistry Department. He thought it a shame for her not to get a major in his department because, he said, she had done very well on her senior project. He talked to his colleagues, and they finally agreed to waive the requirement of an oral presentation.

When I told her the news, I said to her, "You don't have to do it. Now let me tell you why I think you should." Reluctantly, she did finally agree. I went to the talk to cheer her on, and the next day wrote her a note, congratulating her on giving the talk, and suggesting that she should remember the experience. "Use it as a reminder when faced with a forbidding task: You can do it."

Years later, when I retired, she wrote a note to me that included a picture of the note I wrote to her. She told me that it had been taped on the wall over her desk for all the years she'd worked at the Mayo Clinic. She added that she was at that time supervisor of a very large department, had several hundred employees under her, and managed a budget that ran into the millions each year.

My final story involves a high school student. The letter she sent to me is self-explanatory.

> Three years ago, when I was a sophomore in high school, one of my friends told me that I should join the Math League. I was very hesitant at first, because I felt that if I said yes, I would be considered a nerd, and I wasn't sure I wanted that. I was just an average math student, but I decided to do it anyway. Our school didn't have a very big team. In fact, when I joined, I was the second sophomore on the team.
>
> Once we started, I loved it. I may have been stumped most of the time, but when I would see the answer and understand the solution, it was amazing.
>
> At the end of my sophomore year, a terrible thing happened. My father was diagnosed with lung cancer and given only a year to live. This came on top of my uncle having been similarly diagnosed six months earlier. I coped with a life full of stress by trying to keep up with my activities. Sometimes when things got really bad, I would pull out

old Math League tests and work on them, one way to shut out the world at least for a while, and get absorbed in a problem that would eventually have a satisfying answer. On February 12th of my junior year, my uncle passed away, and on March 12th, my father followed.

I write now, one year later, reflecting on the last two years. I think the problems you provided helped pull me through some very tough times. This past year was my last in Math League, for I am graduating. It was a great year; your problems were still as challenging as ever and kept me going.

As for college plans, I plan to pursue my love of math. I may decide to major in math and teach mathematics. You touched my life without even knowing it. Thank you.

A good teacher must, of course, be an asset to his or her institution, and that certainly requires being a good citizen of the college: serve on committees, attend faculty meetings, accept the occasional ad hoc assignment. The good teacher will keep up with changes in the discipline, both in terms of what is taught and how it is taught. And of course, as anyone who has read my critiques of Alice Tucker will anticipate, I must add that a good teacher will be known in professional circles outside of the college.

These things all being essential, I believe the deep satisfactions of teaching come from one's interactions with students. Watching them develop, seeing them succeed at something, getting the occasional expressions of appreciation; that's the real compensation that comes to a teacher.

Reflections of a Teacher

I learned after leaving the office of provost that whenever colleagues get a negative answer from the new provost, they seek out and try to enlist the support of the old provost for their cause. I quite quickly learned to say, "When I was provost, I tried to be the best provost I could be; and now I am trying to be the best ex-provost I can be, which means staying out of the hair of the current provost."

To be sure that I would live up to that aspiration, I let it be known that in my final years on campus, I would not serve on any committees or attend faculty meetings. For good measure, I did not even attend department meetings.

The effect of these decisions was to leave me for the first time in many years with teaching as my only responsibility. I was reminded of how much I enjoyed interacting with students in the classroom, in my office, and as I moved about campus.

Working on a college campus is like working in a well-tended park with tasteful landscaping, flowers and mowed lawns in the summer and cleaned sidewalks in the winter. Within easy walking distance from your office, there is a comfortable library, a well-equipped gymnasium, a student union where one can take care of banking, mailing a package, or picking up a cookie.

It was appropriate that my last stories in this book should be about working with teachers. I have had the privilege of experiencing every activity one associates with college teaching: classroom teaching of course, writing books, working on local and national committees, leading a national curricular reform project, serving in many ways in my professional association, and in administration.

I am grateful for all these experiences. None, however, has brought the enduring satisfactions of working with those who supported the vision of a Math League, and with the teachers and students that have been the heart of the league. My departmental colleagues acted wisely when, in setting up the Wayne Roberts Prize in Mathematics, they specified that it was to go each year to a student preparing to be a teacher.

Epilogue

Starting with my account of how the Cicero race riot affected me as a teenager, I have returned again and again in this book to experiences that raised questions in my mind about my Christian faith. It seems fitting that I end the book by trying to describe the state of that faith after a lifetime of reassessments.

Without a doubt, the most helpful guide to my thinking has been the realization that in any organized system of thought, one must begin with terms that are undefined and assumptions that cannot be proved.

I encountered this fundamental principle in an introductory economics course, in the first pages of my abstract algebra book, in Karl Menger's unforgettable first lecture in formal logic, and once more in a graduate course in topology. Clear realization finally dawned when I heard a lecture in a graduate symposium titled "What's the point?"

It was a liberating moment when I realized that my troubles in trying to articulate a definition of God were not owing to a lack of theological training. Any effort to define all your terms must sooner or later become circular. Similarly, it is not an intellectual capitulation to say at some point, "That's just something I assume." All logical discussions can be pushed back to such a place.

I found that just this idea made conversations about religious ideas much more productive. The tone changes if people are trying to explain their basic assumptions, rather than arguing about the virtues of various religious traditions. It unobtrusively reminds discussants that religious faith is a matter of personal belief, not something that can be forced on people, whether by rules on a campus or by laws advocated by people who have carried their religious ideas into the political arena.

This idea that everything we believe rests on assumptions meshed nicely in my mind with the philosophic concept of

Weltanschauung, a German term defined by James Orr as "denoting the widest possible view which the mind can take of things in an effort to grasp them together as a whole from the standpoint of some particular philosophy or theology."

According to Orr, we all have a Weltanschauung, whether we realize it or not. Indeed, the most deeply held parts of our Weltanschauung are those things inculcated in our earliest years, the things we accepted as "just the way things are."

The idea that I had a personal Weltanschauung resting on things I believed, whether conscious of them or not, suggested a way to examine my Christian faith. I would identify as clearly as I could the basic assumptions I was making. I would write a book: *Assumptions and Faith*.

I am pleased to note when I look back on that book to see that I started by admitting awareness of difficult problems I would probably be unable to resolve: the problem of evil in a world created by a loving God, conflicts between science and religious faith, reconciling ideas of creation with modern cosmology, to name a few.

I then gave careful statements of the assumptions I was making, accompanying each with an explanation of why it seemed right to me. The assumptions, perhaps tweaked ever so slightly, still describe what I believe. The reasons I gave for making those assumptions, largely selected from standard Christian apologetics, still seem reasonable to me, but I realize as I get older that there were more personal reasons for making them than I recognized at the time.

Years of dinner discussions with the many international students at Macalester, enlightening in many ways, also had the effect of making me more satisfied with Christianity. The questions left unanswered by Christian faith are, so far as I can see, left unanswered by other faiths as well.

On the positive side, Christianity has had a remarkably positive influence in the world.

For all that's been written about the conflict between science and Christianity, science has advanced much faster in those societies influenced by the idea that there is in the world a God-imposed order to be discovered. It was Einstein who said that "without the belief in the inner harmony of the world, there could be no science."

Human rights and individual liberty are certainly most evident in countries influenced by Christianity. Even after admitting that Christianity has a regrettably checkered and sometimes abusive record, most faiths of the world put women and ethnic and religious minorities in social situations far more repressive than they have faced in Christian-influenced societies.

The arts, particularly music and artistic expression, seem to me to flourish best under the influence of Christianity, the singing faith. Put succinctly, I am drawn to making the assumptions underlying Christian faith because they seem to support things very attractive to me. The idea of wanting something attractive to live with was most apparent to me when I read Bertrand Russell's book, *Why I am Not a Christian*. He describes "the world which science presents for our belief" in these words:

> That man is the product of causes which had no prevision of the end they were achieving; that his origin, his growth, his hopes and fears, his loves and his beliefs, are but the outcome of accidental collocations of atoms; that no fire, no heroism, no intensity of thought and feeling, can preserve an individual life beyond the grave; that all the labors of the ages, all the devotion, all the inspiration, all the noonday brightness of human genius, are destined to extinction in the vast death of the solar system; and that the whole temple of man's achievement must inevitably be buried beneath the debris of a universe in ruins—all these things, if not quite beyond dispute, are yet so nearly certain that no philosophy which rejects them can hope to stand. . . . . Only on the firm foundation of unyielding despair can the soul's habitation henceforth be safely built.

Interestingly, Russell's daughter wrote an autobiography describing life with her father. It is not a denigrating book; in fact, it is clear that she is proud of her father's intellectual achievements. One cannot read it, however, without noticing that Russell's assumptions did not lead to a happy life for him, nor did it make him considerate of the people, and particularly the women, around him. His daughter became a Christian.

I must admit that more than 50 years after writing *Assumptions and Faith,* I have made no progress on resolving the problems I identified. Indeed, they have in every instance come to seem more intractable.

I have, on the other hand, become more and more convinced that Christian faith does provide a guide to living that is unmatched by any other faith of which I am aware. Where might one turn to find more succinct advice on how to order individual lives in a way that enhances the possibility of life together?

- The Ten Commandments.
- The admonition "to do justly, to love mercy, and to walk humbly with your God."
- The Sermon on the Mount.
- The expectation that we should cultivate the fruits of the spirit: love, joy, peace, longsuffering, kindness, goodness, faithfulness, gentleness, self-control.

My colleague, Jerry Weiss, mentioned several times in this book as my atheistic debating partner, once said to me that his greatest disappointment was that if his assumptions were right, he would never get to say to me, "I told you so." I responded, "If you are right, Jerry, what will I have lost by making the assumptions that I have?"

Far from having lost anything, I feel that my assumptions have given me what humans throughout history have sought: a sense that there is something greater than they see, a sense of awe, a feeling that there is purpose in life. That, I think, is enough.

And if my assumptions are right, the best is yet to come.

ACKNOWLEDGEMENTS

Beginning with my days as a student columnist at Morton Junior College, I continued to write stories and observations motivated by a lifetime in academia. My first thanks must go to my wife, Dolores, who for more than half a century faithfully read the things I wrote before they were consigned to a desk drawer.

The second person to be thanked is George Dugovic. George was a friend from high school and college days. After college graduations, careers took us to different parts of the country, and our principal contact as adults consisted of exchanging Christmas cards. After retirement, for reasons now forgotten, I sent him a few stories out of the desk drawer.

George professed to enjoy the stories I sent to him, and having found an audience, I was happy to send a few more, and pretty soon, a lot more. It was George's encouragement that brought my stories out of the drawer, and his continual encouragement ignited the idea of compiling them in a book.

The third person to play a major part in the creation of this book is Rowland Byerly, a cousin to whom I had been close in childhood. Rowland also became a Christmas card acquaintance after he left home for Purdue and then a career on the East Coast. When he learned that I had a collection of stories that I was sharing with George, he expressed an interest in reading the stories as a way to catch up on my life.

Rowland was principally interested in piecing the stories together as a continuous narrative. Time and again he would ask me to place some incident on a time-line that he created. He is responsible for the chronologic organization of the book, and his questions made it clear to me that I needed to provide more connecting links if my stories were to fit together.

As I worked to make one continuous story from many stories, it occurred to me that I could also introduce some of the ideas that I think should be considered as the costs of higher education soars while public opinion more and more questions its value. Then I might have a book.

With the new goal of preparing a manuscript addressing an audience that extended beyond my childhood friends, I turned to Mary Watson, a friend made in my adult years. Mary is herself a good writer, and our friendship is the kind that enabled her to say just what she thought as she read my manuscript. From an expression that she deemed clumsy to the placement (or failure to place) a comma, from candid recommendations to drop things she thought boring to the accuracy of names and places: Nothing escaped her attention. I improved my manuscript a great deal by responding to her crisp comments.

Based on my experience as an author of several textbooks, I thought the last step was simply to contact a few publishers until I found one willing to publish my book. I soon learned that to even get a publisher to look at your manuscript, you must have a literary agent. Eventually I concluded that if the manuscript was going to get published, it would be by some variation of self-publishing.

In this context, I learned that a completed manuscript is still a long way from a book. Questions of style, creation of front material, acquisition of pictures and diagrams and formatting around them, a well-designed cover, acquisition of copyright and an ISBN number: all things that in my experience had been dealt with by the editorial staff of an academic publisher.

Just when my spirits needed a boost, a friend told me that his brother was an editor who frequently worked with Amazon KDP to turn manuscripts into books. I knew the brother, Dave Healy, by name, but I didn't know that his whole life experience was preparing him to provide just what I needed. My relief was palpable. Dave Healy cared for all the things listed above, and he made suggestions for other improvements that would never have crossed my mind. He turned my manuscript into a book. I am newly grateful for an editor, particularly grateful for this editor.

Made in the USA
Monee, IL
09 October 2023

44228198R00223